Library Automation
The State of the
Art II

Library Automation
The State of the
Art II

Papers presented at the
Preconference Institute on Library Automation
Held at Las Vegas, Nevada, June 22–23, 1973

Under the sponsorship of the
Information Science and Automation Division
of the American Library Association

Edited by

Susan K. Martin
Brett Butler

With a
bibliography compiled by

Martha W. West

 American Library Association
Chicago 1975

Library of Congress Cataloging in Publication Data

Preconference Institute on Library Automation, Las
    Vegas, 1973.
    Library automation.

    Proceedings of the Preconference Institute on
Library Automation sponsored by the Information
Science and Automation Division of the American
Library Association before the Association's 1973
annual meeting in Las Vegas.
    Bibliography: p.
    1. Libraries--Automation--Congresses. I. Martin,
Susan K., 1942-   II. Butler, Brett. III. Amer-
ican Library Association. Information Science and
Automation Division. IV. Title.
Z678.9.A1P7 1973   025'.0028'54   75-20168
ISBN 0-8389-3152-9

Copyright © 1975 by the American Library Association

Printed in the United States of America

Contents

Preface   vii

1   Perspective: Review of 1968–1973 in Library Automation
     Allen B. Veaner   1

2   Technology: Present Status and Trends in Computers
     Diana Delanoy   18

3   User Services: 1973 Applications Status
     Lois M. Kershner   38

4   Cataloging Systems: 1973 Applications Status
     Maurice Freedman   56

5   Acquisitions Systems: 1973 Applications Status
     David L. Weisbrod   87

6   Systems Personnel: What are Our Needs?
     Pauline Atherton   101

7   Innovative Strategies in Systems and Automation
     Walter Curley   127

8   Outlook for the Future
     Ralph M. Shoffner   139

Bibliography   Martha W. West   156

Preface

Upon the creation of the Information Science and Automation Division of the American Library Association, its members voiced a strong concern that continuing education play an important role in the functions of the new division. Before its first year had been completed, ISAD had sponsored an institute on the state of the art of library automation, held immediately before the ALA Annual Meeting of 1967 in San Francisco. After five additional years of experience, and many institutes and seminars on specific topics, the Program Planning Committee felt that it would be appropriate to review the years between 1967 and 1973, and provide a framework and focus for the five-year period to follow. A preconference institute on the state of the art of library automation was planned and held in Las Vegas, in June 1973.

In contrast to the 1967 institute, the Las Vegas institute focused upon operating systems and operational technology. Library automation has matured rapidly in the past five years, despite withering sources of funds—or perhaps because of it. Hundreds of automated systems are operational in hundreds of libraries; these systems are of varying degrees of complexity and sophistication. It was clearly impossible to mention each system. The approach of the institute is one of strategic evaluation: to attempt to identify and discuss trends, using as examples some of the major accomplishments in library automation. The discussion periods have been included in the published proceedings and are a valuable supplement to the prepared talks.

The sessions included a review of the past five years, a hardware review, four applications reviews (public services, cataloging, acquisitions, and "innovative" applications), a statement of personnel needs, and a forecast. It was the intention of the institute coordinators to avoid highly technical information, aiming the presentations at a very broad range of librarians and systems analysts.

Speakers at the institute included:

Allen B. Veaner (Assistant Director for Technical Services, Stanford University Libraries)

Diana Delanoy (Head, Technical Information Center, System Development Corporation)

Lois M. Kershner (formerly Circulation Librarian, University of Pennsylvania; presently Manager, Customer Support, Computer Library Services, Inc.)

Maurice Freedman (formerly Director of Technical Services, Hennepin County Library, Minnesota; presently Coordinator, Technical Services Office, New York Public Library)

David L. Weisbrod (Head, Development Department, Yale University Library)

Pauline Atherton (Professor, Syracuse University School of Library Science)

Walter Curley (formerly Director, Cleveland Public Library; presently President, Gaylord Brothers, Inc.)

Ralph M. Shoffner (formerly Director of Research and Development, Richard Abel Co.; presently Vice President, Ringgold Management Systems)

We gratefully acknowledge the efforts of the speakers and the members of ISAD's Program Planning Committee in making this institute a very successful milestone in ISAD's continuing education program.

Susan K. Martin
Brett Butler

1 Perspective: Review of 1968–1973 in Library Automation

Allen B. Veaner

I confess a degree of jealousy towards my colleague, Ralph Shoffner, on two counts. First, a review of the past is a no-risk proposition; it must deal entirely with facts and known quantities. And by corollary, my second complaint is that his presentation may offer more opportunities for fun. One can speculate almost effortlessly. Evidence seems to indicate that speculation on the role of the computer in the library must be the easiest and most facile activity in library science and bibliography.

Although looking ahead is fun, it is also risky. An illustration of the risk may be found in an article on transoceanic air travel by Paul Gallico.

> When the Sunday supplement artist has nothing better to do, he draws up a half page of fantastic looking flying machines landing and taking off from the roof tops of 25th century buildings. The designs of these flying machines of the future are practically standard and are quite impractical. A bored rewrite man dishes up five columns of quotes from some local crackpot scientist to go with the pictures visualizing flights to Europe accomplished in five hours or less, excursions into stratosphere, dazzling speeds, etc., most of it 18 carat baloney.[1]

Then Gallico goes on to write how Igor Sikorsky, the air pioneer, would realistically get you to China in three days and nights on the gigantic new clipper he built for Pan American Airways. Sikorsky himself, a great scientist and inventor of the helicopter, is no less a victim of his own time in making predictions. In the Gallico article, he cautions the reader that with regard to future aviation developments there are two notions that have to be discarded: the stratosphere flight for passenger traffic and the 500-mile-per-hour aircraft! The 25th century arrived much sooner than expected for Mr. Gallico and Mr. Sikorsky. So much for the risks of predicting the future.

Assistant Director for Technical Services, Stanford University Libraries

Let us review the changes of the past five years—a very short period—in the context of general social and technological change. A characteristic of recent change is that it is extremely comprehensive as well as rapid, as those of you who have read *Future Shock*[2] well know. The broad changes we are accustomed to observe daily have only been made possible by the very rapid world transformation which occurred between 1940 and 1970. Within these three decades the world has gradually seen numerous developments representing orders-of-magnitude increases and improvements in communication, power generation, growing of food, speed of transport, efficacy of contraception, and so forth. Physically, man seems to have approached the technological limits of his ability to manipulate his environment, even to the point where his ability to change the world is rapidly endangering not only the ecological balance but also his political and mental balance. Like it or not, man has made an irreversible quantum jump during this three-decade period. And like it or not, similar quantum jumps have begun to take place in the library community. These quantum jumps are bringing about irreversible changes. The rapidity with which these irreversible changes are occurring is having very significant and highly visible effects upon the library profession. Let us now review some of the specific areas of change over this recent five-year period in library automation. (Incidentally, I really think "library automation" is a misnomer. We're really talking about bibliographic automation and the automation of certain services to the public. The automated library is a concept still somewhat in the distance, but a warning: we are creeping up on it imperceptibly. The text access experiments of INTREX were a start.)

THE R & D PERIOD

The research question of five or six years ago was: Could it be done? Today's question is: How shall it be accomplished? We all know it can be done—technically, mechanically, electronically. But what of the system users, the librarians, the managers, the staff, the support staff, the public? What of the human side? Throughout the past five years, it has been amply demonstrated that the human problems associated with automation far exceed in difficulty and complexity the technical aspects. I do not mean to diminish the importance or difficulty of technology itself, but we have yet to find the properly operating computer that refuses to perform the properly written program or that is tired or is unable to adjust to a new social environment, a different physical location, a new pattern of organization and management. No matter how sophisticated the system, people are still at the center, still the controlling factor in any system. But the computerized environment does not permit them to conduct their business in the same way as in the noncomputerized world. When we leave the manual world, we go from the infinite flexibility and adaptability of people to the rigorous demands of algorithmic procedures of seemingly inflexible machine processing rules. Is the adjustment the same as going from horseback to driving a car? I don't think so. Technological advances in transportation are merely changes in means. Changing from a manual to a computerized system represents a subtle alteration of one's ends or goals. It is partly because the *goals* of the automated system are not quite the same as the goals of the manual system that we have experienced many painful, human problems in installation and application. Now technical processing sometimes has a tendency to become a thing unto itself, self-sustaining in its quest for perfection, out of touch with the real world and sometimes even independent of the needs of library patrons. But the computer gives every librarian—and in particular, it gives the administrator—a very powerful, new tool to achieve *his* goal of service to the public. It is precisely the power of the computer which will not permit us to perpetuate that part of the past which was inefficient or which didn't even need to be done. The computer is forcing us to pay attention to the ends, the goals, the users, the patrons. The computer is telling us that it is more important to make materials available to users as quickly as possible than it is to worry about how the call number is formatted on a particular card. The goal of freeing the professional from clerical work is inherent in automation activities but has yet to be successfully achieved on a large scale. In any case, it is clear that with manual systems there is almost no hope of ever achieving this goal. The computer has "budget visibility"—the cost of its operations are highly resolvable in detail and cannot be hidden. It automatically introduces an element of accountability. So "exposure" results in goal modification, or at least reevaluation—an important consideration in days when institutions are reexamining their priorities, reallocating their resources, and the university's clientele is changing its expectations.

Accustomed to rapid, efficient computer services, many members of the academic library community can no longer be satisfied with plodding, bureaucratic library responses. The library's clientele is changing its expectations. A change in expectations is apparent at least in two areas: in the general public, television has done much to change expectations for getting rapid turnaround and rapid reporting on current events; and in the academic area the rise of the computer center as a consumer of resources and provider of services has extensively challenged the library. The public will no longer be satisfied with any kind of library response that smacks of being plodding or bureaucratic. People want information *now,* not tomorrow or next week. If they can't get what they want from the library, they'll go to the computer facility.[3] So, systems which speed access to all types of learning materials will be welcomed—whether they are printed book catalogs, film booking systems, or on-line query systems.

Changes in federal, state, and local priorities have almost conclusively done away with the idea of local self-sufficiency in collections—a fact which requires cooperation and which, in turn, virtually dictates the need for fast-response computerized union catalogs and their ancillary network apparatus. I believe that Fred Kilgour recently mentioned that in the Ohio College Library Center there are many more query, interlibrary loan, and location transactions than technical processing transactions. If this is the case, I say good! That's why the network exists. Self-sufficiency in development has also come to an end. Economic and technical realities now virtually require network and consortium participation if success is to be achieved. (Intellectual energy—like thermal and electrical energy—is also in short supply.)

CHARACTERISTICS OF THE DEVELOPMENT PROCESS

I think it's fair to say that five years ago very few librarians even understood the concept of development, and some still do not comprehend it. The evolutionary process from basic research to development, to pilot operation, and then to production is a long, slow, and continuous process. The library community was impatient, easily frustrated, wondered why development work occurred so slowly, why so many things had to be done over and over again. The characteristics of an R&D effort are expenditures of a great deal of time and energy learning and making mistakes. Persons not familiar with the development process have tended to be very critical of these costs, believing that with "good planning" most of these expenditures would have been "unneccessary." Any such claim really demonstrates a high ignorance of the development process. But by definition, *development is an iterative process;* in massive intellectual endeavors there is no way to proceed without going through a series of research and experimental stages, some of which indeed begin with fantasies, some of which lead to dead ends, others of which lead to the building of prototypes, the testing and evaluation of pilot operations, and finally—the great day—going into operations with a production system.

I need only point to the United States' aerospace program as an excellent example of the development process in an area which is vastly more complex than our development efforts, and vastly more expensive. At the risk of repeating myself, in library automation we are not trying to build next year's model of a car, because we have 75 or more years of automobile technology behind us. We are trying to build a spacecraft, the next generation of spacecraft. This figure of speech may help to explain why it is so complex to undertake library automation development projects.

Development is *not* a turn-key operation. Development is impossible without the persistent, painful, dogged participation of the staff which is to use the system. Every automated system has manual procedures associated with it and even if one bought a complete package from the outside, considerable exercise, investigation, and development would be required to match the manual and automated procedures in that library. And none of this is "do-able" without hard work.

CHANGES IN THE MANAGEMENT OF COMPUTER FACILITIES AND DEVELOPMENT PROJECTS

Like any other complex resource in the university, the computer has almost everywhere finally been brought under professional management. The day is past when the computer was a plaything of a few favored research faculty, and most computer centers are nowadays no longer run by part-time faculty members. Correspondingly, in this same five-year period, it has been recognized how important it is to have library development projects under full-time professional management. The development of complex systems is a highly specialized art which cannot be undertaken part-time by a librarian who has prime responsibilities elsewhere. An experienced manager is required and many of the outstanding ones have come into libraries from industry. This has had a marvelous effect of cross-fertilization of ideas. So today the librarian plays a much reduced *technical* role in system development, a fact which enables him to give more attention to his goal-setting role.

FROM FANTASY TO THE REALITY OF PRODUCTION SYSTEMS: A RECORD OF ACCOMPLISHMENT

Proposals written five or six years ago, the proceedings of the preconference held five years ago, pronouncements of the computer experts and librarians, all represented more wishful thinking than most of us would care to admit. A wide credibility gap was created in a very short time. But five years ago very few people knew what lay ahead in the way of hard work: the enormous investment in staff time, the realization that no one could do the job for us, the appreciation of the need to express everything in all its excruciating detail, the pain of assuring internal consistency in our documentation. Not too many people understood the degree, the intensive degree, to which the managers of library systems would themselves have to delve into the dirty details of system requirements and system design work. Fortunately, all that has changed. In five years we have learned how to turn fantasy into reality—partly at least. We have real production systems working as dependable, indeed indispensable, library tools.

It has been ten years since publication of the "Red Book"[4] and the "White Book."[5] We have passed from fantasies and dreaming to experimentation, research, development projects, and today, actual production. We have seen the activation of important research projects in the United States like MEDLARS and INTREX, and abroad, LIBRIS in Sweden and BIBLIS in West Germany. We have seen the introduction of on-line production systems at the National Library of Medicine (MEDLINE), Stanford (BALLOTS), Oregon State University (LOLITA), Northwestern University (no name); mixed batch and on-line systems at the University of Chicago and at LC (Order Division, Card Division); and batch systems at Columbia University, Cornell University, and the University of California's Union Catalog Supplement Project. These are probably less than 10 percent of the actual existing systems that are really viable.

We now can better understand and appreciate Dolby's 1969 conclusion about computerized cataloging: ". . . the primary conclusion of this study is that mechanization of the cataloging function is not only necessary and desirable, but also inevitable."[6] One might say that we have gone through the "childhood" period of R&D and have entered a "second generation" of development systems—systems that are more grounded in reality and a surer understanding of technical, financial and human problems of implementation than their predecessors.

Despite this progress a small but strident minority continues to delude itself with the belief that it is useless to apply computers to bibliographic problems.

This reminds me of the state of journalism in this country for several years after the Wright brothers made their first flight. It was attempted from time to time to report that two bicycle manufacturers had built a plane that actually flew. Editors of various newspapers, as late as 1910 or 1911, refused to publish the story because they felt it couldn't be true. Anyone with this attitude toward library automation will find himself bypassed very quickly.

Less than two years ago, even as the Ohio College Library Center was gearing up for production, lugubrious voices declared solemnly that on-line systems for the libraries were just so much science fiction, another starry-eyed, impractical dream, perhaps concocted by those Sunday supplement writers Paul Gallico mentioned. Meantime, back to the real world: a voluminous ADP study conducted as a result of the Dainton Committee's report defined the scope of automation for a new institution, the British Library.[7] In 1971 a White Paper submitted to Great Britain's Department of Education and Science recommended that five institutions—the British Museum Library, the National Reference Library of Science and Invention, the British National Bibliography (BNB), the National Central Library, and the National Lending Library for Science and Technology—should be combined in the British Library. A study made by Scientific Control Systems, Ltd., for one of these units, the British Museum Library, recommended establishing an on-line processing system. As reported by M. B. Line, "Off-line systems were considered but rejected. . . . It is extremely difficult to find one that is significantly superior to a good manual system and the costs are greater. An on-line system has far more to offer and it is on this assumption that detailed planning will take place."[8]

In the wake of successful on-line systems—OCLC, Northwestern University, Stanford—interest in such systems is at an all-time high. The Association of Southeastern Research Libraries has recently established SOLINET to build an on-line network aimed at serving libraries from Louisiana to Florida. Northwestern has indicated interest in upgrading and regionalizing its own system. Stanford is promoting CLAN. NELINET is busy studying the replication of OCLC. Several state agencies have plans to develop or transfer existing on-line systems, and even IBM is getting into the act aggressively, albeit somewhat late in the day.

THE SIGNIFICANCE OF MARC

Without a standardized format for the transmission of bibliographic data, we might not exactly be no place in library automation, but we would certainly all be riding off in different directions, dissipating our resources, and enjoying not the remotest possibility of interchanging bibliographic data or building networks. But MARC gives us more than mere local ability to use centrally produced records and exchange locally produced ones. It opens up the possibility of worldwide bibliographic standardization, since MARC is already an established international standard. ISBD, the International Standard Bibliographic Description, is well on its way to equal rank in importance for achieving international, computerized bibliographic control, the next logical step after the achievement of Shared Cataloging, and is already in use in the national bibliographies of six countries.

It is easy to underestimate MARC. We take for granted this electronic marvel for distributing bibliographic data, which became a production system just *one* generation after the Association of Research Libraries provided the impetus for starting publication of the familiar series of LC-based bibliographic tools, *A Catalog of Books Represented by Library of Congress Printed Cards,* and its successor, the printed *National Union Catalog.* Take a hard look at how far MARC has advanced beyond current English language coverage in just the past year or two: films, maps, serials, and now French language imprints. Counting the recently converted LC popular titles, we now have access to some 400,000 high quality MARC records. Altogether there are six classes of MARC services available to subscribers.

MARC has had a considerable international impact. The Australian National Bibliography is now completely produced through an application of MARC transferred from the British National Bibliography.

A disappointment was the nation's inability to fund the Retrospective Conversion (RECON) Project, a study of which produced several fundamental reports and articles. In retrospect, perhaps it was just as well, since limited resources were badly needed for current activity, both by LC and by MARC subscribers. However, a British group, London and Southeastern Library Region (LASER), plans to convert 1.25 million retrospective records over a three-year period. The University of Chicago is studying its own needs for RECON in connection with its design work for a circulation system. A significant number of RECON titles (including foreign imprints) are already in the OCLC data base. The important thing to stress is the need for all future data base conversion to conform to MARC to the highest possible degree in order that bibliographic interchange will be possible.

And I almost forgot Cataloging-in-Publication (CIP) records! Their presence in MARC is of inestimable value to speeding all aspects of technical processing in libraries.

FINANCIAL IMPLICATIONS

Some (but not all) libraries are operating with budgets substantially below the high levels of five years ago which were made possible by both federal and nonfederal development grants. Most libraries must now support not only production costs, but also their own development work. For several reasons production costs are bound to be high during the initial operation stages of new systems. First, while in a transitional state, manual systems must be run in parallel. So you have to pay at least a slight incremental charge to get into the new game, even if you purchase a packaged system. Second, because the new systems have been in operation for a relatively short time, the programs which make them possible will need further fine tuning to make them more efficient and more economical of computer resources. Both these factors are compounded by growing unionization of employees in libraries and general inflation, which also contribute to cost increases. If manual costs continue to rise and productivity per dollar invested continues to fall—as they must in manual systems—then the provision of library services, at least in large research libraries, may be seriously jeopardized unless computer assistance is assured.

I recently saw a report issued by the McGraw-Hill Economic Department which listed the amount of R&D expenditures expected by industry in 1973.[9] The total amount of R&D expenditures expected is 21.2 billion dollars, or 2.4 percent of sales. Therefore, considering the kinds of development monies invested by commercial organizations to develop new products or services, comparatively little money has been spent in developing major library systems. The cost over the past five years has been no more than a few tens of millions of dollars, an infinitesimal fraction of the nation's Gross National Product and a minute fraction of total library expenditures over that five-year period. I regard the accomplishments to date as actually quite remarkable despite the generally inadequate and sometimes erratic support provided.

CHANGES IN LIBRARIANS' ATTITUDE
TOWARDS MARKETING

A shortage of cash seems to work like magic in getting librarians interested in practical, cooperative efforts. This introduces a new topic which until recently some librarians didn't want to touch. I refer to the realization that bibliographic data bases, products, and services need very much to be marketed. They need to be marketed not only because cash is short but also because, even if cash were available, it would not be a wise use of resources to encourage the development of too many diverse and incompatible networking schemes. The success of the networks we have may be attributed at least as much to marketing as to technical excellence.

This marketing angle is very important; it pushes us into areas of economy and cooperation that we did not consider earlier because we have always felt that there is a degree of nobility about free access to bibliographic information. Yet in the end, the market and a means of marketing may give us the most efficient and most effective access, because even in a free public library access is not free.

RISE OF COMMERCIAL SERVICES

The availability of a national machine-readable data base is drastically changing the pattern of distributing bibliographic data. Today instead of all libraries across the country patronizing one big store, we have a system of wholesalers and retailers. The Library of Congress distributes the MARC tapes to regional and commercial centers which in turn make them available to their users on a retail basis. For the first time the manner in which bibliographic data are disseminated seems to be approaching the way in which library materials are sold. Just as we have book jobbers, we now have jobbers of bibliographic data. They are perhaps too numerous to mention: Abel, Bro-Dart, Baker and Taylor, Information Design, Information Dynamics, NELINET, OCLC, Oklahoma Department of Libraries, the networks proposed in New Jersey, Illinois, the Southeast, Texas, and the Pacific Northwest, as well as the organizations which commercially produce book catalogs, such as Bro-Dart, Science Press, and General Research. Even on-line services are commercially available through System Development Corporation.

HARDWARE

Five years ago there existed no production cathode ray tube (CRT) terminal which fit library requirements for character set, independence from the main frame, economy, and reliability. Today we at least have several programmable terminals with their own internal memory and microprocessor, and they are leasable at reasonable prices.

Minicomputers, which were practically unknown to librarians in 1968, today play important roles. They are in use in circulation at the University of British Columbia, for a major system development project at University of Minnesota's Biomedical Library, and in Stanford's BALLOTS project.

UNSOLVED PROBLEMS: TRANSFERABILITY

Can there be a more elusive goal? With respect to programs, the third generation of computers was very disappointing, although there is some indication that the present generation, commonly known as the "three and a half generation," may be much better. As for the transfer of a complex system, that is a different matter; it has not yet been tried. But it may be the most important task to be defined politically, technologically, and economically over the next five years, since it is clear that in this quinquennium we have reached a watershed—the end of the first period of developmental library automation.

There isn't the money or the energy to continue developing a galaxy of new systems; the problems of transferability must be mastered. Some progress has been made. The work done at the Institute of Library Research on automatic format recognition was of great assistance to the Library of Congress in developing its own AFR programs. This work was also used in the Hennepin County Library, Minnesota. There have been isolated instances of pieces of systems that have been transferred successfully with maintenance, but we must do much more.

THE FUTURE

I'm only supposed to review what's happened in the past five years. But I cannot conclude without making up a shopping list for Ralph Shoffner. My list is taken straight from Henriette Avram's paper in the 1971 *Annual Review of Information Science and Technology*, with the addition of several of my own items.[10]

Here they are:

1. We need LC's authority files in machine-readable form to help us achieve bibliographic consistency nationwide. (In this area the New York Public Library has made excellent progress in applying the computer together with microforms to make subject authorities available to its staff).
2. How do we solve the transferability problem?
3. Getting out of the R&D stage and into production—we're out.
4. Overcoming the problems of using MARC—we've accomplished part of this.

5. Can we agree on computerized handling of serials? On standards? On objectives? A lot of work to be done here, but beginnings have been made with the National Serials Data Program, development of cataloging standards agreements (e.g., OCLC).

6. Management and funding agencies must recognize the hundreds of man-years of systemwide human effort necessary for bringing the conceptual design to operating reality. (This is allied to my earlier comment that development is not a turnkey activity. I believe we have achieved at least some appreciation of this fact, but much more is needed.)

7. Too much danger of using computers to mimic manual systems. Inevitable in early stages—weren't the first automobiles really "horseless carriages"? (How much work was done in the 19th century on the ornithopter, whereby man hoped to achieve flight by imitating birds?) It is for exactly these reasons that funding agencies must continue to support R&D activity in librarianship. What has already been achieved is not the answer but merely the launching pad for still better and more effective systems.

Some of the new and different things I believe should be investigated and developed include the following:

1. Nationwide development efforts to enable *different* network systems to intercommunicate. This is important because it is quite apparent that we will not have one grand system for the entire country.

2. Experimentation with patron use of interactive CRT searches, especially a study of the human factors in searching large files and in the man-machine interaction

3. Derivation and publication of hard-cost data

4. More consideration of off-line storage, particularly computer-generated microforms (COM) for infrequently used records, along with methods of getting these records back into machine readable form on demand

5. Better, easier search logic. Boolean search capability may not be the best for information retrieval applications, according to Lancaster.[11]

6. Better terminals, with reliability as their key feature

7. Improved understanding of the enormous computing complexity of the on-line bibliographic system

8. Some less expensive approach to retrospective conversion, perhaps through optical character recognition and a cheaper alternative to the problem we'd face if we had RECON—storage costs.

SUMMARY

I've heard J. C. R. Licklider quoted as saying it's easy to overestimate what you do in one year and underestimate what can be accomplished in ten years. I think that statement is just as valid for a five-year period. Remember the MARC Institutes? We don't have them any more; they were excellent tutorials. As production systems get into operation, there will be less and less need for tutorials. The progress of the past five years has been almost as fantastic as our imaginations were ten or even five years ago. Five years hence with operational national networks, we may have forgotten the agonies of yesterday. We can then be preoccupied with solving new problems—the activity which keeps man alive and vital.

DISCUSSION

Brett Butler (Information Design, Inc., Menlo Park, Calif.): I would like to open up for questions from anybody; do give your name and affiliation. We'll pick primarily on Allen, but if anybody has general questions, we'll try and draw the whole panel up here, if necessary.

Ralph Shoffner (Richard Abel Co.): I think my name is Gallico. This is a question on interpretation with respect to the expenditure of R&D funds over the last six years. Suppose we had taken all the money that went into that on-line systems work, and put it into retrospective conversion. What part of the nation's library resources would now exist in machine form so that it could be put out in printed form, microform, or what-have-you?

Veaner: I'm sure a large part, possibly all of it. I believe the original RECON estimate was that it would cost ten million dollars to do the entire project; that is my recollection from the final report. However, the publication in printed form of those particular catalogs I don't believe would give us the kind of flexible access that one can get through on-line systems in terms of searching. A second point is that an on-line system has the capability, much better than any manual system I know of, of integrating all of the necessary technical processing operations. I am talking specifically of technical processing here, in effect integrating these operations with the data base. And if a complete technical processing system and a data base can be supported by an on-line system, then I think you are much further ahead than you would be by printing the book catalogs and disseminating them. You still would have the update problem with the book catalogs; you would still have a great many manual operations that would have to either be carried out manually, or through batch computer processes. It seems to me that the real advantage lies in this integration capability. I will confess, at this point, I am speaking from a kind of tunnel vision because I see so closely how finely the BALLOTS system, let's say, integrates the data base and the procedures and the processes, so it kind of all moves together. I should not be using a public platform for that, but it's the one I know best, and from what I have heard of users of the Ohio College Library Center the reaction has been similar.

Butler: Ralph, it seems to me you are questioning whether we would have been better off to put the money into the data base and wait for the hardware, technology, or other things to catch up? I think not. Information Design is a MARC wholesaler, and there are a number of other individual MARC users in the audience. The kind of statistics that we hear today indicate that today's MARC data base handles 70 percent to 80 percent of most libraries' needs, and a much higher percentage for medium-sized public and junior college libraries. If that means that the data conversion we are doing today has gotten us to a 75 percent or 70 percent level for most libraries, I think that's pretty good. The only question is, how expensive and how difficult is it to get from 80 percent to 100 percent, or whatever we need on a current basis?

Shoffner: I think you have made the point already: with the on-line system you pay for the capability right now to respond, and when "right now" is over and the budget is gone, so is the on-line system unless you continue to support it. As I recall at the 1967 ISAD meeting, the major point of divergence was not whether the on-line systems were feasible in any sense, but rather what it meant in the way of alternatives, particularly with respect to conversion, and when the appropriate time was to set up an on-line system. So the point on this is that I certainly would not like to have seen all the money go into the development of publications such as the *National Union Catalog* was, where nothing was left over except the printed record afterward, but we are still sitting with major problems as far as the totality of library resources in the country are concerned, even though we have on-line systems operating for that current small part of the data. I suppose this is most true with the research libraries of the country, rather than the totality of the libraries, and it's also the case that the bulk of library service without question is in providing current materials to people rather than research materials from ages past.

John Kountz (California State University and Colleges): Allen, you made a curious statement there on the connection between networks, and I was wondering, since you would represent BALLOTS obviously, were you implying that the communications capabilities of BALLOTS equals that of OCLC?

Veaner: I don't think I should discuss any technical aspects of BALLOTS here, John, because that's not the purpose of this meeting and I rather regret I made mention of it at all. I think the thing for you to do would be to talk to Hank Epstein, if he is still giving demonstrations over at the Stardust. I believe the equipment will be hooked up for a couple of days. I would just rather not get into it because I think it would not be proper.

Bob Runyon (Johns Hopkins University): I was at the 1967 ISAD Conference and I remember that at that point there was a tremendous amount of discussion from the floor, and from the podium also, about the issue of whether librarians should become programmers, analysts, and technical people, or whether the technical people should be brought in from the outside. As I remember there seemed to be a sort of balance or concession that this was a separate, specialized technical function in which the initiative had to be brought in, that outside expertise had to be relied on to a major degree. I am aware a little bit of the fact that this has indeed occurred in the BALLOTS system, and without asking Allen to speak on that system, I wonder if he would be willing to comment on his view on that particular issue in the development of library systems in the context of his overall review.

Veaner: Sue informs me that Pauline Atherton will be addressing this point to a certain extent. I hope that I did not imply that there was any firm rule or law that says that we have to have outsiders come in to help us develop systems. I think there is a spectrum here. Many fine workable efficient systems have been constructed by librarians. I can point to Harvard University as an excellent example, where to my knowledge, and do correct me if I'm wrong, at least 99 percent if not 100 percent of all the development effort has been done in-house mostly by librarians (all by librarians, Sue informs me). And there have been applications on a much smaller scale, too, individual subsystems that have been done by librarians.

However, I believe that when the project becomes very large and complicated, when it uses up a fair amount of computer resources (particularly when it is an on-line application) even when you have your own machine or whether you are sharing a machine, you simply have to have people with telecommunications systems programming knowledge that you're not likely to find in the library profession. If you have your own machine, multiple demands are made on the resources of that machine at the same time, and a systems programmer, somebody who can write operating systems, has to be available to do all this juggling so that the computer can be the one-man band. That requires the kind of machine expertise that will rarely, if ever, be found in the library profession.

This doesn't mean to say that it *won't* be found, because you can see that the curricula in library schools are changing, and there's more encouragement to take courses in advanced math, science, information science; and even people from information science are coming over into librarianship and vice versa. I think the difference is really in the scale of the operation; there's no absolute rule here. But I think it is very stimulating and beneficial, and there are a great many technical problems which the bibliographically uninformed person can often give a better response to than a person who is an expert library technician or a cataloger, because you see, the computer man doesn't know that you can't do that or are not supposed to do it, so he comes up with a suggestion about how to do something that will increase your public service or data base access capability ten- or twenty-fold, only because he never knew that *Anglo-American Cataloging Rules* said you couldn't do that. I've seen this happen.

REFERENCES

[1] Paul Gallico, "Planes Leaving for Shanghai, Paris," *Vanity Fair* 44, no. 5:22, 63 (July 1935).

[2] Alvin Toffler, *Future Shock* (New York: Random House, 1970).

[3] Anthony Ralston: "The Library Lobby," *College and Research Libraries* 32: 427–31 (Nov. 1971).

[4] *Automation and the Library of Congress*. A Survey Sponsored by the Council on Library Resources, Inc. (Washington, DC: Library of Congress, 1963).

[5] *Libraries and Automation.* Proceedings of the Conferences ... held ... under the Sponsorship of the Library of Congress, National Science Foundation, Council on Library Resources, Inc. (Washington, DC: Library of Congress, 1964).

[6] James L. Dolby and others, *Computerized Library Catalogs: Their Growth, Cost and Utility.* (Cambridge, Mass.: MIT Press, 1969), p. 16.

[7] Dept. of Education and Science, *Scope for Automatic Data Processing in the British Library,* ed. by M. B. Line and A. Phillips (2 vols.; Great Britain: Her Majesty's Stationery Office, 1972).

[8] M. B. Line, "British Library Feasibility Study," *Aslib Proceedings* 24:614–16 (Nov. 1972).

[9] "R&D is Losing its High Priority," *Business Week* no. 2279:198 (May 12, 1973).

[10] Henriette D. Avram, "Library Automation," in *Annual Review of Information Science and Technology,* v. 6. (New York: Encyclopaedia Britannica, 1971).

[11] F. Wilfrid Lancaster, "Evaluation of On-Line Searching in MEDLARS (AIM-TWX) by Biomedical Practitioners" in *Occasional Papers* no. 101 (Urbana, Ill.: Univ. of Illinois Pr., 1972).

2 Technology: Present Status and Trends in Computers

Diana Delanoy

INTRODUCTION

I'd like to begin with my last sentence, which is something of a warning, "If libraries and librarians don't, something and someone else will." New technologies are affecting all aspects of our lives and are forcing change in established institutions. In its traditional role of selecting, collecting, and distributing information, the library faces increasing competition with interactive cable television, on-line information retrieval services, and micropublications that are cheap, easy to read, and disposable. In a feature article in the *Library Journal*, Louis Vagianos argues that information-transfer mechanisms of the future need not be libraries or anything like them, nor must they be staffed with librarians.[1] It is true that less than 10 percent of the nation's libraries use the available technologies at all and that competitive alternative services are being formed as a result.

Librarians must begin using these innovations and defining their roles in what I call the "information business." If they don't, the "learning resource centers" and the "technical information centers," which are being spawned specifically to capitalize on emerging technologies, may take over. Special libraries of large corporations are rapidly being transformed into Technical Information Centers. Ours at System Development Corporation includes responsibility for the company's store of computer programs and documentation in addition to print, audiovisual, and microform materials. There is no reason why academic libraries cannot evolve into Educational and Research Information Centers, and public libraries into Community Information Centers. In a few instances this is happening, but not in the majority.

Head, Technical Information Center, System Development Corporation

During this session, I will address myself to the major technologies that are here and ready to be used by libraries. I will also briefly address myself to the current trends, since they indicate what lies ahead. Other speakers will be concerned with the application of these technologies to specific library operations. I hope that you will obtain from this session a clear understanding of what is available today, what the trends are, and how you can take advantage of them, so that you can begin preparing for your potential future roles.

COMPUTER TECHNOLOGY TRENDS

The results of a recently distributed GUIDE/IBM Delphi Study of experts in technology attempted to identify the uses computers and data processing technology will be put to over the next ten to thirty years.[2] Although the applications varied from industry to industry, the major conclusion was that by 1985, computers will have reached into almost all areas of business, government, and private life, and that one family in every hundred will have a computer terminal in its home. Computer usage in the United States currently accounts for some $20 billion per year, and this amount is increasing by about 12 percent per year. The area of largest growth, now and probably for some time, is that of teleprocessing products and services—the area that offers the greatest potential for libraries. However, the total funds spent on library automation in the United States is at most about $20 million per year, or one-tenth of one percent of the total data processing industry budget.

Moreover, these funds are spent by probably no more than ten percent, and perhaps closer to five percent of existing libraries. These figures indicate that "laissez-faire" isn't the way libraries can afford to operate. However, today's and tomorrow's dollars will buy a lot more computer usage than in the past. And this is a significant trend!

What does this mean for the nation's libraries? Table 2-1 illustrates a few of the major trends in the information business. Those in the 1970 box will be my primary emphasis, since they are the ones you should be considering use of, right now!

TABLE 2-1.   Trends in the Information Business: 1970s and 1980s

1970s	1980s
• Minicomputers for library applications as turn-key systems.	• Widespread use of CATV and computer terminals for interactive information handling.
• Cooperative processing using networks.	• Concept of "information utilities through national and regional networks."
• On-line large file searching of major bibliographic files.	• Dial-access audiovisual libraries for instant reference.
• Packaged software for library applications.	

MINICOMPUTER TURN-KEY SYSTEMS

With the costs of circuitry decreasing due to the miniaturization of circuit units, minicomputer "turn-key" systems that come complete with software tailored to meet specific applications are beginning to appear.[3] The term "turn-key" is applied to these systems because they are designed simply to be plugged in and turned on, like radios. The software application packages, however, although generally versatile, are not always appropriate, and although they may run without problems, they may not do the jobs their purchasers thought they would do. For this reason, a note of caution should be sounded: before buying any system to speed up or reduce the cost of some specific operation, it is advisable that you examine—with the help of a systems consultant—your entire operation as a whole. You will then be in a better position to intelligently evaluate the potential of the available systems.

Because of their expertise in developing software, it is becoming popular for companies like SDC to buy the minicomputer hardware, write the software for applications of a particular industry, and sell the system after it is configured. Except for the large file systems that minicomputers today can't support, these packaged systems could well become so inexpensive that they may be the answer for many libraries with moderate budgets.[4] It is not unreasonable to expect that in five years, the number of installations will increase tenfold and the prices will decrease substantially. Minicomputers currently range in price from $3,000 to $20,000, and there are approximately 50,000 of them installed throughout the country.

In considering a minicomputer—there are over 40 manufacturers—the most important characteristics are that the machine is part of an established and growing product line; the machine as configured is suitable and adequate for your application; the manufacturer-supplied software meets your needs; and the manufacturer's installation and maintenance commitments are clearly specified.

In selecting the peripheral units—tape drives, card readers, etc.—to be included with a minicomputer system, it is important that the devices in question have been installed and used with the minicomputer being procured and that their users' experience has been favorable. It is also important to find out who will service the device and under what conditions.

COOPERATIVE PROCESSING USING NETWORKS

The trend toward cooperative use of computing resources is a most significant trend for libraries, since the only way most libraries can afford to use computer technology is by sharing the costs. Since telecommunications line costs can often exceed the cost of computer time used for a given operation, the trends in newly emerging networks are highly significant.

Computer networks in the United States are increasing in number, size, and geographic coverage, giving alternatives to use of the Bell System and the 2,000 other telephone companies offering data telecommunication via voice grade transmission lines.[5] To highlight a few specializing in data communications, there are the new special-service common carriers—AT&T's Digital Data System, using private leased lines, plans to provide data service to five cities in 1973, increasing to more than 100 cities by 1977; DATRAN plans a digital service across 35 cities, with the first segment to be implemented in 1973–74; and MCI, the pioneer in petitioning the Federal Communications Commission, is initiating point-to-point line service. Tymshare Corporation currently provides commercially a computer-controlled lease-line network to approximately 40 cities, and the Advanced Research Project Agency of the Department of Defense is sponsoring an experimental network that links some 40 computers nationwide for applied research. Western Union is extending its services with cross-country microwave and extensions in TWX and TELEX.

The market trends here indicate an increased competition among carriers, a potential decrease in data rates, and increased use of all digital networks. Also, network design technology is becoming more sophisticated, with computer-controlled distributed intelligence, load balancing, and alternate routings. If these emerging network technologies lower the cost of data transmission significantly—and, with wider bandwidths, this should happen—the cost of communications, which is one of the greatest impediments to network operation, should disappear.

INFORMATION RETRIEVAL SYSTEMS

Of special and major significance to library research and reference activities is the current and growing availability of major large retrieval systems and services.

A list of these companies, institutions, and their systems appears in table 2–2. I can't speak for the plans of the other services, but SDC is in the process of expanding from three to ten data bases, some two and one-quarter million bibliographic records. The major features of these services are that first, the data base arrives through the mail on a tape from a distributor in a prestored format on a subscription or other agreement basis. The data base is then converted into the on-line system and inverted direct-access index files are created. Most of these systems are interactive; they also provide high-speed output on a line printer, using medium to large scale time-shared computers. The *Tymshare* network is often used for communications and most terminals used are CRT, Teletype, or typewriter. Some user training is required to master the search vocabulary and functions. The systems and services are somewhat competitive—for example, offering access to the same data base and therefore competing for customers.

TABLE 2–2.   Major Large Data Base Time-Sharing
Information Services

COMPANY	SYSTEM	DATA BASE(S)
SDC	ORBIT	ERIC, CHEMCON, NLM
Lockheed	DIALOG	ERIC, NTIS, Pandex
Informatics	RECON	NASA, TOXICON
IBM	STAIRS	EI, SUNY BCN
Mead Tech. Labs	DATA CENTRAL	EPA
Battelle	BASIS-70	NTIS, CHEMCON
Infodata	INQUIRE	American Petroleum
INSTITUTION	SYSTEM	DATA BASE(S)
Lehigh	LEADER	EI
Stanford	SPIRES/BALLOTS	MARC
Massachusetts Institute of Technology	INTREX	Bibliographic
National Library of Medicine	MEDLINE	MEDLARS

PACKAGED SOFTWARE

Before you make a decision to develop your own software, you should find out if there is similar software available in packaged form. There are a number of published catalogs that list available software obtainable today. Usually you can save considerable money by leasing or purchasing a package rather than developing one.

It isn't uncommon for a package to take several hundred thousand dollars to develop, yet lease for about $10,000 a year. The amortization of development costs are spread over the many users. How do you find the package you want? If you are an accounting firm, bank, or an insurance firm, it's quite easy, since packaged software is readily available for practically every application that can be computerized. But today for libraries it's still fairly slim pickings except in information retrieval, circulation, and book catalog production. Nevertheless, with labor rates going up and packaged software proliferating, libraries should soon be able to select among a variety of packages that handle both the standard housekeeping and bibliographic functions as well as those that deal with complex text retrieval and SDI.

DECISION-MAKING

All the trends in library data processing—and in computing in general—indicate a continuing increase in contracted computing services, packaged software, and the use of communications networks. It is important to review the major factors of decision-making in dealing with the suppliers of computer services or systems. Careful evaluations of alternative systems must be made in light of your unique requirements. Not everyone speaks the same language. The key is to ask the right questions, understand the real costs, talk directly to other users, and to seek assistance in running good benchmark comparison tests. Additional items to consider with commercial vendors are the length of time a potential supplier has been in business, the number of computer centers it has and their locations, procedures for keeping users up to date, sales volume, and other factors relating to stability and financial soundness.

Additional concerns in decision-making are as follows:

- Following the rule of "When in doubt, ask," consulting with an *objective* expert is a good policy. One day of expert analysis and recommendations can save time, effort, and expense in the long run.

- In evaluating computing services, consider your specific application needs—a scientific vs. a commercial computing environment, file handling and data storage requirements, size of programs to be processed, which computer language you need, system reliability, and response/turnaround time.

- Don't be hoodwinked by the glowing promises of marketing and publicity brochures or the persuasiveness of salesmen. Perform benchmark tests of various system features and performance on paper and in "live" mode until you have established which one or ones satisfy your specific requirements.

- Consider the ease with which the system can be used by the people who will actually operate it, whether they be librarians, secretaries, or students. Find out how much user training is required to use the system effectively, and whether the vendor provides adequate training.

- Closely examine and compare costs. Prices vary from vendor to vendor, machine to machine, and system to system. Important to understand and sometimes very misleading are the basic charge elements in on-line computer processing:
  - Terminal connect time—elapsed time from entry of user identification to telephone disconnection
  - Line charges—expressed in terms of elapsed time, and sometimes also in terms of characters transmitted
  - Computer time—time spent in actually executing program statements
  - Storage space—for programs and data, usually on disk backed up by tape
  - Printing costs—per-page charges for output produced on a high-speed line printer.

- When these charges are added up for your application, the costs will vary considerably from system to system. Sometimes those charges that you weren't aware of suddenly appear as "hidden costs." Make sure that you have a clear understanding of the entire picture!

SUMMARY

What do these technological advances mean for libraries? For the rest of the 1970s, it obviously won't make sense to develop software, duplicating what is available off the shelf at low cost. Instead, it may be cost-effective to slightly modify your manual procedures to align them with the processing of a packaged system. With the advances in communications, it does make sense to join an existing cooperative for computer-provided products and services. Not many libraries can afford to use MARC simply for their own card products or current awareness purposes. Why not throw away the many volumes of specialized abstracts and instead search them on-line using a time-sharing service? Turn-key systems using minicomputers may not be available at low cost for a while, but developments are worth watching.

In relating the '70s to the '80s, cable television as a technology now exists for a broad spectrum of specialized programming for the public. Libraries could share channels with other broadcasters and contribute those resources and services for which they are the source. There is a variety of excellent reading in this area. One by Brigitte Kenney and Frank Norwood[6] that is useful in encouraging librarians to get into the act appears in the July/August 1971 issue of *American Libraries.*

Major networks that provide computer services to the very large bibliographic files will emerge. It doesn't make sense economically to duplicate these locally because it's too expensive. Dial-access libraries, wherein a requester dials a number for a prerecorded audio response to a reference question, now exist in the medical field. It's just a matter of time before other professions get on this bandwagon. What I've been talking about are just a few of the trends as they are appearing. The technologies, networks, cooperatives, time-sharing services, packaged software, and, soon, turn-key systems are all out there ready to be used. You don't have to suddenly jump in and dabble in all these new areas, but you do need to know about them, keep up with the advances, and carefully select those that can support your clientele needs. I hope that a majority of libraries will: (1) rapidly become working parts of cooperatives that use network facilities and services—the cost justification is there today; (2) work toward supporting centralized or regional suppliers of these large-scale system services; (3) continue to influence standardization of information representation and exchange; and (4) assume the roles of vigorous centers that serve not as information repositories but as information disseminators and network agencies of exchange. If libraries and librarians don't—something and someone else will!!

DISCUSSION

Fran Spigai (Oregon State University): I think libraries have a unique problem in that they all need to have many packages and networks. I wondered if you saw any trend toward solving this problem by either vendors or libraries themselves. There doesn't seem to be too much standardization. You were talking about packages and networks information retrieval systems, among the different vendors that you have mentioned, people like SDC, Lockheed, etc. What do you see as a solution to the problem of standardization among packages for information retrieval systems that are being marketed, like ORBIT marketing through SDC, Lockheed DIALOG, etc.? They've each got different kinds of record formats, search strategies, protocols, etc.

Delanoy: That is a problem. If you just look at Lockheed and SDC, both profit-seeking companies, it's illegal to have a gentleman's agreement, such as "You put up that data base and I'll put up this one." The systems are highly competitive and they are very similar, and it gets down to the point of whether you would like to search with the television set or have colored lights flashing at you, the speed of response, etc. It's a horserace, and someone is going to win; maybe several people will win.

There is certainly enough room out there for the ten institutions and companies that are pushing ahead with information retrieval. We are all driving each other's prices down. I used to market the SDC information, and it was very painful. The user doesn't usually see the internal format for any of these systems. They all receive the tape in the same distribution format and then have a conversion program that converts it into their own internal gobbledegook. I don't think any of those systems that are offering retrieval services are at all transferable, and I don't think they are trying to be. There is no reason for them to want to be. With the decreasing costs in communications, nationwide networks are here; you can buy one of these systems at a cost of $10 to $50 an hour, and it is quite reasonable to do so.

David Weisbrod (Yale University Library): Although I think standardization is very important, I'd like to do battle with Fran just for a second right now. I think that in the area of interactive information retrieval systems we are probably in what Allen would call the "early iteration state," where there is a lot to be gained with various systems approaches being tried. Perhaps a good analogy would be the automobile industry where there is now, after fifty or sixty years of common use of automobiles, a trend to have standardized controls and standardized information panels. But this is well after the functions that are called for have been indentified and shaken down. I suspect that we are really too early in the game to do that for information retrieval systems.

Butler: As I understand it, there is a cooperative project among Chemical Abstracts Service, BIOSIS, and the American Physics Institute which is working toward a common output format for these things that would be analogous to MARC. It would not be a MARC format, but analogous in the sense that there would be a standard format.

Sue Martin (University of California, Berkeley): I just have a comment to make which relates to what Diana was talking about—proliferation of packages; the software packages and minicomputer systems that were coming on the market. It occurred to me that right now, for librarians, proliferation may very well be equal to confusion and I'm very glad that she went into more detail about the decision-making aspects. This is really a very important thing to consider when you are faced with the prospect of whether to buy or lease one of these systems, and there are so many of them that you can't make a decision, so perhaps you don't do anything at all.

Butler: I had a question put to me at the coffee break which was a good one and I don't see its author standing up there so I'll rephrase it to the first two speakers, if I can. It's a question of definition and confusion of terms regarding *transferability* of hardware, of software, of programs, of systems, as opposed to the interconnection and communication links between them. Allen, I think this came from your comment about the need to have the ability to communicate between different library networks, or automated library systems, and the question is: what's the relation between transferability of these things and communication ability between them, if they are not transferred?

Veaner: Well, I'll make a stab at that, if I can. I think I might have to lean on some of my fellow panelists for assistance. I think transferability is really not *one* thing; there are several levels to transferability. Perhaps the lowest level of transferability is shipping a program (some small computer program that does one thing) from one installation and running it on another installation. We are talking here probably about a batch program of some kind. I think an illustration of program transferability at a higher level than the simple one-shot program was in the experiment that was done at the University of Colorado to use a serials list program that had been developed elsewhere and run there. I don't recall the exact specifics, but the National Science Foundation sponsored a study to determine the feasibility of this five, six, or seven years ago. That's one level: the programming level.

I think another level would be at the subsystem level. Someone devises a circulation system that works well and it gets transferred in toto to another institution. Now here, I think we start getting into problems right away, and in both Diana's paper and in mine, I think there were allusions to the problems. If you want to take somebody else's subsystem for circulation or acquisitions or what have you, you will have to make changes in that system (which means programming changes), or you will have to adapt your manual procedures to the requirements of that system. If that package says that the circulation period for books is four weeks, you've got yourself a four-week circulation system. There is no way that system is going to make your charge-out period two weeks or two months or a quarter, or what have you, without somebody getting in there, just like a mechanic gets into the guts of your car and makes a change, and that's another level of transferability.

Moving beyond that, the total system or the multisubsystem transferability, which is a job that is so big that at least to my knowledge it hasn't been successfully done as yet. Now as far as the communication aspects are concerned, I think I would prefer to just reveal my ignorance and say that I should not answer this part of the question. Someone who is a communications expert really has to answer this question and I'm not that person, but we do have ample evidence from our experience with the telephone companies that companies with diverse equipment and different procedures and standards have been connected through a national telephone network. It can be done but requires software and hardware modifications. Diana, do you want to add on?

Delanoy: Something in the area of communications that is happening today is the Tymshare network I mentioned before. It's a commercial venture that uses some 40 little computers all over the country. They take telephone calls and switch those telephone calls to a variety of computer systems located in various places in the United States. With our search services, people call through Tymshare and give a little code and get us instead of Lockheed, whom other people are calling through the same network. Tymshare isn't making much money yet; this is the first year they have shown a profit, I believe. But they are on the upswing and it's a very successful network. There will be more of these as time goes on, but this is the first computer-controlled network of its kind and it does hook up to a variety of information retrieval systems.

Veaner: Maybe I can just add another comment on the telephone network, if I can. The reason that it's such a trivial task for you to direct-dial any point in the country is because the Bell System and its associates have done a tremendous amount of support work behind the scenes using switching computers and other devices which allow these diverse parts of the network to be automatically interconnected. What we need is something that will do this for bibliographic records.

Delanoy: We've got it. It just needs to be more economically feasible to use. Tymshare presently runs from $5–$15 an hour to use, which is quite reasonable. However, add the cost of the retrieval system, and you have a gigantic thing to support. AT&T is becoming competitive with Tymshare and its Digital Data Network, a separate network of leased lines for computer transmission. Other people are getting into the act; it should be like a gas war over the next few years in telecommunications, kind of exciting.

Butler: We should stop at this point with a note that there will be a session this evening on systems transfer. Jerry Pennington, who was scheduled to lead it, had a last-minute conflict, but John Kountz from California State University and Colleges will fill in. That's the place to continue this discussion; the session on on-line systems will also relate to some of these things. Dr. Matta, you've been standing there very patiently.

Seoud Matta (Pratt Institute of Technology): Just a question to Ms. Delanoy. The impression you left in your discussion of the minicomputer and the fact that they could be had for $3,000–$20,000 means that any small library can afford to automate; but in order to leave a balanced effect, I would like you, if at all possible, to talk about some of the limitations, even within one subsystem, and see how much these computers can handle, and the requirements in terms of software and planning, just hopefully to erase some of the effect that you may have left by that comment.

Delanoy: The $3,000–$20,000 price is misleading; that is just for the hardware. As I mentioned, some companies buy the hardware, develop the software, and then raise the final price. I can't really speak to minicomputers; they are smaller. With the increased miniaturization of circuits, decreasing cost of circuitry, they are getting much more powerful. All computer languages are supported. They can't handle the very large files, but these are peripheral device limitations, and sometimes size limitations rather than speed. With terminals in the home over the next thirty years, with the cost of computing going down as drastically as it is, minicomputers are a viable thing for libraries to look at. They are not a quarter of a million dollars. They are getting reasonably priced and I saw an ad in *Library Journal* a couple of months ago that had a minicomputer and a spread of cassette tapes with circulation, serials, and five or six other things. Someone is peddling it, and I'm not sure who it was. Minicomputers are going to be rapidly emerging.

Veaner: I don't know any more about it, except that Walter Curley at the Cleveland Public Library is using one of these packaged systems, furnished by CLSI, a New England firm. It uses a minicomputer. I don't know, maybe we can find out and discuss it during the open workshop.

Shoffner: I'm not sure whether this question has just been ruled out or not. It has been my impression that the total development costs for a minicomputer system are the same as for a large system, if you remove from the large system the overhead costs of the very major operating systems that are provided usually by the manufacturer itself. It would seem to me that this would mean that whereas many organizations with large systems may invest in their own development efforts if they are using large hardware systems, it's most unlikely to be the case when we begin to discuss minicomputers and the attempt to install them. Now, the question is to Allen, then: in your survey work did you come across any order-of-magnitude estimates on development costs as they have existed over the last five years, either with respect to the large-scale or the small-scale systems?

Veaner: I'd have to say no, I really didn't look into that specific point, but I agree with you on the general level of development costs, that it doesn't make that much difference whether you're using part of a big computer or a minicomputer. Any development work to be done, you would have to pay for through the nose in order to do it.

Pauline Atherton (Syracuse University): I'm going to go back to an earlier comment that I think I heard. It doesn't have to do with computer technology, it doesn't have to do with the availability of telecommunications, of systems like Tymshare, it has to do with the ultimate user/system interface.

If we are going to have a computer terminal in one out of a hundred homes in ten or fifteen years time, is that home going to have to have five or six user manuals available in order to get onto any data base that might be available from their own public library? In other words, that's the thing that concerns me. ASIS has a User/On-line Interface Special Interest Group; and some of us who have been in this game for a long time with on-line systems are very concerned that to go from SDC to Lockheed to something we might generate in our own library, we literally need a month's instruction before we can get through all the user/system-query language idiosyncracies. Now I heard Allen say that the thing that saved library automation development in the last five years was MARC. If we didn't have MARC we wouldn't have had a common data base format that would bring us as far as we are. I heard Diana say that if we sit still and wait (I think it was one time for a gas war and the next time a horse race), that we would see something come out of it that couldn't be touched right now by libraries. We just have to observe it. Sue says we are confused, therefore we won't make any decisions. I say: do we sit and wait until somebody decides what is going to be the ultimate user/system query language? Or do we as librarians who have had to sit back while encyclopedias were organized differently and we bought them and put them on the shelf, and various indexes were arranged in various ways, do we also sit by during this machine age in libraries and let the producers of the new information networks decide how long we'll use five different systems, with five different user manuals? Or do we get involved and try to come up with a common system-query language?

Butler: I don't think anybody on the panel wants to answer that comment; it's an excellent comment.

Delanoy: James Martin, who is a prolific writer in the computer field, has just written a book called *The Human Interface in Data Communications.* He says that the user is going to be driving the systems of the future. The systems are going to have to be configured to meet his idiosyncratic specialized human-type requirements, and that's probably true. I know that at least three or four of the on-line systems that are available today have been painstakingly tuned to be human-engineered and to be viably usable. I know that at least one takes about a day to be curious about, another day to really use pretty well, and then in a week or so you are right on it. They don't necessarily take a couple of months to learn. They are being tuned to meet the needs of the people that are going to be operating them.

As far as terminals in the home, I hope that terminals in the home will be dialing up to the local libraries, the local "community information centers" that will be supplying them with their periodical printouts and cable TV. Those are the kinds of things that will be bypassing libraries if libraries don't get into the act now. I didn't say to sit around and wait.

Veaner: I think Pauline's points are very well taken and I would just like to add that in a sense we have been struggling with this problem but not calling it by that name for some time. It has taken the form of variant file organizations, various filing rules, and choices of entry, and things like that in the manual system. One almost never knows where to go into a file in a particular library—in the conventional card catalog, or even in the multitude of book catalogs produced both here and abroad. So this is not a storage problem to us, but I also agree with Diana that the future systems will be user-driven. The systems we have just gone through, over the past decade, at least, have had a lot of their characteristics determined by the limitations of the machine or the software, or the desires or wishes or whims or beliefs of the designers. Now I think we are mature enough and have enough experience to know that no successful system can be designed that doesn't start backwards. All good systems analysis starts backwards, at the end product—what does the user want to accomplish—and when you find *that* out, then you can jump back and start doing some systems design. But you don't start out with any ex cathedra statements about what the user wants or needs.

Butler: There is certainly some hope that the competition that is mentioned is going to make it easier but we are still faced with the multiplicity of user manuals.

Weisbrod: Returning to the earlier topic of intersystem communication versus system transferability, there was an important thing that didn't get said that I would like to say. Communications seems to have been interpreted by the panel as electronic instantaneous communication. That is not the only kind of communication. MARC is a communications format and, indeed in the library arena, is an extremely important functioning intersystem communication. The major difference between mere intersystem communication versus transferability is that in communication you limit the interfaces to a few critical points of contact rather than trying to pick up a complete Gestalt and transferring it into another institution.

Kountz: I think one of the things that appears to be implied in all of this is the ability to specify what is required, and I rather suspect that our growth curve or maturation here is to the point now where we can become quite sensitive to the users' requirements. These are areas where we as librarians had been somewhat derelict in the past; hence Pauline's encyclopedia analog and things of this nature. It is extremely important that we know what we want, especially with regard to automation. It is not a cheap game by a long sight, and I think the past five or perhaps ten years, which have been alluded to, are good representations of people not knowing exactly what they want, and not being capable of specifying and making the hard decisions to live with it long enough to see whether it works or not. Getting into production (and in large measure I'm going to suspect that you are watching here the struggle of individuals who are offering approaches), it's incumbent upon the individual who accepts those approaches to know what he wants, quite frankly.

Veaner: John, those are good comments. Knowing what one wants is very often tied to knowledge of what one has had over the past and this tends to color, even to obfuscate and defocus, not only what you really want, but what you may even need, and that's why I think we really can't find out what we want without going through some of this pain, this agony, doing it and realizing "Oh, gosh, that was awful, that was stupid, that was a bad mistake." I don't see how we can avoid it; if we knew exactly what we wanted, we'd be God, but none of us is God.

Shoffner: I did want to point out there is another phenomenon which is called death, which is an extremely good thing for change because it removes from the board the people who cannot modify their behavior and allows us to replace them with people who can. If one looks at the history of education here in the country, around the point of pre-World War II it looked as if the citizenry could add and subtract. At the present time they can multiply and divide. The supermarkets have trained them to do that. You know, a friend of mine used to buy a cigar after lunch: in fact they were 5 cents apiece, but he always bought them in quantity because it was a special bargain—4 for 25 cents. And he really did this for a couple of years before he realized it. So now people can multiply and divide.

There was a major change after World War II in the teaching of mathematics. It took many years, but everybody going through grade school from about 1960 on has been learning set theory or whatever you want to call it, modern algebra, and the result of this is that my kids understand retrieval of things in a way that most of you in this audience don't. Now my kids don't yet understand that they understand this because they don't have the application. But in fact there are really two different kinds of retrieval; one is straight boolean and the other is modification to provide numeric characterization, and that's all there is. And by the time we are writing these user manuals it's going to be very easy to communicate with one in one hundred people in this country. It may well be a matter of a selection as to who the people are who buy the terminals.

So I think that I agree with you, Pauline, very much, that there is a major problem here, but I would suggest that the major problem is in the training of the citizenry, rather than in the issue of standards as such, because once you have the power of that "understanding what's behind it," it's a fairly straightforward process to evaluate and select with respect to these and to learn to handle these systems.

Russ West (Torrance Public Library): After those remarks I'm not sure if I want to ask the question. I'd like to go back to another subject. If you have an in-house system at present and are forced by the obliteration of your present service bureau or your in-house hardware to seek a commercial venture, or commercial vendor, is your present system obsolete?

Delanoy: No.

West: It goes back to transfer of systems; please don't merely say "no," but amplify a little bit.

Delanoy: Well, the only thoughts I would have on that are that it doesn't make sense to install in-house these very large file bibliographic search systems that take many, many expensive disk-packs to get up there and a lot of computer energy to search. It does make sense to either go outside if you want to embellish your reference activities and have ERIC and NTIS and Chemical Abstracts and MARC and all the rest of them on-line. The only way you could possibly afford to do that would be to use a low-cost available service. You could not afford to either develop the retrieval system or hang on all those disk-packs that the files take up. It makes sense to pay for a terminal; what you pay for is a terminal from $80 to $300 a month, depending on how fancy you want your terminal to be. You pay the telecommunications cost, which now aren't telephone company maximum $29 an hour cost, but are $10 an hour average using Tymshare. It costs some $20 to $40 an hour to do interactive searching to get some six to twelve good searches accomplished retrospectively, through millions of records. That's significant in today's terminology; that's low cost.

Veaner: I can say "no" too, because I remember what Dan Melcher said at the Conference five years ago, which was: "Don't ever ask if it's possible to do anything by computer, because the answer is always yes."

West: The problem relates to a city department, a city data processing service, and the city government in its infinite wisdom is now going to declare it obsolete and remove it. You have developed all of your files throughout a five- or six-year period, you have developed your system, you have developed your programs. Now you must seek another vendor. All of that money that you have invested into the systems and into the programs. Are they obsolete, or can they be compatible with the vendor?

Butler: You've definitely got a specific situation that's a problem. Ralph had one comment and I do think we need to cut this off, unless there is one last question that somebody has to get in.

Shoffner: Obsolete and obsolescent: the way you phrased your question, I think the answer is "yes" rather than "no", and by definition. The point of an obsolete system is that it is no longer possible to run it economically as compared with a known alternative that you understand to the same level of risk. An obsolete system is the last stage after obsolescence. An obsolescent system is one that you would not choose to have if you didn't have it already. Now this is terribly important if we are going to be serious about the problems of economics and investment because a system has to have a useful life in order to pay itself back, and all of us all of the time are on varieties of obsolescent systems. But what we pray is that we do not *select* for installation an obsolescent system and what really sends shudders through us is the selection of an obsolete system.

Butler: We'll try and get that quote printed up for you as quickly as possible.

Butler: Several people have asked about the University of Nevada Serials System. Let me give you somewhat more complete information about it from an abstract issued by the library: "University Serial System is operated on the CDC 6400 located in Reno: Serials data are stored on magnetic tape and disk and include information from the Las Vegas and Reno Libraries, as well as other libraries within the State participating in union list of serials projects. Master package for each item includes information pertinent to that title, as submitted by the various libraries. Printouts are produced from the tapes. The system has recently been re-designed so that the serial files are available through direct interaction on teletype or CRT. Documentation is not public at this time." The people to contact are Bob Andrel, the head of technical services, who will be back here this evening hopefully with our print-outs, and Bob Allande, who is the serials librarian, who may also be here this evening. They will have the whole serials file up on-line during the week, although normally it's a batch system. They do the up-dates on-line, so they will have a little more to show than they do in normal everyday operation.

REFERENCES

[1] Louis Vagianos, "Libraries: Leviathanic Vagrants on a 'Titanic' Trip," *Library Journal* 98, no. 9:1449 (May 1, 1973).

[2] Kenneth E. Wylie, "Summary of Results GUIDE/IBM Study of Advanced Applications," *GUIDE International Corporation and IBM Data Processing Division, 1973*, pp. II/1-7.

[3] John R. Hilligass, "The Minicomputer—Getting It All Together," *Computer Decisions* (Jan. 1973), pp. 10-13.

[4] "The Minicomputer's Quiet Revolution," *EDP Analyzer* (Dec. 1972), p. 12.

[5] "Developments in Data Transmission," *EDP Analyzer* (Mar. 1973), p. 3.

[6] Brigitte L. Kenney and Frank W. Norwood, "CATV: Visual Library Service, *American Libraries* 2(no. 7):723-26 (July/Aug. 1971).

3

User Services: 1973 Applications Status

Lois M. Kershner

User services in libraries are those with which individual library patrons directly interact in their use of the library or library materials, or, as defined by this conference, user services are those which are neither cataloging nor acquisition services. Within this very broad structure, therefore, this paper will attempt to review, organize, and describe selected examples of automation applications in reference and circulation, with a brief comment on interlibrary loan, reserve book, and current periodical activities, and note several observations and trends in automation of these services in United States libraries.

CIRCULATION SERVICES

Since the 1967 paper on the state of the art of automated circulation systems, technology has proven that the desirable circulation operations can be handled successfully. Emphasis has changed from "what do we want and how can we do it," to "can we do what we want at an acceptable cost to my library," and "what decisions do we need to make about the functions we want to automate and those we don't want to automate?"

Circulation system requirements which are highly repetitive and individualistic have been met by multiple configurations of hardware and software capabilities throughout the country. Systems have been installed by individual libraries, and by multiple-library systems. Development has taken place generally within the limited political boundary of single-library authority. There has not been very much emphasis on cooperation outside political units.

Circulation Librarian, University of Pennsylvania Libraries

Circulation system transfer at the program code level has not taken place outside these political limits as is documented by the Inforonics Survey of automated library systems prepared for the California State University and Colleges. But system transfer at the functional level has been accomplished as is evidenced by the similarities of final design of the IBM System/7 installations at American University, Georgetown University, and the University of Pennsylvania, and also many systems using Colorado Instruments equipment.

Technology has now demonstrated the handling of circulation control functions:

- Charge, discharge, renew all types of library materials for varying loan periods
- Recall and hold desired items; validate requestor upon charge
- Validate patrons or detect restricted patrons
- Provide current book status—location, borrower, date due, times renewed
- Display fees and permit entry of payments
- Produce notices, statistical, and bibliographic management reports.

Applications of circulation systems can be dependent on hardware capabilities and are most commonly categorized as off-line batch processing, on-line direct terminal connection, or minicomputer distributed logic systems. The minicomputer system offers control over library circulation in a highly cost-effective manner when compared with on-line operation. Whether or not the minicomputer system is preferred to off-line processing must depend on the individual library.

CIRCULATION APPLICATIONS

Off-line

The majority of pre-1970 system development was off-line batch processing which has economic advantage but which is not up to date; file maintenance usually is accomplished daily, and cannot detect book reservations or delinquent borrowers. However, the majority of operating systems in 1973 are still off-line.

In off-line systems, data are read into the computer by magnetic tape or punched cards with post-processing outputs being printed lists, printed cards, reports, and punch cards. Good examples of well-documented off-line systems are Lehigh University, Southern Illinois University, and the University of Missouri at Columbia Library, all using the IBM 357 Data Collection System. Since 1970, Colorado Instruments has installed about 50 systems in libraries, that can be considered off-line.

On-line machine-readable shelflist

The more recent systems are on-line for reasons of immediacy of on-line capabilities, decrease of on-line costs, and benefits derived, such as the detection of book reservations and delinquent borrowers. These systems are immediately up to date, a factor which requires continuous computer connection with the library and adequate computer storage. These requirements are reflected in the high cost which is the disadvantage of an on-line system.

Two types of on-line circulation systems characterize those currently operational in the United States today: that which utilizes the complete machine-readable shelflist file, requiring conversion of the shelflist; and that which utilizes a complete circulation transaction file, created as books circulate and may or may not be used as the basis for creation of machine-readable shelflist.

Notable on-line circulation systems are operational at Northwestern University, Illinois State Library, Eastern Illinois University, and Bell Telephone Laboratories—the BELLREL system. The most sophisticated system, the Ohio State University Library Circulation System (LCS), provides on-line real-time, remote entry circulation control for over 2.5 million volumes located in the main library and 23 departmental libraries. This is done through a network of IBM 2260 display stations and 2740 typewriter communication terminals connected to a System 370 computer via telephone line.

The emphasis of the LCS is patron needs and services. By telephone a library patron can learn whether a book is in the system, where it is located, and whether it is available. Also by telephone a patron can request that a book be charged to him and held at the library, mailed to his campus address, saved for him until available, or renewed. Certainly this does stress the user and user needs; Ohio State has made the decision to provide this service.

To permit this type of service, on-line files are stored in a 2319 disk storage. The Master file contains a shelflist of the entire collection and is accessible by call number; a main entry/title access file is accessible when the first few characters of the main entry/title or author's surname are known; the patron name and address file is accessible by patron ID number or name; the circulation/save file contains a record for each book in circulation; and the log file contains a record for each on-line circulation transaction.

When a patron requests a book, a circulation operator keys the first four characters of the main entry and the first five characters of the first significant word or words of the title. The response to this, displayed on the CRT terminal, is one line of data for each matching main entry-title in the master file listing line number, author, title and publication date. The feature of this technique is the display of all works of one author that are currently in the library's collection. By keying in the line number desired, a display of the item's entire master file record and circulation/ save record is produced. (By keying the charge command, patron ID number, and line number, a charge is entered.) A book may be charged at the circulation desk by keying in the call number on a 2260 or 2740 terminal along with the charge command and patron ID number. A 2740 terminal in the library owning the book automatically prints a paging slip listing call number, volume, copy, library location, patron ID number, author, title, and date due.

Without going into further details of the other functions, the LCS handles discharges, saves, snags, renewals, fine payments using procedures not unlike other on-line systems, and produces off-line the desired reports and notices. Operational results of LCS indicate in 1971–72, the first year of total operation of the system, a 16.9 percent circulation increase over the previous year as compared to 12.4 percent in 1970–71 and 1 percent prior to 1970. Ohio State believes that ease of access and current knowledge of circulation status will increase the flow of materials. It may also mean that some 'students are using more books now than they did when the campus was in an unrest situation. (I think we have noted, too, that there was a drop in circulation when campus activities were not particularly favorable to library use.)

On-line circulation transaction file

Contrasted to the on-line system utilizing the machine-readable shelf-list is the on-line system utilizing a complete circulation transaction file such as exists at the Northwestern University Library. For book charging, this system, like most other systems, accepts an 80-column punched book card and a punched plastic user identification badge which are inserted into an IBM 1030 terminal. A printer (IBM 1033) types a date due slip, complete with the book's call number and date due, which is the reader's authorization to take the book from the building. A unique feature of the system is the self-service charge of books at satellite terminals located on each of the library stack floors. Other circulation functions such as processing renewals, discharging, charging for nonstandard loan period, or charging to users without badges are performed at the circulation desk master terminal. This terminal accesses the general purpose file which contains record entries for all books not in their proper place on the shelves. Inquiry to this file, using an IBM 2740 typewriter terminal, is made by keying in the command code and partial call number of the book desired.

Like the Ohio State system, off-line processing is used for statistics and management reports.

Minicomputer systems

Recent interest in library circulation systems involves distributed logic computer systems, using what is commonly called a minicomputer. The basic structure of such a system consists of input and output devices (terminals, tapes, printers, etc.), the minicomputer (which contains the high-speed memory and controls and processes data input to it), peripheral mass storage devices (disks, tapes), and software which determine the operational flexibility of the mini.

With these combined features the advantages of off-line and on-line systems are provided:

- Access to recent circulation transactions possible by interrogation into the recent transaction file maintained by the mini
- Immediate detection of book reservations and validation of borrowers
- Avoidance of expense of continuous connect time and storage dedicated to the library
- On-line file search, for reserve collection circulation, or restricted borrower, may occur with no reliance on the main computer.

Some libraries currently using minicomputer systems are: Bucknell University using a disk-based PDP–8L in concert with a Sigma 7; American University, Georgetown University, and the University of Pennsylvania using IBM System/7 in concert with an IBM 370; University of Maryland using a Singer System 10 configuration; and Providence Public Library using a system designed by Computer Library Services, Inc.

The University of Pennsylvania Libraries cooperated with IBM in the development of the System/7 software which is now available for use by other libraries as an IBM Field Developed Program. The University of Pennsylvania system was operating in November 1972 in the main library with four 2791 input terminals and by February was operating in three departmental libraries, each having one 2791 input terminal. Each 2791 terminal has an operator guidance panel with a matrix of 36 messages giving step-by-step instructions for each of the 24 transactions provided by the terminal. This particular feature facilitates the training of terminal operators, who in an academic library are usually student assistants working for only a few hours at a time. The terminal also provides entry and display of numeric data for keying of ID numbers, display of numeric codes for number of reserves placed on a book, library and reason code for restricted patron, or display of ID badge punches.

Book-charging requires use of a punched book card and punched ID badge. When these are entered in the terminal they are checked against the on-line call number and restricted files located on the disk resident in the System/7. If a match is made the transaction is aborted. All transaction activity is recorded on the System/7 disk transaction file. At the close of the working day and after processing, a library clerk types on an IBM 5028 typewriter terminal the simple instructions for transmission of data to the computer center or receipt of updated files from the computer. These transmission connections with the main computer take approximately 30 minutes daily and constitute the only on-line connection with the computer.

Library batch processing programs provide complete listings of the issue file, patron notices, punched cards, statistics and management reports, and the daily circulation listing which is the public record of books not in the card-catalog assigned locations.

PRESENT DEVELOPMENTS IN CIRCULATION SYSTEMS

There are two developments of systems utilizing minicomputers of which libraries planning circulation systems should be aware. One is the installation of a total circulation system by a firm which has procured equipment from another manufacturer and prepares a software package for each library installation. The Providence Public Library has an acquisition and circulation system prepared by CLSI, who designed the system specifications to meet the individual library requirements, installed the hardware, wrote the software, and implemented the system. This type of service is designed for the library which does not have or does not wish to establish a specialized systems staff, yet wishes to obtain the benefit of highly skilled technical expertise.

The second development is the introduction to the United States of the bar encoded label for optical scanning. The Plessey Company circulation system which has been in use in academic and public libraries for over a year in the United Kingdom and Sweden is now being marketed in the United States by Checkpoint, which will use Villanova as a study site for the system. As its most significant feature, the Checkpoint System utilizes an infrared optical scanning head configured as a "Library Pen" which reads a bar coded label of nine to fourteen characters in length. The pressure-sensitized label is interpreted optically for human reading; however, with the limited label length, the number must be linked with the actual call number and book identification by separate computer index files.

MANAGEMENT REPORTS

Circulation systems, whether off-line, on-line, or distributed logic systems, have proven the usefulness of the management reports produced from the manipulation of data captured in log or history files. Peter Simmons of the University of British Columbia reports on the application of circulation loan records to book selection. The University of Pennsylvania notes the integration of a special collection into the main library stacks after indication that the greatest usage was by. the generalist rather than the specialist. The University of Missouri (Columbia) Library reports studying the length of journal circulation by borrower status with resulting recommendations for a policy change. Georgetown University is studying the transaction activity by terminal location and time of day in efforts to provide adequate and effective staffing. The BELLREL system produces a semiannual Zero-Loan list including a summary of previous loans to help in decisions in weeding. Many libraries produce lost or missing item lists used for replacement or withdrawal, and lists of items in high demand for purchase of additional copies.

With the demonstration of high levels of achievement, circulation system emphasis in the future should be directed toward:

- Study of cost-effectiveness of circulation operations
- Study of user responses to circulation activities
- Less development effort by individual libraries and more application of systems offered by library oriented commercial firms
- Greater use of management reports

- Greater integration of circulation systems with processing systems
- Changes in line responsibility of circulation departments from public services to processing services.

CONVERSION AND COST

Any library desiring to automate a circulation system must tackle the task of conversion, either keypunching book cards or converting the entire shelflist; it can be done either before or after the book circulates. It can be done gradually or all at once. Every library must make its own decision concerning its conversion strategy.

Major costs in circulation systems have been development costs of new systems, and I think this is reflected largely in the personnel budget. I have not tried to compare any of the circulation systems in terms of cost because it is most difficult to do this in meaningful terms, and it must be done in explicit detail in order to be meaningful. What is feasible for Ohio State with over 1 million charges per year is not necessarily feasible or justifiable for our library with only 200 thousand charges per year. Each library must establish for itself what is affordable, based on transaction loads and the degree of service it wishes to provide. Generally, the ongoing costs can be equated with the number of transactions. The greater the number of transactions, the less it costs per transaction. Generally, libraries implementing automated circulation services have not reduced their personnel costs, but they have maintained the existing personnel to perform additional functions.

REFERENCE SERVICES

Catalogs, collections, and COM

Much has been accomplished and much has been reported by libraries engaged in computer-assisted production of book catalogs, listings of special holdings, and data base dissemination services. These reference services directly demonstrate the usefulness of the computer to the user and particularly lend themselves to cooperation among libraries.

Book Catalogs by Maurice F. Tauber and Hilda Feinberg (Scarecrow, 1971) is a good state-of-the-art review of these catalogs, reviewing the virtues, costs, problems, and prospects in 1971. Since then, the move to computer-produced catalogs has become a reality, with one splendid example being the *New York Public Library Dictionary Catalog of the Research Libraries*. Generated from a magnetic tape-oriented batch-processing system which accepts MARC II records and original cataloging, the catalog is a bound cumulative volume issued annually with monthly cumulative supplements of authors, titles, and subjects representing books and book-like materials added to the collection since January 1, 1971.

A catalog much smaller in size but broader in geographic coverage is the recently published Washington State Library Network's *Resource Directory*, representing a pilot project listing English monographs purchased by six county and regional libraries and the Washington State Library from July 1 through September 30, 1972. This system too generates entries from MARC records and records input locally by Washington Library Network libraries.

The attractiveness of computer-produced listings has induced some reference areas to utilize on-line technology to produce holdings lists of limited collections. Two examples of such projects are *The Newspapers in Philadelphia Area Libraries*, an arrangement by title, city, and state of origin of United States newspapers or city and county for foreign newspapers, and *Scientific Serials Currently Acquired by The Libraries of the University of Pennsylvania and Drexel Institute of Technology*, arranged alphabetically by title, listing library holdings, and giving appropriate bibliographic data and call number. The computer production benefits of flexibility of format and manipulation of data into various format configurations which is evident in printed listings and catalogs is more noticeable when applied to microform output. Computer-Output-Microform, COM, has advantages of being inexpensive, compact, quickly produced and easily duplicated.

The three new campuses of the University of Texas at San Antonio, Dallas, and Permian Basin plan a COM catalog on microfiche, an application particularly feasible for a new campus with no existing catalog to convert. The fiche catalog, designed to supplement a planned on-line catalog, is now used at University of Texas, Permian Basin.

The *Louisiana Numerical Register* (LNR), issued by the Louisiana Library Association, is a new computer output microfiche union catalog in Louisiana containing locations for 1,100,000 volumes in 21 Louisiana libraries. The catalog, listing LC card number and the libraries holding a copy but no bibliographic data, is particularly useful as a location tool for interlibrary loan.

In the report sector, COM is used by the University of Michigan for its circulation transaction listing, because it is less expensive and more easily distributable than a printed listing. The Los Angeles Public Library Automated Library Technical Services (ALTS) project reports successful results with COM production of their Patron Directory, Delinquent Report, Book History Report, and Systems Open Order Report, with savings of $82,000 during the first year of the COM application.

INFORMATION DISSEMINATION SERVICES

Data base information dissemination services go back to about the mid-sixties with the simultaneous occurrence of increasing availability of computer facilities, application of computers in computer-aided type-setting generating machine-readable data bases, expansion of world litera-ture, and increased cost of labor and labor intensive services. Since then a variety of machine-readable data bases, which have been proven technically feasible, have become available, largely from industry and society-based or discipline-oriented organizations. A majority of the tapes available are produced in the science area: CA Condensates (Chemical Abstracts), CAIN (Cataloging and Indexing System file issued by the National Agriculture Library), COMPENDEX (Computerized Engineering Index), BA PREVIEWS (files distributed by Biosciences Information Service), to name a few.

Two approaches to remote use of tape are the formulation of questions submitted to data bases such as MEDLARS or the 1970 Census tape and the formulation of a user profile for search of current bibliographic data bases.

Selective Dissemination of Information (SDI) services or current awareness services using bibliographic data bases are being developed by organizations generally known as Information Dissemination Centers representing industry, government, and educational institutions. These centers, of which thirty now exist under the membership rules of Association of Scientific Information Dissemination Centers (ASIDIC), process two or more machine-readable data bases produced by outside suppliers. Centers serve statewide or regional areas and cooperate in extending resources to other centers. To illustrate this point, the Uni-versity of Georgia has provided links to the University of Pittsburgh, Lehigh, Georgia Tech, and Georgia State University who may enter profiles through CRT terminals and receive search results via remote printers. Also, the University of Georgia, which does retrospective as well as current searches for the 27 colleges and universities in Georgia, extends the retrospective searches to the University of Florida, which in turn provides use of its 1970 Census tapes to Georgia.

Emerging recently is the on-line search of data bases held by an agency, an example being the National Library of Medicine MEDLINE service extended to 200 medical libraries in the country. The MEDLINE data base, listing 2400 journal articles indexed in *Index Medicus* since 1970, is accessed by a trained information specialist through a CRT keyboard terminal. Up to 30 citations meeting the parameters of the profile request are displayed on the terminal and may be directed to a connecting typewriter printer. Up to 300 additional citations, should they be desired, may be remotely printed for later delivery, usually two days, to the library.

This service is user-oriented as is evident by the approach taken in many of the medical libraries handling MEDLINE. The doctor or researcher may place a search request by phone, mail, or in person by giving an outline of requirements, specifying subject matter, stating points to be excluded, defining terms with special meanings, indicating language and time period to be covered. Typically the requester is notified later in the day to pick up the printout of search citations.

The library information specialist, following the MEDLINE worksheet, constructs the search statement to be entered on the terminal during the on-line search of the MEDLINE data base. The average on-line search takes 14 minutes, but the librarian may spend from as little as five to as much as 45 minutes per profile.

Should the requester wish a monthly current awareness search of his request, the librarian saves the request and worksheets for use in searching the SDILINE which indexes the current month of *Index Medicus* and is on-line about two weeks prior to the printed issue. Or, by searching the COMPFILE, which is on-line once a week, search of approximately 1000 additional journals in foreign languages, dentistry, and nursing may be obtained. Should the request warrant it, the librarian may also do a personal literature search of journals not covered in the data bases.

The University of Pennsylvania Medical School Library reports an enthusiastic response to MEDLINE, performing 600 searches in 6 months since installation of MEDLINE, compared with 175 literature search requests the previous 12 months.

Studies done by libraries utilizing SDI services generally maintain usefulness of data obtained by SDI for researchers using the service. However, provision of the data base inquiry service by individual libraries has recognizable impact on its operations and staff: time and effort must be actively applied to inform and sell potential users of the service; some persons on the staff must be knowledgeable in the subject literature, the scope and characteristics of the data base, and the user needs in order to construct adequate search profiles; since the projects are usually not self-supporting and tapes are generally procured by lease agreement, the center or the library must pay for the service or shift all or part payment to the user.

Several consequences of SDI services for libraries are yet to be determined: the cost/benefit ratio for the library and for the user; the effect of service on borrowing loads, acquisition policies, and organizational structure; accessibility of high demand items; and followup procedures for provision of materials not locally owned.

All of these factors will be objects of much study because of their direct relationship to the growing responsibility of the individual library to prove in economic terms its abilities to meet and satisfy user needs.

PERIODICALS, RESERVE, AND INTERLIBRARY LOAN SERVICES

Five years ago in the institute on state-of-the-art of automated circulation systems, the routing of periodical issues was cited as one of eight major circulation operations feasible with a computer. The generation of computer data bases of staff routing choices and printing of routing slips is now being done, particularly in special libraries. However, the operation is more commonly a facet of serials control systems.

A rather unusual approach to periodical routing and processing is PEARL, Periodical Automation Rand (Corp.) Library, which produces monthly routing labels, stubs, and corresponding batch of prepunched claims cards for issues expected to arrive that month. The stubs and their routing labels with title code, title, volume, issue, part number, etc., are matched against incoming items. When a match is made, the routing label is pulled and affixed to the issue. At the end of the month, the claims cards corresponding to the stubs with routing labels remaining are pulled and input into the program. In other words, PEARL is a negative reporting system merging check-in and routing steps in one operation.

Few advances have been made in automating reserve book collections, existing largely in academic libraries, since the reporting in 1969 of the Columbia University Computer Based System for Reserve Activities. Reserve processing activities have benefited from advances made in circulation or cataloging system development, particularly where the shelflist is converted to a machine-readable format permitting access by main entry. Holdings lists by author, call number, course number, and professor have been produced by many libraries. Studies of reserve book usage, or lack of usage, have resulted in reporting to faculty of book usage and removal of books from reserve. One approach taken at the University of British Columbia is the return of books to the stacks when the books fail to meet the minimum circulation quota in the annual circulating reporting.

Benefits have been gained too for interlibrary loan processes where bibliographic verification and locations can be obtained by on-line query of MARC record data bases, such as provided with OCLC terminals installed for cataloging activity. Where book catalogs are distributed throughout a library system, such as the Illinois State Automated Microfilm Catalog, ILL requests are based on verification of up-to-date listings of holdings. And where circulation is automated, established procedures handle book loan as well as provide statistical loan activity for type of material and status of borrower. However, the on-line direct request for materials is still handled by TWX.

CONCLUSION

In user services, emphasis in the future will be placed on automation of reference services which are being influenced by recent developments of on-line technology and production of bibliographic data bases. The emergence of information dissemination centers indicates the trend toward network cooperation in reference services and recognizes the growing awareness of the library obligation to its users.

Circulation systems have now been developed by individual libraries to perform all the desirable circulation functions. Unlike reference service, circulation service to date has not had much relationship to overall library network cooperation. Future development of circulation will be adaptation of circulation systems to emerging technology and greater emphasis on management evaluation for better service to library users.

DISCUSSION:

Unidentified speaker: Can you tell us what problems a library may encounter in using a minicomputer system? What are some of the limitations?

Kershner: For one thing, if the mini is down, you may or may not have backup for it. You might have to rely on a manual backup.

Unidentified speaker: I guess I was thinking partly of file limitations. You reach a certain size collection and then you can't function easily on a mini.

Kershner: It is difficult to generalize about the technical restrictions of file size in the minicomputers. They do vary, and you can extend them. I think there comes a point where it's not economical to put large files on a minicomputer. There are times when you want to be on-line, for instance, if you are talking about large files of patrons, or entire circulation files.

Brian Aveney (Richard Abel Co.): I worked on that system with Lois. One very clear disadvantage, or at least limitation, of it is that the minicomputer system is not capable in general of storing your entire file, so you don't have an on-line environment. In general, with a minicomputer you are storing a subset of the file that you think is important to have to interrogate. You have a list of bad borrowers you want to match against, or a list of books that people are waiting for, you can afford to keep these up to date. There isn't anything that approaches the kind of immediate availability of absolutely up-to-date information that you have in the Ohio State system. I think it's pretty inherent in all minicomputer systems; I don't know of any that have the software available and the support available to support really good-size files.

Bob Harris (University of Colorado): I just want to suggest that if you have a minicomputer system, and it breaks down, you shouldn't be going manual; you should be relying on your magnetic tape backup, for a minicomputer.

Kershner: If you have it.

Harris: If you have it, yes; you probably should. You mentioned the lack of cooperation with circulation systems. I would suggest that the main barrier is the registration. A book is a book is a book, so you can catalog and cooperate. A user is not a user if he's from another school. The Colorado academic libraries all cooperate in terms of policy, but when it comes down to being practical, we have to register the students from another school. It's a matter of having an address, is what it boils down to; in that particular case, a centralized address file would make a difference. That's probably the one biggest barrier to that type of cooperation.

Kershner: I agree.

Butler: I have one comment on the benefits of mini- or maxi-computers, or anything else. Probably the biggest consideration as to what's an advantage is what is available to you, more than anything else. To a certain extent we can talk about it for a while, but you're going to have to go back and use what's available, or what you can rent or buy.

Helena Rivoire (Bucknell): We have some cooperation with the libraries in the ACLCP consortium. We lend them all books on the same basis as our own students, and enter them into our patron file. They have to apply for patron cards, but our system will permit any kind of borrower that we want. They are in our system.

Joe Ryus (University of California, Berkeley): You know that there have been worries, or even an actual situation I was involved in, with wanting to know who had borrowed which books. With a manual system, you usually have to get rid of your records simply because of space. With a machine system, there is the potential of keeping records to the point of "big brother is watching." Have you built anything into your present system to avoid this, or have there been any reactions from the borrowers about the fact that they can be traced?

Kershner: I think that the individual library must take one stand that they will not reveal information of this type to outside agencies, even if they do wish to maintain particular identification of borrowers for use studies. I think the library must refuse to issue this information.

Maurice (Mitch) Freedman (Hennepin County Library): Ohio State University's circulation system automatically erases borrower identification when a given period of time has elapsed after the material has been returned. It's impossible for anyone, after a certain period of time, to find out what particular human being took what book out of Ohio State University. You can in other words build it into a system.

Joe Gantner (SUNY, Stony Brook): We did have a problem with our computerized system. We had printouts—it's a batch system—and made them available throughout the library, with the borrowers identified by Social Security number. Those were available all through the library, and we did have a bad reaction from students and faculty because we were making these records available. The problem was that the FBI was looking at a student's records and had his Social Security number, and was able to tell what books he borrowed by just using our printouts for the last year. We had to discontinue making the printouts available until we could wipe out the Social Security number after each borrowing record, at least those printouts made available to the public.

Susan Hess (University of Wisconsin, Milwaukee): I have two questions to ask, although I don't know if you want to go into this much detail. I was wondering if you have any statistics on the time it takes to complete a transaction. You said you have to go through a step-by-step process on the minicomputer, and if you have to wait for these various lights to come on when you're going through the transaction, do you have specific timing statistics, or would you like to comment at least on what you think would be proper for that? Also I was wondering if you have any statistics on the cost per transaction on the System/7?

Kershner: First question. The response of the instruction is immediate, so just as fast as the operator can enter the patron ID badge, he can then enter the book card. It takes three to four seconds. We've not done any specific study. It goes just as fast as the operator moves his hands, so there's not been any necessity to study that. We have not done any study on cost per transaction. I guess we intend to do that, but you have to define so clearly what costs you include in trying to determine how many cents it costs you to charge a book that I think it's very difficult to come up with a figure that another library would find meaningful.

Aveney: We did a real crude cost analysis one time, trying to pick up about everything we could, including personnel costs. We found that if we took every cost that we could identify, and divided by the actual number of charges (excluding renewals, excluding any other transactions), we came out on the order of 50 cents. We started bringing in other transactions (excluding discharges and those things that were simply repetitive of a charge) we started coming down to 25 cents. Now there are some things that are awfully hard to cost, like how much cost can be assigned to a reservation that you're holding for someone; how can you assign costs to bad-borrower checking and things. We are also influenced very much by the fact that we have a clerical union and we pay very nice salaries for clerical employees in the circulation department, and the major portion of our costs in the circulation system are salaries to clerical employees. The actual machine costs and hardware costs are considerably less than half the cost of running the system, even when you start including paper and all of your consumables. An awful lot of that is hard to transfer to any other situation, because your hardware is going to cost the same, no matter how much you use it. So a person who gets a lot of transactions through comes up with this marvelous figure, and a person who gets few transactions comes up with a horrendous figure, so you really have to say: "If I'm going to identify unit costs, how many units do I have and then what can I tolerate and what kind of system can I get for that sort of money?"

Hess: You mentioned that for the discharges you can just process those through right away, one after another. Do you have a capability on there that you can lock something in, say a discharge transaction, and then just put in the book card?

Kershner: We just feed the book cards through, that is correct.

Butler: This evening we will have, I think, people from most of the big systems that were discussed in Lois's talk. Specifically, I was just talking to someone from the University of Maryland, which looks like a particularly interesting application.

Kountz: I was wondering, Lois, did you indicate or did I interpret correctly, where circulation would be a locally implemented application, that you didn't see this as something wherein cooperation could occur?

Kershner: I believe by the nature of circulation services that they can be handled very effectively at the local level and that you don't necessarily need to have central data bases of many universities and many shelflists in order to handle circulation. I know that you are hoping to develop a system for the California State University and Colleges. Will you have central data bases and central patron files—every time you charge a book you'll go directly into the central base? Or will it be local?

Kountz: No, what I was indicating was that insofar as circulation is really a form of local inventory control, and if you have inventory visibility on a broader base, then it's probably one of the most powerful tools available to us as a means by which to field what we're now calling interlibrary loan. In other words, it will preclude the hit-or-miss requirement to try to determine who has which book and whether it's in circulation when your loan goes into that particular library. If you have inventory visibility on a broad base, and local circulation linking mechanically into that, I think a lot of our problems are closer to solution than they would be without that.

Butler: I think that point of view represents John being involved as a systems person for a number of libraries, and Lois's comment means that it's easier to work on a local library basis unless you've got an overall system like that.

4   Cataloging Systems: 1973 Applications Status

Maurice Freedman

I would like to begin with some acknowledgments. I am not a systems librarian, and I haven't had any hands-on experience with machines. Brian Aveney, John Knapp, and Mike Malinconico are the people who have helped educate me to the realities of hardware. I am especially indebted to Jerry Pennington, the assistant director of technical services at the Hennepin County Library and systems analyst there, without whom nothing would have worked.

INTRODUCTION

The applications status of cataloging in 1973 is quite difficult to characterize by such evaluative terms as good, bad, healthy, hopeful, of concern—it is all of these things, depending upon one's focus. In the past five years there have been substantial controversy and concern primarily over the automation of cataloging, perhaps the most complex area to have been seriously dealt with by systems librarians. In some respects it is ironic that the successes finally started to come at the same time the most reactionary statements were being made. An effort will be made to identify some genuine causes of concern, highlight some of the successes, and point out some of the directions which must be pursued. Let us begin with some general observations.

Perhaps the most obvious thing which can be said is that the days of the massive megabuck research enterprises are, for practical purposes, behind us. The granting agencies just do not have the same quantities of funds available to subsidize research they had in the past. As well, some of the research results, obtained at great expense, need not be duplicated

Director of Technical Services, Hennepin (Minnesota) County Library System and are available to all. In the next five years, it will in the main take hard dollars directly from library budgets to pay for cooperative or individual efforts. The past five years of automation have seen some substantial commitments: the Stanford University Libraries through the period of 1967–74 will have spent grant money totalling close to $3 million on the BALLOTS-SPIRES projects, while The New York Public Library, unable to obtain outside funding, spent about $4 million of its own funds to develop its various bibliographical control systems, just to mention a couple of the heavyweights. Finding the money in the period of 1973–78 will take cost justification, greater ingenuity, tenacity and, in all probability, more self-sacrifice than was needed in the past quinquennium.

Continuing in a general mode, that the computer can be successfully used as an aid to the cataloging enterprise has been amply demonstrated. There have been spectacular successes proving that the computer technology is viable and that the blue sky is no longer beyond the horizon but is unquestionably the atmosphere we live in and breathe.

Notably the Ohio College Library Center has performed the feat of providing an on-line cataloging service for libraries all over Ohio and elsewhere for libraries in Georgia, Pennsylvania, and New Hampshire. Printing the catalog cards at night for titles requested or cataloged during the day, OCLC is providing a cataloging service apparently less expensive and far more efficient than its participants can provide for themselves. By the summer of 1973, an OCLC user will have on-line access to a data base of almost 1 million records.

Although less glamorous but at least as significant, The New York Public Library has solved the problem of authority control through the use of computer technology, thereby permitting automatic control of all subject and name authority terms which occur within bibliographic records, as well as cross-references, scope notes, and other authority components intrinsic to professional cataloging. Those of you who have received letters from LC explaining why changing such terms as "aeroplanes" to "airplanes" is too expensive should appreciate that a single input transaction to NYPL's authority control system can accomplish this kind of change, thereby liberating catalogers from the tin can of outmoded terminology to which they've been tied.

The most widely felt effects of the successful application of computers to cataloging are on two cataloging products: the book catalog and the catalog card. Commercially and noncommercially produced book catalogs can be found in such disparate places as Ventura, California, and New York City. Such commercial organizations as Science Press and Autographics and, in the noncommercial sphere, the Orange County

(California) Library and The New York Public Library have produced book catalogs based on a variety of principles, but all are successfully continuing to produce them with regularity. Critics of automation should take note that in 1968 it was doubtful whether a book catalog exceeding 100,000 titles was possible. The extraordinary *University of California Union Catalog Supplement, 1963–67* with its 750,000 titles and 2.6 million entries demonstrates the current capability, not potential, of the digital computer. Book catalogs can provide the least expensive, most efficient, and most timely means of access to a library's resources for the greatest number of people.

Line-printed catalog cards produced by commercial or institutional organizations are found in libraries all over the country. Such competing firms as Josten's Catalog Card Corporation, Richard Abel, and Baker and Taylor are using line printers to provide card sets to their customers, who at least in part are incidentally purchasing books they job. The University of Chicago, an original MARC Project participant, has printed over 2 million cards for its own use, and OCLC, a nonprofit corporation, has a fantastic card service. It is clear that computer-generated cards have enjoyed a sound fiscal and technological base.

In 1973, the question is entirely decided that the computer can be used as a tool to facilitate, change, and improve cataloging techniques, processes, and services. In 1968, this point might have been questioned: hardware considerations notwithstanding, few could have envisioned an Ohio College Library Center or the *University of California Union Catalog Supplement* as realizable in the next five years. This is not to say that there have been large expenditures for automation projects where the results have been primarily of research value, or where the results are not yet known.

MARC AND LC SERVICES

From the present perspective, the work titled *The MARC II Format*, written by Library of Congress staff members Henriette Avram, John Knapp (now with Richard Abel Co.), and Lucia Rather, has been the single most important event in the automation of cataloging. With a national standard for the communication of bibliographical information, the feasibility of sharing machine-readable cataloging data was permanently established. Since the inception of the MARC distribution service in 1968, the Library of Congress has disseminated over 300,000 machine-readable English language monographic cataloging records in the MARC

II format, and currently includes Cataloging-in-Publication data. The direct or indirect dependence of the library community on the MARC service is a reality. Whether libraries get card sets from commercial firms, OCLC, or their own line printer (as the University of Chicago and Columbia University do), or whether they, as does the New York Public Library's 82-library branch system, get the majority of their catalog records from MARC for ultimate reproduction in a book catalog, the MARC service is a necessary component in the nation's cataloging service. Information Design, Incorporated, founded a searching and cataloging system which was originally based wholly on the MARC service. This firm takes the MARC tapes, extracts and builds title, series, and card number indexes from them; it also has a Videocomp create a set of card images on microfilm from which the full set of overprinted cards can be made.

The Library of Congress, which has supplied a variety of bibliographic services to the country since 1901 when it began to distribute catalog cards, has not yet been able to accomplish all of the things in automation it set out to do. In the 1960s, LC, through its various services, found it increasingly difficult to meet the mushrooming demands of the national library community. The demand for catalog cards created an opportunity for card services that commercial suppliers leaped to fill, and prompted LC's Processing Department to recognize that automation was the best approach toward solving LC's card distribution problem. LC's inability to fully implement Phase II and produce cards on demand for all records in machine-readable data has had several serious implications for the library community, some negative and some positive.

MARC service subscribers have been seriously affected. The Library of Congress has had the capability since September 1971 of producing photocomposed catalog cards of such quality that the average person could not distinguish them from the hot-type printed card. But LC is still following a procedure which, to the outsider not fully appreciative of LC's internal complexities and problems, seems paradoxical: the English monograph records are first printed using the traditional printing methods, and only after the finished printed card is approved by a proof editor does the conversion to a MARC record begin. It is painfully clear to both LC and the MARC subscribers that eliminating the hot-type process would probably eliminate the delay in distributing MARC records.

Furthermore, libraries purchasing either card sets or card services, such as NEWS sets or proof slips, either pay for the service with extended waits or, in the case of the NEWS set, with exorbitant costs. The NEWS-set service currently costs about $325 per month, and provides a library or firm with the English-language catalog card output of LC on a daily basis, and on the average two to three weeks in advance of the offset-produced proof-slip service, which includes most of LC's foreign-language and English-language cataloging. The success of Phase II of the Card Division's system is a necessary precondition for lowering costs and hastening deliveries of the basic card services.

On the positive side, resourcefulness, ingenuity, and creativity characterized the library community's response to the problem. In the commercial area, Information Dynamics Corporation and Information Design, Incorporated, have adapted LC catalog products by combining microfilm and computer technology to provide services which enabled libraries through micrographics to produce their own catalog cards. In addition they include multiple indexes to the LC cataloging data, thus instantaneously improving over the manual single-access files of proof slips maintained by individual libraries, and eliminating the file maintenance problems associated with traditional card files.

As mentioned earlier, the high-speed line printer has come into full bloom as a card-printing device. Through consultation with the American Library Association, IBM implemented the ALA print train which contains not only upper- and lowercase characters, but also all the diacriticals required by various Roman alphabet languages. In 1973 computer-generated catalog cards are routinely produced in all sectors of the nation, the MARC records being a chief input source for these suppliers.

At least one commercial book catalog firm, Science Press, is using MARC records as an input source, primarily for public libraries. The Oklahoma State Department of Libraries' MARC-O service provides a MARC-based SDI service, as well as listings of MARC records. The Richard Abel Company and the University of Massachusetts use the MARC service as a source for providing catalog cards and processed books. Still other uses of the MARC service are made. Some of these will be considered in the discussion which follows.

SOME PROJECTS OF SPECIAL SIGNIFICANCE

The Ohio College Library Center has developed the nation's best card delivery service. One of the major preconditions for OCLC was the difficulty and cost to libraries in the sixties to adequately solve their basic cataloging problems: namely, how can the library quickly and cheaply get authoritative cataloging information? A nonprofit corporation was formed in Columbus, Ohio, and as of June 1972, OCLC had 49 members in Ohio plus experimental users at Dartmouth College, the Cooperative College Library Center in Atlanta, Georgia, the Pittsburgh Regional Library Center, and the Union Library Catalog of Pennsylvania with terminals at Drexel, Temple, and Pennsylvania Universities. OCLC under the direction of Frederick Kilgour and backed by massive funding from the State of Ohio and grant sources established a center for computer-based technical services which up to the present has produced arranged catalog card sets on demand and on-line union catalog information.

Although already described in a variety of places, some of the basic features of the system are worth examining and evaluating. OCLC has a Xerox Sigma 5 computer with its own operating system, an OCLC-developed system specially geared to efficiently deliver products and services. The OCLC file of cataloging data has been growing at the rate of 30,000 titles per month and is creating one of OCLC's severest problems: the capability to store new cataloging data. In the first third of 1973, the secondary memory will be doubled, but it will be only adequate for one year. It will also be difficult for OCLC to take advantage of any new equipment manufactured by other firms because of the dual problems of rewriting the portions of the operating system required to operate the new devices, and building the black boxes required to physically connect them to the Sigma 5. (OCLC once solved similar problems when it successfully connected the IBM 1403 N-1 line printer to the Sigma 5.)

OCLC has two input streams to its cataloging data base. The first is the input of MARC records from LC. The other is the addition of original cataloging on-line when no MARC record exists for the given title. Two separate problems arise from this. It is difficult to control the quality of the record which is originally input. The first record of a title becomes the permanent one with the exception that a MARC record can bump an originally cataloged one. Furthermore any user may decide to add a record, irrespective of the existence in the file of a record describing the same bibliographical entity, thus further exacerbating the storage problem. Unfortunately, the sharing of cataloging of various levels of quality has real limitations and problems. Another way of characterizing this deficiency in the system is to note that there is no built-in control of name and subject authorities entering the system via OCLC input.

The other problem, which has a tremendous impact on cost, is the storage of all LC MARC records on-line. As of January 1973, 62 percent of the LC MARC records had never been used by OCLC members. Of course, it is difficult to know which 38 percent will be used, but some alternatives might be sought. (The University of Chicago announced at one time that it found that it was only practical to save the current six months of LC MARC output. Further discussion of this problem will occur later).

There are three methods of access to the data base of OCLC: by LC card number, author-title (the first three letters of the author's surname and first three letters of the first significant word of the title), and title only (by keying in the first three letters of the title's first significant word and the first letters of the next three words of the title). The implementation of this truncated search method is one of the great accomplishments of OCLC. In a matter of seconds the entire data base is searched and the record (or records), if found, displayed.

Among other things which happen each evening, in Columbus, Ohio, catalog card sets are printed in a single arrangement for all of the records for which a given library requested cards. During the day holdings records are instantly created for each institution cataloging a given record. So OCLC is truly creating a powerful on-line Ohio union catalog, as well as an excellent card service. And at least two networks have plans to replicate OCLC. In 1968 most librarians were not really believing this would be possible.

The other major MARC-based on-line system is BALLOTS (Bibliographic Automation of Large Library Operations using a Timesharing System), a project which began in 1967 at the Stanford University Libraries. The coordination of two Stanford automation projects, BALLOTS and SPIRES (Stanford Public Information Retrieval System) has allowed the BALLOTS system to extensively use and incorporate several features of the SPIRES management and searching software. BALLOTS-MARC is the first of eleven modules of a comprehensive BALLOTS system to be fully implemented by the end of 1974. (This discussion, as with OCLC, is restricted primarily to that which is operational. Since I've been here, I've been informed that module 2, a process information file, is operational; module 3, which includes a file of permanently cataloged records, is going to be operational next week). BALLOTS-MARC offers its sole user at this time, Stanford University, neither authority control nor a large data base. But it does provide a fantastic search capability. It presently contains only a small portion of the LC-MARC data base and provisions for original input will come in subsequent modules. BALLOTS-MARC is used both in the acquisitions and processing modes, as well as in cataloging. When a MARC record is found, BALLOTS-MARC has the capability of producing a purchase order, a vendor invoice, seven possible different file slips, two book labels, and an average of ten different catalog cards. The BALLOTS-MARC capability is particularly effective in the area of information retrieval. The search method is interactive and negotiable. There is on-line access by virtually any form of, or combination of, name(s); by one or more title words; or by combinations of name and title words; and by LC card number. If more than one title meets the search request, then the number of titles meeting it is displayed. The user then has the options of either expanding or decreasing the information in the search request, or displaying each individual citation. This ability to readily manipulate the search request is unprecedented in the use of searching general library catalog files. It is questionable whether other automated cataloging systems will in the near future be able to afford to duplicate Stanford's search capability on a large file.

An interesting sidelight of the Stanford research was its conclusion that capturing diacriticals in machine-readable form and displaying them on CRTs was not cost-effective. Research libraries which regard these marks as an absolute necessity might ponder Stanford's results.

The other automation projects which should be discussed in some detail in a 1973 review are the New York Public Library bibliographical system, the *University of California Union Catalog Supplement*, and the Hennepin County Library book catalog project. Each of these is especially significant for different reasons.

The New York Public Library's automation effort produced the first wholly computer-controlled bibliographical control system. NYPL was forced to automate because of the deteriorating condition of its card catalog and the continuing increase in the cost of manually maintaining the catalog. The NYPL system currently has as its major features: a provision for MARC input and original input, maintenance capability, authority control, sophisticated sorting and filing capability, and the power to regularly produce a photocomposition driver tape for printing book catalogs. The three basic files the NYPL system maintains are: (1) an authority file of names, subjects, series, and conventional and uniform titles, which includes the filing form of all authorities as well as catalogers' notes, cross-references, and other such information one normally associates with manual authority files; (2) a bibliographical file of records in a MARC-like format which contains the full catalog record with MARC tags, indicators, and subfield codes, and also pointers from each authority term to the control number of that term on the authority file; and (3) the MARC service data base, which is periodically searched as LC card number queries are made of it.

One of the refinements of the NYPL authority control system is the automatic authority search performed for all new entries added to the file. It works as follows: all new terms are passed against the existing authority file and either are identical or not identical to terms on the file. If identical, the term is automatically accepted. If it matches a cross-reference, it automatically gets switched to the valid term. If not identical to a term or cross-reference, it is sent back to the cataloger for maintenance or approval. NYPL built in the feature of automatically accepting all authority terms entering the system from MARC records.

The system of bibliographical control NYPL has developed is the most comprehensive mechanized bibliographical control system in large scale at this time. This writer has seen printouts from a prototype authority control system which has operated at Richard Abel Company. It is understood that in the State of Washington the MECCA system has automatic authority features and that Science Press advertises automatic authority control with its MARC-based book catalog service.

In the process of developing its authority list, NYPL created an invaluable file of data which in either hard copy, machine-readable form, or microform can be an invaluable aid to catalogers around the country. It will continue to have such value until LC can make its authority information available.

NYPL has done extensive work in the area of automatic filing. Most filing forms are automatically generated, but provision is made for the insertion of special filing forms for which algorithms could not be utilized. For example, the Revolutionary and Civil Wars file automatically by date and not by spelling. (Altogether there are 54 chronological subdivisions automatically recognized). But, numbers in filing positions in titles have to have sorting forms manually inserted.

The NYPL bibliographical system's chief deficiency is that it is a batch system. There is the laborious process of sending proof copy back and forth to the computer, but this is true of all batch input systems which, of course, cannot provide for interactive cataloging.

The *University of California Union Catalog Supplement, 1963–1967* (also known as UCUCS) represents a notably different strategy of library automation. Ralph Shoffner, Project Director, Institute of Library Research (ILR), University of California, Berkeley (and now with Richard Abel Co.), developed a strategy which had as its target the conversion of a catalog card into a machine-readable record with the MARC II structure, but with less specificity than required by MARC for catalog records. For printing purposes, the *Supplement*, a book catalog, did not need to distinguish personal name main entries from corporate or other name main entries; hence all nontitle main entries were assigned the MARC tag 100, which normally is used only for personal name main entries. Other such simplifications were introduced with the additional consideration that an error rate of one error in each five entries would be permissible. It was the ILR concept that machine methods could be introduced at subsequent dates for the purpose of refining MARC tagging and coding, and automatically identifying and/or correcting errors. The obvious corollary is that the initial product has many more errors than one associates with research library catalog products, and the data base is of less value to potential customers than if it had been more precisely tagged.

Underlying the project was the demand that costs be kept at a minimum. The concept of automatic field recognition (AFR) was introduced as the tool for the conversion of 750,000 titles comprising the catalog. AFR, as implemented at Berkeley, bypassed the batch input process which usually begins with a human editor explicitly identifying and tagging the various data elements on a catalog card or work sheet. Instead of the computer having the incoming information properly labeled, AFR automatically tagged and coded the data elements by identifying certain cataloging elements defined as constants. For this to work, the input operator had to follow certain conventions (e.g., always begin with the call number), but then did type directly from the catalog card. The Berkeley AFR program, although far cruder than the one developed at LC for the RECON project, did allow for a cheap conversion of a catalog record to the MARC II format with codes and delimiters sufficiently specific for the production of the UCUCS catalog. (The RECON project at LC utilized a format recognition program geared to produce a pure and precise MARC II record. RECON tested the feasibility of the REtrospective CONversion of existing catalog records, working directly from the cards for a relatively small number of titles. LC has no immediate plans for a large-scale retrospective conversion.)

In addition, a maintenance program called FIX was developed which had the dual characteristic of allowing one to change something as specific as a single character within a given subfield or as general as deleting an entire field or record, and then building a new MARC record. Sort keys were then built for all of the filing fields and a tape (actually several tapes) was produced which ultimately drove a Videocomp to photocompose the page masters.

Looking at UCUCS itself, one will find a host of typos and problems. On the other hand, it is inconceivable that a clean catalog could have been created in the short period of time for the relatively low cost: 750,000 titles, 42,000 pages, 47 volumes, and 250 class-A bound sets cost a total of 1.25 million dollars, or $1.16 per title. The machine-readable data base generated in the process should prove to be of value to other libraries or commercial firms despite its condition. UCUCS's usefulness as an acquisitions and cataloging tool for the various University of California libraries is obvious, and assuredly should manifest itself at some point in the literature.

Previously mentioned was the fact that NYPL had expended $4 million for research and development. The Institute of Library Research of course expended a significant amount of money on research and development, as well. But the Hennepin County Library (HCL), a public library serving suburban Minneapolis residents, developed an automation program predicated on the transferability of software and the universality of the MARC record. Unable to allocate substantial amounts of money for research and development, HCL negotiated the transfer of the ILR software. Implementing and modifying AFR and FIX to meet local cataloging requirements, Hennepin converted its shelflist of approximately 85,000 titles to the MARC II format. Having budgeted $1.50 per title, just for the conversion, but spending considerably less, HCL, using FIX, tried to create a clean data base. (Several years ago, Richard De Gennaro had published an article in *Library Trends* saying that the price of getting a clean MARC record was $1.50. You will recall that the University of California had a catalog of 750,000 titles for $1.16 per record.) Controlling the flow of printouts was one of the biggest problems. The printouts for each record and the various pages of corrections ran into the hundreds of thousands of pages, which had to be stored, retrieved, and replaced on an orderly basis. This problem in part has been solved by dumping all approved records on upper- and lowercase COM microfiche, thus obviating the need to refer back to the hard copy. The other major problem was the fact that HCL's production deadline of a June 1972 book catalog seemed like an impossibility because the remaining ILR programs for sort-key generation and printing had not yet been fully tested and debugged. This of course made transfer to Minnesota wholly impractical. With one full-time programmer and one systems analyst, HCL had to wait. In the meantime, the New York Public Library was in the process of announcing the publication of its *Research Libraries* and *Mid-Manhattan Library* book catalogs and the successful implementation of its bibliographic control systems.

Through a series of negotiations, NYPL agreed to make minor modifications to its software to enable it to accept an HCL/ILR/MARC record and thus produce the Videocomp driver tape for printing the 2,800 page catalog. For the first edition of the Hennepin County Library Catalog, NYPL actually processed about 80,000 records through its system. In the process, HCL, using the NYPL authority file, and incidentally getting the benefit of all matches, cross-references, scope notes, etc., was able to clean up many of its variations in entry with simple authority transaction. (This was a key element; we are a suburban library that has evolved from a very small library. The procedures involved over a period of thirty years were almost infinite in variety.) The resulting catalog of course would not have been possible working through the ILR system. On the other hand, passing 80,000 records through the system at once with little time for review because the publication deadline had already passed had at least two negative effects: (1) many filing and authority errors did get through, and (2) a minor error occurred in the call number field (any call number over 12 characters in length was converted to fiction).

At present, the Hennepin County Library is in the process of transferring the entire NYPL system as it is constituted for NYPL's branch libraries to Minnesota. HCL's current plans are to use the MARC input portion of the NYPL system, but to continue to create MARC records through AFR and FIX for original cataloging rather than the more complex and expensive input utilized by NYPL. This should, once accomplished, establish the transferability of entire complex computer systems and interrelatedness of large systems through the MARC format. In reality this task is proving tougher than anticipated. Hennepin County will have to add a second programmer to concentrate entirely on the transfer. Lastly, because of the remote processing, the supplements are taking far too long to produce.

In terms of its originality, the HCL project introduced little that was new—basically it used the products of other original library automation efforts. Its willingness to use and modify the software developed elsewhere will enable HCL to have the capability of the New York Public Library's system and the Institute of Library Research system without the concomitant development costs.

It should be noted that the Institute of Library Research and the New York Public Library both gave their software to the Hennepin County Library without a fee. The chief implication of successful software transfer is that a library with access to a computer and a small but qualified systems staff can, in principle, use and maintain a system developed at great expense, but by comparison require only minor expenditures of staff and money to operate. It seems to this observer that from a cost standpoint this is certainly one of the most practical approaches libraries embarking on automation programs can consider. One critical concept implicit in this is accepting the wheel someone else has invented, albeit less perfect than the one you could not afford to invent on your own. Another is that library institutions other than ILR and the New York Public Library try to be as generous and cooperative in terms of software exchange. The third concept is the power of MARC, without which none of this could have been possible.

In the area of practicality, note must be taken of the automation program of the University of Massachusetts Library processing center. A complete technical services system was developed which includes on-line order input and computer generated catalog kits. The University of Massachusetts system has few of the refinements and subtleties of the Ohio College Library Center, the New York Public Library, or BALLOTS; on the other hand it purchases and delivers to participating Massachusetts colleges the book selected by the college with a set of ready-to-file cards, a book pocket, and appropriate labels for a cost of $1. Established strictly as a processing operation, the simplicity of the University of Massachusetts system offers a most inexpensive processing service to its many member academic libraries.

Computer-output microfilm (COM), a magnetic tape-to-film process utilizing a cathode ray tube (CRT), will have an ever-increasing impact on library automation. COM catalogs have been created in such disparate places as El Centro Junior College, Dallas, Texas, and Tulsa Junior College, Tulsa, Oklahoma. Each of these libraries took its machine-readable cataloging records in magnetic tape form and had a COM service bureau convert those data into microfilm and microfiche, respectively.

The most exciting application of the microform technology to cataloging is at the Georgia Institute of Technology's project LENDS. The library's card catalog was filmed, using traditional microfilming methods, and converted to microfiche. New cataloging data was captured in machine-readable form and published in a COM microfiche format supplement. The supplement is periodically replaced with a newer cumulative supplement. Altogether Georgia Tech currently has 50 copies of its main card catalog and its most recent cumulative supplement available throughout its processing areas, in various department libraries and offices, and even at a remote campus. The net effect of this project is the successful and inexpensive access it provides to Tech's collections. This use of microfiche is the cheapest method yet of breaking away from the location of the centralized library catalog without losing the valuable information it holds.

In relation to COM, another far more sophisticated device has been alluded to several times, the electronic photocomposition device. Videocomp, Fototronic, and Photon are brand names for the devices which at high speed set the cold type for the LC Phase II catalog and card plates, the Information Design microfilm, and the page masters for most of the book catalogs being printed these days. The per-page cost of these typesetting devices has plummeted in the past few years. One can now have a book catalog of graphic art quality, as opposed to line printer quality, without incurring excessive costs.

SUMMARY AND CONCLUSION

Let us review what has been discussed up to this point. Several general points were made at the outset asserting that the use of the computer technology in the last five years demonstrated its viability and usefulness when applied to catalog processes and products. Line-printer cards and computer-generated book catalogs can be found all over America. It is entirely beyond question that computers can be used for cost-effective cataloging processes. As well, the various systems discussed demonstrate that for practical purposes the technology imposes few constraints: both on-line and batch systems have been found useful and operative. The chief cost problems seem to be associated with the effort to provide on-line access to huge quantities of data, the requirements of ultrasophisticated search capabilities, and the difficulties of getting clean data using batch input methods. We have noted that it is possible to transfer complex programs; and that a field recognition program geared toward producing a generalized MARC record is capable of minimizing the cost of creating a MARC record.

The national dependence on the Library of Congress' success in automating its technical processes was also emphasized. Automation efforts around the country are critically dependent on LC's ability to provide prompt machine-readable cataloging records and will be measurably enriched when LC successfully implements its plans for the distribution of MARC name and subject authority data. Through the New York Public Library's success in the area of authority file development and control, it is clear that at least the technology is already available for this process.

The Institute of Library Research's publication of the LC subject supplements in a cumulative edition has been of great value. Nonetheless it is still distressing to note that the cut-off date for data for the most recent edition of the LC list of Subject Headings was June 1964.

It is difficult to predict the next five years. Clearly there will be more and more automation of cataloging: more institutions will be engaging in it, and more will be receiving products of such efforts. I will close with my hopes for the future.

I hope that the success of OCLC is not converted into an OCLC replication movement which will cut off the development of alternative network systems. Such other systems should include at least one which begins its implementation with some form of rigorous bibliographical control built into its initial stage, and one which would attempt to utilize standard operating systems and standard programming languages. Certainly this latter goal, if successful, should contribute substantially to the successful transfer and maintenance of the system.

In a lighter vein, I hope that the LC card number will continue to be used by LC and other American libraries for identifying catalog records. Invented at the turn of the century to identify printed catalog cards, and having successfully withstood and repulsed the future shock of the check digit, the LC card number appears to be the principle form of access to even the most sophisticated data base systems of today.

I hope that a central data bank will be created, preferably under LC's control, to which all networks can have on-line access for titles which their member libraries do not have holdings. Obviously the burden of an individual network's carrying large numbers of titles not held by its members is costly, and should not be necessary.

I hope that the next five years see far greater utilization of the same software in different libraries. Libraries not subsumed by networks can have a high quality system with a limited expenditure. As well, all libraries should try to be as cooperative and generous as the New York Public Library and the University of California have been.

I hope that automation librarians investigate the possible application of the COM technology. COM is cheap to produce and cheaper to duplicate; it is easy to use; and it has a fast turnaround time.

I hope that systems librarians will neither have to waste their time defending library automation in the future, nor, at the same time, make outrageous claims or promises. There was altogether too much of the latter in the 1960s and of the former at the outset of the 1970s. The sequence is not coincidental. (I might add that I was a little distressed this morning to hear hierarchical notions invoked regarding systems analysts and programmers, who might in some way be "better and smarter than librarians," intrinsically finding solutions that librarians couldn't find. I had hoped that we were beyond putting down librarians for not being systems people.)

I hope that the Library of Congress will be able to expeditiously deliver the products and services which it has promised and which the library community so desperately needs. It should also be recognized that until LC *does* meet the library community's needs, libraries must more aggressively and openly make these needs felt, as well as cooperatively develop realistic alternatives.

And toward that end, I hope that all of the libraries, institutions, and businesses creating data bases make as a major order of business the development of a program which can convert their internal record into a MARC II record. This seems to be the real key to shared cataloging.

Finally, I thank you for giving me your attention for so long a time. My last hope is that this talk has been of some value.

DISCUSSION

Butler: Thanks very much, Mitch. That was a lot of material in a short period of time. We'll take questions from the floor for a few minutes, and we'll start the open forum later.

Bill Larsen (North Suburban Library System): Mitch, you mentioned the problem that you had with your supplements. You have also mentioned the potential of COM. Have you considered putting out your supplements in COM?

Freedman: Yes, I think there's a long way to go with taking COM microfiche and putting them out for general public use. We are using COM internally, for staff, but I have some doubts about the technology in terms of display devices, storage and access and retrieval of fiche in a public library situation. The problem isn't the speed of turnaround and printing. The problem is that we're sending material to New York; they run it through one part of their system; it comes back to us; we have to edit it and send it back again to run; and every time there's a hang-up, we've got a week in the mail. That's the primary reason the supplements have been slow in coming.

Judith Hopkins: Since any library which automates its procedures tends to automate in terms of its existing procedures and when it considers its future needs, I'd be interested to know, in line with your use of software developed by other libraries, what changes in cataloging procedures were required at Hennepin County? Do you feel these changes were beneficial to your cataloging in general, or made because of the adoption of the software but didn't improve your cataloging?

Freedman: No changes at all were necessary to our cataloging in terms of the conversion to a MARC record. We started with a unit record card which had already been in existence in our shelflist, and as far as what we're doing right now, we're using unit record cards for MARC cataloging procedures. [I think it's like a red herring, though, because we're following the Anglo-American Cataloging Rules, using the LC List of Subject Headings, and the manual procedures used in taking the intellectual cataloging record to the application of those rules and putting it on some kind of hard-form document for an input operator are lower level in terms of significance, I think, than had we not been following standard cataloging rules. With the NYPL system, the authority control file has actually helped our cataloging. We've had a variety of authorities, and we adopted the position that we would not recatalog the whole collection. A public library turns over in five to ten years anyway, with the exception of basic reference works. It has helped us without our having to make major changes. When we install the NYPL system, it is my hope that our catalogers will interact with it and write out transactions to change authorities on the file. This all required new procedures, not necessarily changes in present operations. They are doing authority work every time they catalog a book.

Mary Kay Daniels (Card Division, Library of Congress): I would like to state that LC *is* trying to help you, Mitch, as well as all our subscribers throughout the library world. I have quite a few comments that I would like to make, because I felt there were some statements that do need elaboration.

Insofar as the card distribution service is concerned, MARC titles are indeed made available on demand, in effect. Some of them *are* handled through inventory but on a demand basis; in fact, this demand is handled on a daily basis. Every order that we receive, if it is available in a card format generated from a MARC record prior to being printed through the Government Printing Office, is made available to our subscribers through that method first. Whichever card is ready first, that's the card that is received.

Freedman: Isn't it true that if the MARC record has not been received, the record is pulled out of the original linotype stock?

Daniels: Yes. If what you are alluding to is that there are two job streams going on at the moment for processing new card copy for English language materials, you are right. This is primarily occurring for one, and only one, reason at this time: because the printing and cutting capabilities within the Card Division that are linked to the photocomposed card copy cannot handle the volume that will be induced by the requirement for providing new card copy for these titles. It is expected that this equipment will be available in the Division by December 1973.

At that time these two job streams should no longer exist. As of now, all newly cataloged film copy and sheet map materials are not going through this duplicative process. They are going directly through photocomposition, and your depository cards, your NEWS set cards, are photocomposed cards.

Then you also mentioned the time involved in getting bibliographic materials, and I thought I would like to bring your attention to some of the current timings. The rates of turnaround have increased dramatically in the last four years, as most of our subscribers, I think, would readily admit. At present we are on a seven-day turnaround time for cards which are in inventory, and this covers about 75 to 80 percent of the titles that we receive. Interestingly enough, 50 percent of these receipts are in MARC, which shows you something of the volume of how MARC is helping us, as well as everyone else. Insofar as reprinting, anything that's in MARC we can now do on a one-day turnaround basis, using this photocomposition and offset printing of these titles by Card Division staff. Anything that's not in MARC, that therefore must be reprinted for inventory through GPO, is now on a five-day turnaround. Really, any longer timings that may occur are normally caused by orders falling into the category of preassigned card numbers for which cataloging has not been completed, into the category of reprinting cards via Copyflo for titles not in MARC that are not maintained in inventory, or into the category of orders requiring a search by author and title to determine the card number for a title prior to an order being filled.

Freedman: I welcome LC getting back into it, because I think the LC card with its authoritative data is superior to the lineprinter card.

Daniels: You also talked about some of the relative timings involved in procuring various types of cards that are available. I'd like to point out that I don't think you can say that one type of card is consistently two or three weeks behind or ahead of another type of card. The distribution of all of these types of cards is built on cycles, and the only thing you can positively predict is the sequence in which these cycles start. Anything along the line can interrupt an individual card within an individual cycle, or an entire cycle. The normal sequence of the cycle is that after all of the new copy is printed, depository set cards are pulled, are alphabetized by title, and should be the first type of card mailed out. But, concurrent with alphabetizing of the depository cards, there is the pulling of cards for NEWS sets; so that this cycle is started immediately after the first step of the depository card set cycle. For those of you who might not be familiar with the term, "NEWS set" is used to designate English-language monograph titles. Then, proof sheet copy, which is really no longer a proof copy but is actually an offset copy of the printed card, is usually the third category of materials sent out. So, in terms of 1-2-3, it's normally depository–NEWS set–proof sheet. I've often seen in the literature various studies of the timeliness of proof sheets vs. MARC tapes, but really that is not the most valid comparison of LC data going out in a card image vs. a tape record form.

There is one other thing that perhaps is not widely known and that should be more widely known. The Card Division is now really the sole subscriber to the MARC Services. In essence, we get all the tapes produced by the MARC Development Office. We are doing the cumulation, selection, and copying necessary for the MARC subscribers. As a part of this process we are attempting to overcome some of the problems that deal with duplicate LC card numbers, particularly as you get into having more than one interactive data base, such as serials and books, where you might wish to recatalog a monograph as a serial, and you would want to delete it from one data base and add it to another. Unless carefully managed, a MARC subscriber getting two tapes on the same day with this type of information might well be misled.

Butler: Mary Kay, that has been very helpful. Mitch mentioned briefly, in passing, feeling the necessity for the completion of Phase II and didn't really explain Phase II. Maybe you could summarize? What are the remaining steps?

Daniels: Perhaps we should look at Phase II the way initially announced, the way presently in operation, and the way it should be or will be in the immediate future. Initially, the grand concept was that all the titles would be in machine-readable form, everything would be handled on demand, and would be prepared like clockwork. However, everything is *not* in machine-readable form, nor is there enough time in a 24-hour day to produce all titles on demand in individual sets, given the current configuration of equipment. As a result there have been reevaluations of what is the best way to handle all the card copy we do handle. Consequently, we now have two new copy card distribution systems, as I noted before, and four card reproduction systems: (1) offset printing in GPO of cards not in MARC, (2) photocomposition and offset printing within the Card Division of titles in MARC (except that modified records are not printed for distribution through photocomposition, but are printed for distribution through the GPO branch, in order that the complete information that appears on LC's Official Catalog card may be given). Both of these first two reproduction systems are for "popular" titles, that is, for titles which the Card Division maintains in inventory. Other titles, whether in MARC or not, are considered "nonpopular" and are not maintained in inventory but are reprinted on a demand basis. To provide a little further background on this practice of popular vs. nonpopular titles, we based this split of inventory vs. demand items on ordering statistics we have maintained in the automated card procedure since 1969. So we now have approximately four-and-one-half years of data. Once a year, usually in the fall, we realign what is in inventory based on these statistics. We are presently using the algorithm that if a card has not been ordered three or more times over a period of two years, we delete it from inventory. If a card has been ordered four or more times over a period of one year, and is not already in inventory, it is added to inventory. The two remaining card reproduction systems used thus cover the redistribution of nonpopular items by: (3) photocomposition and offset printing within the Card Division of titles in MARC that are not maintained in inventory, and (4) the photographing of a master record card, and printing of Copyflo cards for titles not in MARC that are not maintained in inventory.

As to where we are going in the immediate future, the most pressing concern is increasing the amount of equipment on hand needed to process the new copy printing requests for all records being entered into MARC. We can now do all the integral parts of Phase II, including generating new copy, reprint copy and demand copy. Insofar as new copy, we can produce not only the unit card used for depository sets and individual card orders, but also overprinted cards for LC's official and public catalogs. We can also produce all the book catalog format cards required for those catalogs which are produced manually, including main entry, subject heading, added entry, see reference and added entry in reference formats. In December of this year we do expect that we will have the additional equipment, and all the MARC that can be processed through the system, will be processed through the system.

Freedman: For those of you who want to know more about LC's automation program, there's an excellent article in the Spring 1972 issue of *LRTS*, which covers all phases of what LC is doing, what they promise to do, with the deadlines.

Daniels: I'd like to make just one more comment. We have talked briefly about subject headings and book catalogs. In May of this year the Card Division was given the go-ahead to actually use our film data base to produce the film book catalog. Right behind that, we will also be responsible for doing the subject headings' 8th edition.

Bruce Warren (Autographics): I don't mean this to be a loaded question, but once you've successfully transferred software from ILR and NYPL to the computer center at Hennepin, do you perceive any operational, political, perhaps communication problems, with Hennepin itself being responsible for the production of the book catalogs, especially in the supplement area?

Freedman: Do I see any problems internally for doing it?

Warren: Right.

Freedman: The only problem is, we have to do it. That's all. We do it or we don't do it, and making it work is what we've lived with since we started. We started with a dependence on ILR, and ILR, like most other automation projects in this world, wasn't proceeding on the time basis that it had planned. We were stuck waiting for the rest of the software, and we were just lucky that NYPL had a system that produced a book catalog and that took a MARC record, so we were able to match up with them. We had to make it work; we could have gone to a commercial firm as well, which we would have done, too. The commercial firms are now using MARC input to their systems, and that's the real key. It's freedom for the client as well as for the vendor. The vendor will have lower input costs, but the client should have the sense to require a MARC tape back from the vendor so it's not tied to the internal processing format of a given book catalog vendor. It can take its tape and go elsewhere if it has a chance for better service or better price, but it's liberating for both of them.

Unidentified speaker: Is the computer a part of the Hennepin County Library System itself?

Freedman: In October, Hennepin County is installing a two megabyte device. Right now it has one megabyte; we've never had any problem getting time or adequate core for anything we wanted to do.

Margaret Williamson (University of Houston): In the NYPL authority file, do they also contain and generate all cross-references needed?

Freedman: Let me put it this way: their authority file controls authorities. Their catalogs have input, either from the LC List of Subject Headings or authority work or original subject headings. Whatever they have on there, where our terms went in and got a match, either a match to a cross-reference or to the valid term, we got everything associated with that authority term from NYPL. We got scope notes that are unparalleled in public libraries, like the NYPL scope note on Indonesia. It's a paragraph about the history of the country, etc. It's powerful, and I've been urging the NYPL people to make it available, not necessarily for profit, but at least on some kind of basis for libraries around the country to utilize. I should have pointed out that it's LC subject headings-based; it's not as though they're doing original subject cataloging.

William McGrath (University of Southwestern Louisiana): I want to respond to your response to the question earlier on COM. I'm not sure of the context of your reply; I think it was to the effect that COM was not yet a feasible medium in public libraries?

Freedman: We use it in Hennepin County Library all over our system. I see some user limitations of the current way we store the microfiche and the current devices that are being used.

McGrath: Were you referring to library users, then?

Freedman: Yes, that's all. We have 23 libraries in our system, so I think at some point we'll try doing something experimentally.

McGrath: But you are using it throughout the 23-library system?

Freedman: Every one of our branches gets on a weekly basis a listing of everything on order and everything that's been ordered through our automated acquisition system, by author and by title. Everything that has ever been ordered is listed biweekly, and those lists are invaluable. In effect, they are putting money back in our pockets, because they give systemwide information at a given location.

McGrath: In your earlier response I thought I detected a skeptical tone, but what you're saying now is more encouraging.

Freedman: I prefer microfiche to microfilm, but the one thing that computer output microfilm gives that COMfiche doesn't give is that you can take a reel of film and encase it, and essentially make it public. El Centro Junior College has COM readers available to its public, and it's very easy and simple to use: one entry at a time, one hundred entries at a time, high speed searching, slow searching. With automatic retrieval microfiche, the cassettes I've seen don't impress me, at least in terms of public use.

Butler: I think the distinction there was between the use of COM by library staff and use of COM for public use, which are two very different things.

Harold Roth: You discussed the fact that some of the subject headings are essentially out of date, haven't been brought up to date.

Freedman: Also racist and sexist!

Roth: Forgetting the racist and sexist aspects, now, that's another problem, I'm concerned with the method of updating. Are there any arrangements in the system for input of updated subject headings as you go along without having to renegotiate the whole process?

Freedman: What do you mean by "update," Harold?

Roth: Suddenly a new subject heading is used which requires a change in everything else, or might require such a change. What arrangements do you have in your system to make that change?

Freedman: I'm not sure I understand your question, but let me try answering it. With the authority system that NYPL has, you can in principle make any changes you want; you can add in principle anything you want, as long as what you're adding does not conflict with what's already on the file. If it *does* conflict, then you have to do maintenance. That's basically it. There are many things in the LC subject headings, such as the terms for American Indians or Negroes, that we will not accept; we change the file. That's one of the problems with the system: it's very difficult to change an LC subject heading.

Roth: How do you negotiate that maintenance?

Freedman: We just fill out the appropriate authority transaction.

Roth: And you change everything that has the old term, to bring it up to date?

Freedman: Yes. A single transaction changes "Aeroplanes" to "Airplanes." If there are 400 bibliographic records on that file, one transaction will change it from the undesirable to the desirable, and those 400 records will be automatically updated and have the new term forced into them.

Unidentified speaker: I have some information that I received yesterday before coming over, and I thought that I would mention it because of your hope that OCLC would not be replicated around the nation.

Freedman: No, that wasn't accurate. I hoped that the replication of OCLC wouldn't prevent any other kinds of networks from being developed.

Unidentified speaker: That was my misunderstanding. However, for your information, in Texas, New Mexico, Oklahoma, and possibly Louisiana, there is a 98 percent chance that there will be a linkup to OCLC this fall, for the academic libraries involved. One particular group, the Inter-University Council of North Texas, is responsible; they have already committed the member libraries, and they have invited all the other libraries to join in with them.

Freedman: I want to indicate, on the OCLC matter, that I see a bandwagon going on, and I just don't want to see it snuff out any alternative possibilities. There's no perfection anywhere around, and I'd like to see at least one other try based on different premises.

BIBLIOGRAPHY

Abel, Richard & Co. *Card Catalog and Book Processing Services.* Portland, Ore.: Abel, 1973. (Information packet, including pricelists, flyers, and brochures.)

American Federation of Information Processing Societies (AFIPS). Information Systems Committee. *Interactive Bibliographic Search: The User/Computer Interface;* ed. by Donald E. Walker. (Proceedings of workshop, "The User Interface for Interactive Search of Bibliographic Data Bases," held in Palo Alto, Calif., Jan. 14–15, 1971.) Montvale, NJ: AFIPS Press, 1971. 311 p.

American Library Assn. Information Science and Automation Div. Preconference Institute on Library Automation, San Francisco, June 22–24, 1967. *Library Automation: A State of the Art Review; Papers Presented at the Preconference Institute on Library Automation...,* ed. by Stephen R. Salmon. Chicago: The Association, 1969.

Avedon, Don M. *Computer Output Microfilm.* 2d ed. NMA reference series no. 4; Silver Spring, Md: National Microfilm Assn., 1971. 232 p.

Avram, Henriette D. "Library Automation: A Balanced View," *Library Resources & Technical Services* 16, no. 1:11 (Winter 1972).

Avram, Henriette D., and others. *The MARC II Format; A Communications Format for Bibliographic Data.* Washington, DC: Information Systems Off., Library of Congress, 1968. 167 p. "Supplement One," 1968. 7 p.

Berman, Sanford. *Prejudices and Antipathies: A Tract on the LC Subject Headings Concerning People.* Metuchen, NJ: Scarecrow Pr., 1971. 249 p.

Byrum, John D., Jr. "Informational Report on Cataloging of Data Files." Revised, abridged version of address delivered at RTSD/CCS Program Meeting, 29 June 1972, during 1972 ALA Annual Conference at Chicago. 11 p. (1972). Reprinted in *International Cataloguing* 2, no.1:6–8 (Jan./Mar. 1973).

California State University and Colleges. Library Systems Project. *Report on a Cost Study of Specific Technical Processing Activities of the California State University and Colleges Libraries.* Los Angeles: Div. of Academic Program and Resource Planning, Off. of the Chancellor, California State Univ. and Colleges, 1973. 1 v. (various paging).

California. University of, Berkeley. Institute of Library Research. "Largest Computer-Produced Book Catalog Completed by University of California." 4-p. press release, dated 20 Sept. 1972.

California. University of, Berkeley. Institute of Library Research. *UC Union Catalog Supplement Project; Project Summary and Statement of Requirements for Photocomposition and Book Manufacture.* Berkeley: The Institute, 1971. 72 p.

California. University of, Berkeley. Institute of Library Research. *University of California Union Catalog Supplement, 1963–1967; Fact Sheet: Book Catalog* (1973). 2 p.

California. University of. *University of California Union Catalog of Monographs Cataloged by the Nine Campuses from 1963 through 1967; A Supplement to the Catalogs of the University Libraries at Berkeley and Los Angeles Published in 1963.* (Authors & titles: v. 1/A–ANA) Berkeley, Calif.: Institute of Library Research, Univ. of California, 1972. (24 p. sample)

CARDSET Cataloging Systems: Users' Manual. Menlo Park, Calif.: Information Design, Inc., n.d. 9 p.

Cartwright, Kelley L., and Ralph M. Shoffner. *Catalogs in Book Form: A Research Study of Their Implications for the California State Library and the California Union Catalog, with a Design for Their Implementation.* Berkeley, Calif.: Institute of Library Research, Univ. of California, 1967.

CAT 34T-S. Portland, Ore.: Richard Abel & Co., 1973. (Computer printout of prototype "subject authority control system" test listing.)

Collaborative Library Systems Development, ed. by Paul J. Fasana and Allen Veaner. Cambridge, Mass.: M.I.T. Press, 1971. 241 p.

Collaborative Program in Library System Development. *Final Report to the National Science Foundation.* Washington, DC: National Science Foundation, 1971. 28 p.

"Computer Library Services Has Two Happy Users," *Advanced Technology/Libraries* 2, no. 3:5-6 (Mar. 1973).

"Cooperative Network Boxscore," *Advanced Technology/Libraries* 2, no. 3:4 (Mar. 1973).

Council on Library Resources, Inc. "Assisting the Development of a National System," in its *14th Annual Report.* Washington, DC: The Council, 1970. p. 17-32.

Council on Library Resources, Inc. "Automation," in its *13th Annual Report.* Washington, DC: The Council, 1969. p. 12-21.

Council on Library Resources, Inc. "Automation," in its *13th Annual Report.* Washington, DC: The Council, 1969. p. 12-21.

Council on Library Resources, Inc. "MARC and RECON," in its *15th Annual Report,* Washington, DC: The Council, 1971. p. 22-23.

Council on Library Resources, Inc. "National library services," in its *16th Annual Report,* Washington, DC: The Council, 1972. p. 17-25.

"Dartmouth-NELINET-OCLC Test," *JOLA Technical Communications* 3, no.5:3-4 (Sept./Oct. 1972).

De Gennaro, Richard. "Automation in the Harvard College Library," *Harvard Library Bulletin* 16, no. 3:217-36 (July 1968).

Epstein, A. H., and others. *Bibliographic Automation of Large Library Operations Using a Time-sharing System: Phase II, Part 1 (July 1970-June 1971). Final Report.* Washington, DC: U.S. Bureau of Libraries and Educational Technology, 1972. 207 p.

––––––. "An On-Line Network—Cooperative Planning with Several Libraries," in American Society for Information Science. *Proceedings.* 34th Annual Meeting, Denver, Nov. 7-11, 1971. Westport, Conn.: Greenwood Pub. Co., 1971. p. 227-31.

––––––. *A User's View of BALLOTS: No. 1: The MARC Module.* rev. ed. Stanford, Calif.: BALLOTS Project, Stanford Univ., 1973. 31 p.

Fairfax County Public Library. *Catalog.* Ephrata, Pa.: Science Press. n.d. 3 p. (specimen pages)

Fasana, Paul J. *Automation Efforts at the Columbia University Libraries. Part I. Progress report for period January 1968-December 1969.* Washington, DC: Office of Science Information Service, National Science Foundation, 1970. 17 p.

––––––. "Collaborative Library Systems Development: An Experiment in the Joint Design of Automated Library Systems," in American Society for Information Science. *Proceedings.* 34th Annual Meeting, Denver, Nov. 7-11, 1971. Westport, Conn.: Greenwood Pub. Co., 1971. p. 233-36.

_____. *Utilization of MARC Data in the Columbia Automated Technical Services System*. New York: Systems Office, Columbia Univ. Libraries, 1970. 15 p. (Technical note no. 1, rev.)

Fasana, Paul J., and Jerome Yavarkovsky. *Automation Efforts at the Columbia University Libraries. pt. 1. Progress Report for the Period January 1970 through June 1971; With Proposed Areas of Development Work for the Period July 1971 through June 1973*. New York: Systems Office, Columbia Univ. Libraries, 1971. 14 p.

Fischer, Mary L. "The Use of COM at Los Angeles Public Library," *Journal of Micrographics* 6, no. 5:205–10 (May/June 1973).

Freedman, Maurice J., and Jerry G. Pennington. "Introduction," in Hennepin County Library's *Catalog*. Minneapolis: Technical Services Div., Hennepin County Library, 1972. p. iii–iv.

Georgia Institute of Technology. Price Gilbert Memorial Library. *Library Extends Catalog Access and New Delivery Service*. Atlanta: The Institute, 1972. 4 p. (brochure).

Grutchfield, Walter, and Michael Malinconico. "The Central Role of an Interactive Authority File in an Automated Bibliographic System." New York: New York Public Library, 1970. 7 p. (typescript).

Hawken, William R. *Copying Methods Manual*. LTP Publication no. 11; Chicago: Library Technology Program, American Library Assn., 1966. 375 p.

Hayes, R. M., and R. M. Shoffner. *The Economics of Book Catalog Production: A Study Prepared for Stanford University Libraries and the Council on Library Resources*. Sherman Oaks, Calif.: Advanced Information Systems Div., Hughes Dynamics, 1964. 110 p.

Henderson, James W., and Joseph A. Rosenthal, eds. *Library Catalogs: Their Preservation and Maintenance by Photographic and Automated Techniques*. A study by the Research Libraries of the New York Public Library under a grant from the Council on Library Resources. M.I.T. report no. 14. Cambridge, Mass.: M.I.T. Press, 1968. 267 p.

Hennepin County (Minn.) Library. *Cataloging Bulletin* no. 1– (3 May 1973–). Bimonthly.

Herling, John P. "The Ohio College Library Center." New York: METRO, 1973. 10 p. (Typescript of speech given at METRO conference on centralized processing, New York City, May 1973).

"Information Design Press announces the first titles in an innovative list of original microfilm publishing. . . ." Menlo Park, Calif.: Information Design, n.d. 6 p.

Information Dynamics Corp. *Technical Applications & News Announcements*. Reading, Mass. (Periodical house organ.)

"Information Dynamics Unveils BIBNET for On-Site Processing," *Advanced Technology/Libraries* 2, no. 2:1–2 (Feb. 1973).

International Business Machines Corp. Data Processing Div. *Massachusetts Central Library Processing Service*. White Plains, NY: IBM, 1973. 14 p.

_____. *Storage and Information Retrieval System (STAIRS/VS); General Information*. White Plains, NY: IBM, 1973. 35 p. (Program product 5740–XR1.)

"Ivy libraries to use OCLC," *College & Research Libraries News* 34, no. 3: 101–2 (May 1973).

Kennedy, John P., with the assistance of Elroy W. Eckhardt. *The Feasibility of Establishing an OCLC-type Center in the Southeast; Final Report.* Atlanta: Georgia Institute of Technology, 1973. 81 p.

Kilgour, Frederick G. "Computer-Based Systems, a New Dimension to Library Cooperation," *College & Research Libraries,* 34, no. 2:137–43 (Mar. 1973).

_____. "Evolving, Computerizing, Personalizing," *American Libraries* 3, no. 2: 141–47 (Feb. 1972).

Kilgour, Frederick G., and others. "The Shared Cataloging System of the Ohio College Library Center." Columbus, Ohio: OCLC, n.d., 34 p. (typescript reprint).

_____. "Title-only Entries Retrieved by Use of Truncated Search Keys," *Journal of Library Automation* 4, no. 4:207–10 (Dec. 1971).

Kountz, John C. "Biblios revisited," *Journal of Library Automation* 5, no. 2:63–86 (June 1972).

Library Catalog Report. Ephrata, Pa.: Science Press. *See* nos. 1 (Jan. 1973) and 2 (May 1973).

"Library of Congress Subject Supplements Machine File Cumulated and Published by the University of California," *JOLA Technical Communications* 3, no. 5:4–5 (Sept./Oct. 1972).

Long, P. L., and others. "Large On-Line Files of Bibliographic Data: An Efficient Design and a Mathematical Predictor of Retrieval Behavior," in *Information Processing 71.* Amsterdam, The Netherlands: North-Holland Pub. Co., 1972. p. 473–78.

Long, Philip L., and Frederick G. Kilgour. "Name-Title Entry Retrieval from a MARC file," *Journal of Library Automation* 4, no. 4:211–12 (Dec. 1971).

_____. "A Truncated Search Key Title Index," *Journal of Library Automation.* 4, no. 1:17–20 (Mar. 1972).

McCune, Lois C., and Stephen R. Salmon. "Bibliography of Library Automation," *ALA Bulletin 61,* no. 6:675–94 (June 1967).

Malinconico, S. Michael, and James A. Rizzolo. "The NYPL Automated Book Catalog Subsystem. New York: New York Public Library, n.d. (45 p. typescript with figs.)

Mason, Ellsworth. "Computers in Libraries," *Library Resources & Technical Services,* 16, no. 1:5 (Winter 1972).

_____. "The Great Gas Bubble Prick't; or, Computers Revealed—by a Gentleman of Quality," *College & Research Libraries* 32, no. 3:183–96 (May 1971).

Massachusetts. University of. Central Library Processing Service. "BCL-72 Project Description." June 23, 1972. 5 p.

Montague, Eleanor: *Summary of a Feasibility Study on the Participation of Four Colleges and Universities in a Stanford University Library Automation Network.* Stanford, Calif.: SPIRES/BALLOTS Project, Stanford Univ., 1971. 72 p.

"OCLC to Offer Assistance as Library Computer Nets Spread," *Advanced Technology/Libraries* 2, no. 3:1, 3–5 (Mar. 1973).

Ohio College Library Center. *Annual report, 1970/1971.* Columbus, Ohio: OCLC. 10 p.

_____. *Annual report, 1971/1972.* Columbus, Ohio: OCLC. 18 p.

_____. *Newsletter.* nos. 52–58, July 25, 1972–Feb. 27, 1973.

_____. *Standards for Input Cataloging.* Columbus, Ohio: OCLC, 1972). 28 p.

"Ohio College Library Center will extend its services...," *LC Information Bulletin* 32, no. 21:188 (May 25, 1973).

Oklahoma Dept. of Libraries. "MARC-O; Cataloging Data Search & Print Service: Users Manual." 3d ed. Oklahoma City: The Department, 1973. 10 p.

———. "MARC-O; MARC Record Search & Copy Service: Users Manual." Oklahoma City: The Department, 1973. 77 p.

———. MARC Project. "Proposal for Oklahoma College and University Libraries to Consider an Experimental 'Selective Notification of Intent to Purchase Project.'" Provided cooperatively by participating academic libraries and MARC-O; presented by MARC-O to the OLA Administrators Workshop, February 9, 1973 (Oklahoma City). 5 leaves.

———. MARC-O Project. "SLICE/MARC-O: A Project of the Southwestern Library Association. Description of Services." Prepared cooperatively by Oklahoma Dept. of Libraries and SLICE Office Director. 2d rev. ed. Dallas: SLICE Office; Oklahoma City: MARC-O Project, 1972. 16 p.

Parr, Thomas, ed. "Library Automation at The New York Public Library and the Association of New York Libraries for Technical Services." Costa Mesa, Calif.: LARC Assn., 1970. 104 p. Special issue of *LARC Reports* 3, no. 3 (Fall 1970).

Payne, Charles T., Robert S. McGee, [and] Ellen R. Fisher. "The University of Chicago Library Bibliographic Data Processing System: Documentation and Report as of October 31, 1969" Report to the National Science Foundation; Chicago: Univ. of Chicago Library, 1970. 287 p.

Payne, Charles T., and Robert S. McGee. "The University of Chicago Library Bibliographic Data Processing System: Documentation and Report Supplement." Report to National Science Foundation; Chicago: Univ. of Chicago Library, 1971. 159 p. (looseleaf).

Pennington, Jerry. "An Overview of the Book Catalog at the Hennepin County Library; Justification, Production Techniques, and Anticipated Usage." Minneapolis: Hennepin County Library, 1972.

Ranz, Jim. *The Printed Book Catalogue in American libraries: 1723-1900.* ACRL monograph no. 26; Chicago: American Library Assn., 1964. 144 p.

Robinson, C. Derek. "PRECIS; An Introduction," *CB Newsletter* no. 7:10–16 (Mar. 1973). Don Mills, Ontario: Centennial College Bibliocentre.

Roberts, Edward G., and John P. Kennedy. "The Georgia Tech Library's Microfiche Catalog." Atlanta: Georgia Institute of Technology, n.d. 16 p. (Typewritten draft of article for *Journal of Micrographics*).

"Rutgers trying out CAPTAIN; Finds Software Snags," *Advanced Technology/ Libraries* 2, no. 4:2–3 (Apr. 1973).

Sansing, Maxine, and Nancy Slanger. *U.C. Union Catalog Supplement Record Structure.* Berkeley, Calif.: Institute of Library Research, Univ. of California, 1972. 16 p. (technical paper)

Schneider, John H., and others, eds. *Survey of Commercially Available Computer-Readable Bibliographic Data Bases.* Washington, DC: American Society for Information Science, 1973. 181 p.

Science Press. *Some Questions and Answers about the MARC-Science Press Data Base.* Ephrata, Pa.: The Press, n.d. 2 p. (brochure)

———. *The True Cost of Library Automation: A Practical Library Management Tool.* Ephrata, Pa.: The Press, n.d. 10 p.

Sherman, Don, and Ralph M. Shoffner: *California State Library: Processing Center Design and Specifications.* v. 1: *System Description and Input Processing.* Berkeley, Calif.: Institute of Library Research, Univ. of California, 1969. 254 p.

―――. *California State Library: Processing Center Design and Specifications.* v. 2: *File Maintenance and Output Processing.* Berkeley, Calif.: Institute of Library Research, Univ. of California, 1969. 274 p.

Shoffner, Ralph M. *Catalog Supplement Project.* Berkeley, Calif.: Institute of Library Research, Univ. of California, 1971. 9 p. (Memo to J. Richard Blanchard, Chairman, Library Council, dated Dec. 29, 1971)

―――. *Catalog Supplement Projects. Phase III: File Improvement and Publication. Request for Working Capital, Oct. 7, 1970.* Berkeley, Calif.: Institute of Library Research, Univ. of California. 57 p. plus 4 unpaged appendixes.

―――. *Catalog Supplement Project: Report to the Library Council, Nov. 11, 1971.* Berkeley, Calif.: Institute of Library Research, Univ. of California. 36 p.

Shoffner, Ralph M., and others: *Catalog Supplement Project: Report to the Library Council, April 23, 1971.* Berkeley, Calif.: Institute of Library Research, Univ. of California. 44 p.

Simmons, Peter. "Library Automation." 57 p. draft text of chapter 5 for v. 8, *Annual Review of Information Science and Technology* (8:167–201).

Southwestern Library Interstate Cooperative Endeavor. *First Annual Report. . . , Covering the Period October 1, 1971 to December 31, 1972, and Final Report for Council on Library Resources* (1972). 11 p.

SPIRES/BALLOTS Project Staff. *System Scope for Library Automation and Generalized Information Storage and Retrieval at Stanford University.* Stanford, Calif.: Stanford Univ., 1970. 157 p.

Spreitzer, Francis F. "Developments in Copying, Micrographics, and Graphic Communications, 1972," *Library Resources & Technical Services* 17, no. 2: (Spring 1973). (unpaged offprint)

Stanford Physics Information Retrieval System (SPIRES). *Annual Report to the National Science Foundation (Office of Science Information Service), 1967.* Edwin B. Parker, Project Director. Stanford, Calif.: Institute for Communication Research, Stanford Univ., 1967. 56 p.

"Stanford's BALLOTS Look to Network Operation," *Advanced Technology/ Libraries* 2, no. 2:3–4 (Feb. 1973).

Stewart, Robert C. "Cataloging with a Computer—OCLC Comes to Pennsylvania," *PLA Bulletin* 28, no. 1:9–15 (Jan. 1973).

Summers, F. William. "State Libraries and Centralized Processing," *Library Resources & Technical Services* 14, no. 2:269–78 (Spring 1970).

Swanson, Gerald: "ISBD: Standard or Secret?" *Library Journal* 98:124–30 (Jan. 15, 1973).

Tauber, Maurice F., and Hilda Feinberg: *Book Catalogs.* Metuchen, NJ: Scarecrow Press, 1971. 572 p.

UCUCS. "Significant Cost Elements." Berkeley, Calif.: Institute of Library Research, Univ. of California, May 1, 1973. 1 p.

United States. Library of Congress. Information Systems Office. *Format Recognition Process for MARC Records: A Logical Design.* Chicago: Information Science and Automation Div., American Library Assn., 1970. 150 p. plus 12 separately paged appendixes.

_____. *MARC Manuals Used by the Library of Congress.* 2d ed. (Chicago: Information Science and Automation Div., American Library Assn., 1970. 3 v. in 1. Looseleaf.

_____. Processing Dept. *Filing Rules for the Dictionary Catalogs of the Library of Congress.* Washington, DC: Card Div., Library of Congress, 1956. 187 p.

_____. RECON Working Task Force. *Conversion of Retrospective Catalog Records to Machine-Readable Form; A Study of the Feasibility of a National Bibliographic Service;* ed. by John C. Rather. Washington, DC: Library of Congress, 1969. 230 p.

Waite, David P. *Library Networks: Book 1.* Reading, Mass.: Information Dynamics Corp., 1972. 49 p.

Waldron, Helen J. *Book Catalogs: A Survey of the Literature on Costs.* P-469; Santa Monica, Calif.: Rand Corp., 1971. 26 p.

Washington State Library. *Book Catalog of King County Library System, North Central Regional Library, Timberland Library Demonstration. Sample pages.*

Weber, David C., and Allen B. Veaner. "Project BALLOTS: A Progress Report on Library Automation," *Library Report.* p. 1-4.

Westby, Barbara M. "Commercial Processing Firms: A Directory," *Library Resources and Technical Services,* 13, no. 2:209-20 (Spring 1969).

My special thanks to Sanford Berman, who prepared the descriptions in the bibliography, and Jean Ranisate, who typed it. MF.

5   Acquisitions Systems: 1973 Applications Status

David L. Weisbrod

INTRODUCTION

It would be inappropriate either to tell you what goes into an acquisitions system (SDC[1] has already done that, and so have Hayes and Becker[2]) or to list the various publicly recorded acquisitions systems (LARC[3] did it in 1971), and ASIS SIG/LAN (American Society for Information Science, Special Interest Group on Library Automation and Networks) has a more current version under way in conjunction with ALA/ISAD, SLA, and ERIC/CLIS. Besides that, I probably would not do as good a job as these others have, and, moreover, the time for this presentation is too short.

Instead, having looked at a few trees, I will attempt to describe the forest. But before doing that, let me first make public my orientational preoccupations and handicaps. My background is in computation, not libraries. I have worked for the last eight years in a large research library in a university and am most familiar with the world of ARL-type libraries. Finally, I make no claim to intimate and authoritative knowledge of every computer-assisted acquisitions system ever implemented in a library in the United States—to say nothing of the rest of the world.

DEFINITION

The major problem with reporting on acquisitions systems is that I don't know what one is; i.e., there exists no standard operational definition, "X is an acquisition system if it exhibits characteristics A, B, and C."

Head, Development Department, Yale University Library

Instead, we see a wide range of systems, all having something to do with the library acquisitions function, but having not one single element guaranteed in common. These systems range from book fund accounting systems to order writing systems to order monitoring systems. And we also see conflict over "turf": is a serials system an acquisitions system? Is a cataloging system that monitors work flow through technical processing really a schizoid acquisitions system? There exists a number of systems that perform more than one of these functions, but I know of none that performs all.

I will beg the question of definition, admitting only that the remainder of this presentation will concern itself mostly with acquisitions-type functions, primarily monograph-related.

DESCRIPTION: FUNCTIONS AND SCOPE

To the amusement of the cognoscenti and the befuddlement of the rest, I will attempt briefly to state what acquisitions systems are all about. Basically, they are about getting materials into libraries. This obviously simple chore can be decomposed into a number of complicated tasks, such as materials selection, order preparation and control, fund control, materials receiving and tracking, and overall supervision. Since many of these tasks involve the filing and subsequent retrieval of data, and entail the processing and arranging of data according to fixed rules, computers can be used to speed up the work, to assure consistency of treatment, to correlate data too scattered for convenient manipulation by humans, to increase worker productivity, and to help control costs.

Functions

Connie Dunlap's report, "The Automation of Acquisitions Systems," at the preconference institute on library automation in 1967 enumerated a number of acquisitions-related computer functions that either had been implemented as of June 1967, or for which plans were then in existence.[4] A more recent tabulation of this sort appears in the section "Automation of Acquisitions Functions" in Markuson et al,[5] which I recommend highly as a useful volume. It would be a waste of time to repeat here what these authors have already published. I will, however, enumerate a few functions that both seem to have skipped:

- Automatic checking for duplicate orders
- "Parent–child" record scheme for handling separately the distinct groups of materials arising out of partial shipments
- Control of cataloging arrearage (backlog)
- Automatic generation of LC card orders or requests for NPAC (National Programs for Acquisitions and Cataloging) cataloging
- Lists of materials to be ordered, awaiting availability of funds
- Status reports to book requesters
- Reissuing of an order to a second vendor, if the first cannot fill it.

Each of these functions has been implemented in at least one acquisitions system somewhere in the United States.

Scope

The matter of system scope is intimately related to the matter of system functions: enlarging the scope generally entails the addition of functions. The scope of an acquisitions system may vary in quite a number of parameters including, for example, the following:

- Types of materials handled: monograph, serial
- Methods of procurement initiation handled: unitary order, standing order, blanket order, gift, exchange, membership, approval agreement
- Modes of payment handled (may be tied to method of initiation of procurement): "normal" invoicing, prepaid order, deposit account, membership
- Languages representable in the machine-readable file: alphabetic (Roman, Cyrillic, etc.); nonalphabetic (e.g., Chinese).

BRIEF OVERVIEW OF LAST SIX YEARS

To the jaded eye, nothing much has changed in the six years since Connie Dunlap's report. Most of the functions or techniques or approaches that I believed at first to rank as innovations after that date I found, upon checking, are indeed mentioned there: on-line systems, integrated systems, and processing centers were just the first three on my list. And networks were the topic of Joe Becker's keynote address right at the start of the institute.[6]

Although I perceive nothing radically new that has happened in acquisitions over the past six years—nothing to change our conceptions right down to their very roots—some things have changed. During these years we have demonstrated that we are now able to realize what we could only hypothesize and write about then. We have moved from tabulating systems driven by "card jockeys" to computer-managed multiple-file data bases and have built honestly innovative capabilities far beyond those of earlier systems that were largely functional replicas of manual procedures. We have added to the menu of functions that may be selected for inclusion in a system a few ideas that are genuinely new.

MAJOR CURRENT TRENDS

With acquisitions systems going off in all directions, as I suggested before, it is a little difficult to identify any major trends. A few minor tendencies can be described under the headings of on-line interactive systems; packages; processing centers; and integrated systems.

On-line interactive systems

When Connie Dunlap made her presentation six years ago there was not one on-line interactive acquisitions system in operation (at least, none that I know of). She identified two on the drawing board: one at the University of Chicago, the other at Washington State University (it is worth noting that both of these were designed as general, comprehensive technical services systems, of which acquisitions was but a part). Since that time both of these systems have become operational in varying degrees and for varying lengths of time. Other on-line acquisitions systems (or subsystems) have also been implemented: BALLOTS at Stanford University, LOLITA at Oregon State University, ELMS at IBM/Los Gatos, and one (sine nomine) at Northwestern University, just to start the list.

On-line interactive systems share certain attributes: immediate query access from an arbitrary number of locations to common, up-to-date files; ability to maintain these files from an arbitrary number of locations (i.e., to add to them, to modify them, and to delete from them) with the result of such file maintenance immediately viewable at all other locations. This sort of capability has already begun to have profound effect on library operation and organization.

On-line interactive systems have been given added impetus by two technological developments during these six years: the rapid decrease in unit cost of large capacity direct access computer storage equipment and the decrease in unit cost of communications terminals, especially CRT (cathode ray tube) display models, some of which incorporate small computers right inside the terminal itself, giving rise to the catchy phrase, "intelligent terminals."

The viable networks of the future will be on-line interactive systems: the retail-level consumer (order librarian, cataloger, reference librarian, or library patron) wants immediate feedback. Batch systems, even if well designed and brilliantly efficient, just do not provide this, except with anticipatory listings.

Packaged systems

Packaged systems have always existed, inasmuch as library A has always had open the option of asking library B for its programs and documentation and of using B's system "back at the ranch" at library A. What has changed is that we now have entrepreneurs specifically offering their systems on the open market.

Packaged systems that are known by your reporter to include an acquisitions module are being marketed by CLSI (Computer Library Services, Inc.); IBM; Baker and Taylor; SDC (System Development Corporation); and Information Design, Incorporated.

Four major questions arise regarding packaged systems: Do the functions included satisfy the needs of the prospective user? Can the system be configured to handle the prospective user's processing load? What equipment is required, either for purchase or for rental? What is the system's cost? The vendor of a packaged system is banking on his ability to offer a package for which the answer to all four of these questions is satisfactory to a big enough segment of the library market to keep him in business. These four questions are the same ones that should be asked when an in-house system analyst/designer presents the library with a trial design. I believe, however, that one's natural prejudice is to turn thumbs down on the packaged system because "they couldn't possibly know all my problems" and to turn thumbs up on the presumably tailored design because "it was done especially for us, and, besides, look how much we've already got invested." Every decision-maker should be aware of these trends and try to overcome them (note that I did not say overcompensate for them; that would be just as bad). It's never too late to recognize the existence of another truly intelligent being in the universe, and it's never too late to stop throwing good money after bad.

Processing centers and processing services

Book processing centers—i.e., centralized book ordering and cataloging operations serving a number of libraries related usually either by
administration or geography—are making increasing use of computer
technology. The one at the University of Massachusetts is a case in point.
Book processing centers tend to be operated on a "not for profit" basis.
Book processing services offer pretty much the same product and/or
service, except that they tend to be operated by entrepreneurs on a profit
making basis (hopefully!). Except to ideologues, the presence or absence
of the label "not for profit" is not a reliable indicator of good performance or reasonable price; each processing center or service should be
judged on its own merits.

Taken together as a group, book processing centers and services offer
the individual librarian whose library matches the "target" clientele of
the service/center the opportunity to share in some of the benefits of
large scale computerization (and perhaps large scale purchasing, too)
without having to do all the system development himself.

Integrated systems

Integrated system is an overworked catchword that refers to a system
in which potential relationships between subcomponents are exploited in
the interest of overall effectiveness or efficiency or economy. Consider an
example from the world of nonautomated library procedures: The results
of preorder bibliographic searching are retained, so as to minimize the
need for redundant postreceipt searching. We would describe this
coordination as indicative of the integration of technical processing
procedures into a rationally and efficiently organized whole.

Libraries have always been integrated systems to some degree, as the
above example suggests. What we are interested in here is computer
mediated integration. This is usually characterized by data reuse and by
functional coordination, which are really opposite sides of the same coin.
The archetypal example of system integration is the sequence: acquisitions, cataloging, circulation. The idea in its most straightforward form
is that bibliographic data collected in machine-readable form for the first
function, book ordering, are reused by the cataloging function, by
adding subject and call number data in machine-readable form to build a
complete catalog data record from which the production of 3x5 cards or
of a book form catalog takes place. The call number data in machine-
readable form are reused to produce punched cards for a circulation

control system, and the full descriptive entry might also be reused by the circulation control system to produce overdue notices. This data reuse avoids the cost of duplicative reentry and assures consistency throughout the system.

The important potential of system integration as it affects the acquisitions function was seen and documented by Connie Dunlap in 1967, but, with the exception of the purest of straightforward cases, such as the one at Lorain County Community College in Ohio, it seems that we first had to build small systems and learn how to make them run well before putting them together as subsystems in a comprehensive, integrated system.[7]

FORECAST: THE NEXT SIX YEARS

It seems that all the speakers who preceded me were unable to discern that the number of years between the previous preconference institute and this one is actually six and not five. I am timing the scope of this forecast to hold us through the next ISAD Preconference Institute on Library Automation six years from now in 1979. My forecast falls into three areas: technology, system functions, and library organization.

TECHNOLOGY

This subsection treats both specific hardware developments and the question of orientation toward technical decision-making.

Computer Output Microfilm

Computer Output Microfilm, or COM for short, is an alternative to paper as a vehicle for computer-generated hard copy, i.e., as a vehicle for printouts or listings. Actually, Computer Output Micro*form* is a better expansion of the acronym COM, because it can take the format either of roll film (most commonly 16 or 35 mm) or of cards, i.e., microfiche.

COM has a number of advantages over paper copy: it is more compact, it can be produced faster, it can be reproduced faster and less expensively, it can be distributed more easily. If the amount of COM work being done at an installation is too small to justify the acquisition of such equipment, many service bureaus offer tape-to-film services, using as input magnetic tapes written on the customer's own computer. COM is proving to be an effective medium both for the dissemination of current material and for the retention of archival material; e.g., at Yale we were able to liberate about fifty linear feet of shelving that had been used to hold "archival" acquisitions listings by consolidating the source data, which we still had in machine-readable form, and putting it out on computer output microfilm, the four reels of which occupy a total of four linear inches of shelf space.

COM is presently being used in acquisitions systems at the University of Michigan Library, at the Hennepin County Library in Minneapolis, at the Los Angeles Public Library, and at Yale University. (Special librarians may recall Lockheed's computer maintained microform catalog, which has been in existence for several years).

In brief, I think COM will turn out to be nothing short of a new lease on life for large batch systems that might otherwise have had to be converted to on-line, interactive systems because of problems of information dissemination or of information bulk.

Minicomputers

Minicomputers, or "minis" for short, are smaller versions of the room-filling equipment with which most of us are familiar. The processing speed of most minis is just as fast as (and sometimes faster than) that of its bigger counterparts, but the capacity of its immediately addressable memory is usually considerably smaller. This memory can be, and usually is, supplemented from the standard menu of peripheral storage equipment: tapes, drums, disks, etc. Important about minis is that they occupy less space, require less power, and cost less than their bigger brothers.

Minicomputers will become increasingly important as the basis for small, economical, self-sustained local acquisitions systems and also as local processors tied into regional centers, permitting libraries to store and process locally data of only local interest (e.g., book fund accounting information) while at the same time implementing access to common data stored at the regional center (e.g., MARC).

Technical decision-making: hardware selection

It was the case, once upon a time, that a librarian wishing to use electronic data processing in his library would look around, discover what machine was locally "available," and use it. Thus, typically, college and university libraries would use the university computer center, special libraries would use the company data processing facility, public and school libraries the municipal facility, and so forth. It mattered not whether this computer was the one best suited to the application; it was available, and it was used. Many of the earlier applications of computers in libraries were dubbed "experimental"—as much, I believe, because of the uncertainty as to how long the machine on which they were running was going to remain available as because of the system's unknown operability. There were exceptions to this generalization, but not many.

This approach of starting with the computer and then doing the best one can with the application will be reversed: the designer will start with the application and then acquire the most appropriate equipment. This reversal will be made possible by two developments: (1) minicomputers and (2) networks and regional centers. Minis make it possible for the small system to have its own appropriately selected hardware. Networks and regional centers will concentrate enough work to put libraries into the market for "standard" sized computer installations. This predicted trend away from putting the cart before the horse—i.e., away from starting with the computer and following with the application—will have a beneficial effect in the area of system transferability, which was discussed earlier at some length in connection with Allen Veaner's presentation. This trend will also make the designer's lot a more difficult one, inasmuch as design features previously thought of as "given" will now become variables requiring explicit treatment.

The idea of designing the computer assisted library system as an experiment, i.e., in such a fashion as to be able always to revert to the manual system, is not so important now. Library computer applications nowadays are almost never described as experimental—just as operational. In fact, some libraries with efficiently and smoothly running computer-based acquisitions systems realize now that they could not afford to revert to a manual system—certainly not to an *equivalent* manual system—and that reversion to any manual system at all would entail both degradation of services and problems of reorganization. The potential problem of losing access to the computer on which the system runs will be reduced by the library's assuming control of its own hardware and, thus to some degree, of its own destiny.

The major technical problems of the future are going to be system reliability and system extendability. With regard to the first, reliability, I heard only within the last few weeks the first story of a *library's* duplexing its computers for the sake of reliability. The matter of extendability is too complex for treatment here.

SYSTEM FUNCTIONS

This subsection treats one specific acquisitions-related function that I believe will become extremely important, followed by a quick look at the potentials arising from system integration.

Acquisitions coordination

Acquisitions coordination can mean something as innocuous as dissemination of acquisitions information among two (or more) coordinating libraries, so that each can know what materials the other has on order and may modify its own acquisitions accordingly, if it so chooses; or acquisitions coordination can mean an explicitly stated coordinated acquisitions policy among two (or more) coordinating libraries ("You collect in area A, and we'll collect in area B"). Although the latter may be more exciting as a means to try to control costs, I am now going to discuss the former.

The former mode of acquisitions coordination—based on the sharing of information—is currently being done on a manual basis by the libraries of the seven divinity schools comprising BTI, the Boston Theological Institute. The BTI library office maintains a file of order slips from all seven libraries for all items ordered since the start of the coordination program. Each of the libraries sends its newly generated order slips to the BTI library office instead of directly to the vendor. The slip has one of three mutually exclusive boxes checked:

- Order unconditionally, i.e., regardless of which other libraries may have ordered this item.
- Order exclusively, i.e., only if *none* of the other libraries has ordered this item. If any other order exists, return this order to us for cancellation.
- Order conditionally, i.e., only if *none* of the other libraries has ordered this item. If any other order exists, note the name of the ordering library on this slip and return to us for reconsideration.

Since this is essentially a file maintenance and entry matching operation, it has obvious potential as computer application, especially for integration into the acquisitions subsystem of a regional network or processing center.

Just to confuse matters a little, as a postscript to this critical analysis of acquisitions coordination I would like to inject a distinction between *acquisition coordination,* which deals with book selection decision-making, and *coordinated purchasing,* which has to do with simultaneity of ordering, i.e., ordering in quantity. Coordinated purchasing does imply acquisitions coordination in a trivial sense, inasmuch as selection decisions must all be submitted to the coordinating office before the group order can be placed. But that's as far as the resemblance goes. Brett Butler has suggested that coordinated purchasing, which apparently is a familiar phenomenon to public librarians, is the special ingredient without which processing centers are doomed to failure. I am not personally familiar with a number of case histories of processing centers, both successful and unsuccessful, large enough to judge this hypothesis, but the few supporting instances of which I know make this an idea to ponder seriously.

System integration

System integration is a most tantalizing area to write about: it is very easy to hypothesize all sorts of future developments but less easy to realize them; actual implementation of such ideas requires extreme care and great foresight. To build a bridge of twice the span is not just a matter of doubling the length of each part.

The trend toward integrating the major library functions of acquisitions, cataloging, and circulation into a comprehensive electronic data processing system was mentioned earlier in the discussion of integrated systems among the trends now current. But the simple picture of unidirectional flow of data from acquisitions through cataloging to circulation, while by no means inaccurate, ignores the benefits that can be derived (a) from data flow in the reverse direction, e.g., from cataloging to acquisitions, and (b) from the integration of minor or ancillary functions, such as book fund accounting, vendor file maintenance, and patron registration. Ripe opportunities for system integration that will become increasingly common within the next six years include:

- The sharing of MARC files between cataloging and acquisitions subsystems. Acquisitions will use the data for order writing and for acquisitions coordination.
- The sharing of patron registration files between circulation and acquisitions subsystems. Acquisitions will use the data for addressing status reports, notices of materials now available, and routing slips.
- The sharing of vendor files between the accounts payable system

(frequently outside the library altogether) and the acquisitions system. Acquisitions will use the data for addressing orders and claims notices.

• The sharing of book fund accounting files between acquisitions and serials subsystems. The encumbering of year-to-year serials commitments is one of the most perplexing problems of book fund accounting, especially in times of inflation. Only an integrated system can hope to bring this under control on a nonstatistical basis. Acquisitions systems are usually monograph oriented; serials systems usually periodical oriented. Monographs in series, especially standing orders, tend to fall in the sloppy gray middle area. A well integrated system should handle this entire continuum with ease.

Other new functions

We will witness development of new acquisitions functions along evolutionary lines; revolution is too expensive for libraries. The innovative functions I enumerated in the six-year review will come to be commonplace. Increased (but not exclusive) dependence on the ISBN and the ISSN as identifiers for ordering will develop as increased use of them is made in publishing.

More radical is the potential for linking together publishers, vendors, and consumers in an electronic communications network. Los Angeles Public Library presently communicates with Baker and Taylor in this manner. The Standard Account Numbers project of ANSI Committee Z39 may expedite this development.

LIBRARY ORGANIZATION

Organization in the sense of the *organization of procedures* has already been affected in many libraries by the introduction of computerization into acquisitions: manual filing and purging chores in many areas have been eliminated, freeing personnel for other work; searching chores have been reduced through programmed duplicate order detection; and so on. This trend will continue and gain momentum.

Library organization in the sense of the *existence of entire functional areas* will be affected by the growth in the next six years of networks, processing centers, and processing services. That is, entire functions now performed in-house will be transferred out of house for reasons of cost and/or effectiveness. This does not in any way imply the wholesale termination of library personnel: consider the model of what automatic switching did for telephone communications.

SUMMARY

We stated that there exists no standard definition for a computer-assisted acquisitions system and that any specific function generally associated with the area of acquisitions might or might not be implemented in a specific library's system, depending on the designer's perception of his client-library's need.

The recitation of a designer's "cook book" for acquisitions systems was omitted on the grounds of duplication and insufficient time. Instead, we identified some current trends and prophesied some future ones.

The acquisitions process will continue until libraries are no more. As long as it continues at current levels, the need to know and to control what is happening will require computers in the service of man.

DISCUSSION

Daisy Brightonback (Rutgers University): At Rutgers something called CAPTAIN is being developed. I have a very minor question. I'm a little disturbed because we don't find out more about costs—regular dollars-and-cent figures, not the million and a quarter here and whatever there. One of the minor amounts that was mentioned was the cost of BCL (Massachusetts Processing Center) of $1.00 a book, and I wonder if anybody from Massachusetts is here to tell us what costs are included in the $1.00 figure.

Weisbrod: Would you like to talk about that, Don? Don Hammer has had an intimate relationship with BCL.

Donald Hammer (ALA): I'll start by saying I have had nothing to do with that figure, that's one thing. As far as I could gather in the time I was there it was a pretty valid figure. The only question that remained in my mind about it is how much overhead is in that figure, but that was a situation where so much money was allocated by the legislature and merely by dividing the amount provided for processing into the number of books or materials processed gives them that figure. So it's a pretty

well grounded figure, I think, but there is some University of Massachusetts overhead on top of that, that's not been included in that figure.

Weisbrod: This is one of the examples of Brett's hypothesis: in
particular, BCL is one of the operations where they send down checklists
and wait for all libraries to return the lists saying "Yes, we want book X."
So they place an order for 35 copies of book "X" effectively, with the cost
of processing one transaction. The number is pretty much the same as
any place else, maybe even a little bit higher, but the denominator in the
cost ratio is very large and that's what determines that beautiful unit
price.

REFERENCES

[1] Barbara Evans Markuson et al, *Automation and the Federal Library Community*
(Santa Monica, Calif., and Falls Church, Va.: System Development Corp., 1971).
241 p.

[2] Robert M. Hayes and Joseph Becker, *Handbook of Data Processing for Libraries*
(Sponsored by the Council on Library Resources [New York: Becker and Hayes, Inc.,
a subsidiary of John Wiley & Sons, Inc., 1970]). 886 p.

[3] Library Automation, Research, and Consulting (LARC) Association, *A Survey of
Automated Activities in the U. S. and Canada* (2d ed.; Tempe, Ariz.: The LARC
Assn., 1971).

[4] Connie R. Dunlap, "The Automation of Acquisitions Systems," *in* Stephen R.
Salmon, ed., *Library Automation: A State of the Art Review;* Papers presented at the
Preconference Institute on Library Automation . . . June 22–24, 1967 . . . (Chicago:
American Library Assn., 1969), pp. 37–43.

[5] Barbara Evans Markuson et al, *Guidelines for Library Automation: A Handbook
for Federal and Other Libraries* (Santa Monica, Calif., and Falls Church, Va.: System
Development Corp., 1972). 401 p.

[6] Joseph Becker, "The Future of Library Automation and Information Networks,"
in Stephen R. Salmon, ed., *Library Automation: A State of the Art Review. . . .*
pp. 1–6.

[7] Jack W. Scott, "An Integrated Computer Based Technical Processing System in a
Small College Library," *Journal of Library Automation* 1:149–58 (Sept. 1968).

6 Systems Personnel: What Are Our Needs?

Pauline Atherton

Before I tell you about people in library systems work, I want to find out who is in the audience; to do so I would like to take a poll right now. It will give you a chance to stand, to show us—some of us—the double lives you are leading and to give us a better feeling for who is in this audience. Some remarks have been made about the people in the audience or the people in library field, and I would just like to know who you are. So, would you stand if you call yourself a systems person—either a programmer, a systems analyst, or a librarian directly involved in the library automation effort. You are at least a third, if not half, of the group. Who is a library administrator? You are about a quarter, a quarter to a third. Now, as I used to say, "I'm just a librarian, but.... " Who is the audience whould call themselves "a librarian" not directly involved with library automation?—You are obviously interested, but are you that kind of person—a librarian who is not at the present time directly involved in automation? I would say about 30 people. Now, how many of you are my colleagues in library education? That means teaching courses in library school or on the faculty of the school—a smaller number, probably 20. Now, if you call yourself a systems person, rise if you are in a consortium, if you are a commercial firm providing these kinds of services that we have been hearing about—about 20 people.

Now, how many of you are ISAD members? Members of the division sponsoring the conference? O.K., I'd say about four-fifths of the audience is standing. How many of you were at the 1967 conference—we've talked a lot about that—I'd say approximately 40. I remember, when I was at the 1967 conference, being very excited about the young people I saw there—how many were there and how I felt ISAD was

Professor, School of Information Studies, Syracuse University bringing new blood into the library profession. I think we all look older now and not just six years older either.

I will admit something to you at the outset; I may disappoint many of you in the audience with this paper. I reviewed myself this morning—my early plans for the topics to cover in this paper—and I will discuss some of those topics, but what my paper consists of primarily is opinion statements. As I looked at the paper again, I decided that I haven't done the subject justice for several reasons, and I admit this right now. I did not have enough input from library administrators. I could not collect nor could I find data from the field to back up some of the topics I wanted to talk about. No recent manpower research in library automation exists, to my knowledge, that would really cover some of the topics of great interest to us in this area. So I for one strongly recommend that ISAD consider undertaking such manpower studies before long.

All through the 1960s we heard or read the following statement which was used to emphasize the growth of science in modern times and the concomitant information explosion: "The number of scientists alive today is equal to 90 percent of all the scientists and research workers who have existed since the beginning of history" (attributed to Pierre Auger). I feel that I could paraphrase this quote with regard to library automation systems personnel and not be concerned about refutation: "The number of library systems staff alive today is equal to 90 percent of all the library systems workers who have existed since the beginning of history." Is there a concomitant event we should be dreading or beginning to prepare for? Is there something we need to consider that we have been ignoring? There just may be.

During a twenty-year period (1950–1970) we have increased the ranks of librarians three-fold. From 41,000 professional librarians in 1950, we have grown to about 125,000 professional librarians in 1970, 85 percent of them women, most working full time. One-fifth of these librarians are in colleges and universities, one-quarter in public libraries, two-fifths in schools.[1] Dake Gull in a paper presented at a 1965 conference assumed that by 1970 there would be 60 college and university libraries, each of which would have approximately five staff members involved in library automation, making a total of 300 EDP (electronic data processing) personnel working on library needs—90 systems analysts, 135 programmers, and 75 operators—by 1970.[2] Probably, according to Gull, each could handle the output of 100 librarians, 6,000 librarians in all. Although his estimates are very suspect for 1970, from the 1973 vantage point (for example, the Stanford BALLOTS alone employs more than 20 people), it does provide us with a ratio of 1:20 systems personnel to librarians. A little arithmetic with Gull's numbers gives us a ball park figure, not of 300, but of 6,000 systems personnel who may be alive and well and working with computers in libraries today! We can safely assume that hundreds were working in individual libraries and commercial processing centers in 1968. One of my ISAD oracles (which I'll explain shortly) predicted thousands of workers by 1978, and another predicted fewer than are presently in individual libraries and many more in consortia, library systems, and networks. Who are these people? How many are trained librarians? How many are computer specialists or supporting staff? What are their problems? I hope to explore all of this in this opinion paper, coming in a state of the art review conference, which is the second in a series at six-year intervals.

I for one want to put emphasis on *people in library automation.* The 1967 Preconference on Library Automation had very little to say about the people in systems work. Except for a few pages in Chapman's paper on "Systems Analysis and Design Related to Library Operations" and a remark by Charles P. Bourne in his "Trends" paper, we heard only that the systems staff probably included: a library officer as supervisor, a librarian with management-analysis techniques, a librarian skilled in EDP, and some clerical staff/machine operators.[3] At one conference, held at Columbia University on November 26, 1955, William S. Dix, Librarian at Princeton University, was frank enough to admit his feelings about people and library automation:

> This morning we talked about recruiting and getting people into libraries. This afternoon we talk about automation and getting people out of libraries. This is my very rough layman's conception of what automation means.[4]

I am glad that the organizers of this year's conference have agreed to consider the relationships that do exist between people *and* library automation. My personal opinion on this subject was very well stated at the same conference in 1955 during which Mr. Dix made his remarks. Harold D. Jones, then Chief Circulation Librarian at Brooklyn College, said:

> Automation will not drive people out of libraries, particularly not librarians. It will upgrade them,... it will enhance the position of librarians and relieve them ...of much of the idiotic and tedious fiddling around that passes for librarianship, but is really elementary clerical work.[5]

Only a few authors since Weber[6] and Hammer[7] have emphasized the personnel aspects of library automation. My attempt to do so is a pioneer effort and is appropriately being presented in the Frontier Hotel. Please keep that in mind as I explore this uncharted land.

To help with the assignment given me by this conference's organizers, I wrote to a group of library automation leaders—a baker's dozen. I asked them to answer a series of questions (*see* the Appendix following this paper) about the kind of staff they had on their projects in 1968, what kind they have now, what they expect to have in 1978. I asked them about the skills and personality characteristics of these people and something about the organizational structure then and now. In addressing the question of needs for such personnel, I asked for both a quantitative assessment (number estimates) and qualitative assessment (qualifications, training, skills). Those who responded will be referred to hereafter as "the ISAD oracles"; they must of course remain anonymous. I will interweave their remarks into the paper so that I can elaborate on several topics. I hope this paper will elicit remarks from the audience today, in discussions here at the conference, or in subsequent papers. There is truly a need for more to be written on this the most important of issues, namely the human resources in our libraries.

For a proper assessment of our needs for personnel, we must first state our goals for libraries. This is obvious but rarely done. For too long we have been ignoring some important goal changes and danger signals from within our ranks. For example, the article by Philip Ennis, "Technological Change and the Professions: Neither Luddite nor Technocrat,"[8] and the report by Robert Presthus, "Technological Change and Occupational Response,"[9] have not received the attention they deserve from library administrators. Ennis, in his *Library Quarterly* article published in 1962, said, "The decisive effect of technological innovation is that it is irreversible. Once knowledge and skill are applied to a problem it is almost impossible to return to a state of simple ignorance." Presthus found, in his 1970 study, that there was only a marginal degree of job satisfaction among two-thirds of the librarians who were working in 385 different libraries. In fact, given another chance, they would not choose librarianship as a profession. He makes the point that "it seems it has become easier to computerize a library than to cope with the employees involved in the process." There has been an extraordinary turnover in directorships of academic libraries, some directors retiring early, "some with sorrow, some with relief, and a few with bitterness."

Obviously, the most important class of consequences of technological change may not be faster book processing but the breeding of subsequent and self-generated consequences affecting library personnel. We have paid all too little attention to the consequences of library automation and networks. Ennis pointed out *in 1962*(!) that when the technological innovation applies to the world of work and is of any significance, it will shake up the allocation of specific tasks to specific people. For an early case illustrating this in ancient cultures, he draws upon the remarks of V. Gordon Childe, who reminds us that when the wheel was first anchored in a horizontal position and used to turn a lump of clay into pottery, the task of pottery-making then shifted from being the responsibility of women to that of men. What is the equivalent shift in library tasks brought about by the shift from typewriters to computer terminals? No doubt the technical services area of library operations must be feeling some mild tremors by now, but that is only the first of several predictable shakeups.

Many people have said it, but it bears repeating again. A library is primarily an organization of people intended to get things done. Therefore, individuals and groups of people must be motivated to achieve organizational goals. As Allen Veaner says in his conference paper this year, "changing from a manual to a computerized system in a library is a change in the ends or goals. Because the goal of the automated system is not the same as the goal of the manual system, we have experienced painful, human problems in their installation and application." When the objectives of the enterprise and the objectives of its employees (including the top administrators) do not coincide, the satisfaction of the objectives of one, at the expense of the other, will not be in the best interests of either. Because we have changed policies and procedures very rapidly in the past few years, we have apparently unleashed a series of consequences that we have not given proper attention. It is very difficult to address our needs for personnel when the very system for which they are "needed" is undergoing changes unperceived by the policy makers in major libraries who have remained silent on the subject of automation, by and large. (The recent article by McAnally and Downs[10] is no exception).

Abraham Heschel, the great Jewish scholar, in writing about human nature said something appropriate about librarians when he remarked that "need" denotes *the absence or shortage of something indispensable to well-being.*[11] This may be an authentic or artificial need. We librarians, like other humans, often make our judgments, decisions, and directions for action dependent upon our needs. He considers this an alarming fact that man is becoming "a fighter for needs" rather than "a fighter for ends," as defined by William James. Relating this to developments in library automation, I find that we are possibly fighting for needs to feel well ourselves and forgetting the ends or goals we have. We often find ourselves apologizing for the developments of the past five years with so many false starts, so many dashed hopes and unfulfilled promises. What have we been trying to accomplish? Why are we so unhappy with the results today? Some explain our false starts as the result of the pioneering aspects of development, but it is just possible that a better explanation comes from one ISAD oracle who said:

> Those in charge of library automation efforts in libraries in the late 60's, the top administrators—the ones who should have been directing and providing guidelines—were totally unable, unwilling, and inept. The result too often was that *systems were developed that did not correspond with the true objectives of the library.* They were often baroque, inefficient, and tended to focus on too small a part of the overall operation. In essence, the systems person in charge lacked insight to the executive/administrative levels and fell back on his experience and knowledge, usually limited and incomplete. This was exacerbated by the fact that funds were plentiful; budgets had not yet gotten tight. Therefore, there was an attitude which I think is best characterized as being irresponsible—fiscally that is.

Have the objectives of the libraries today stayed the same? Who knows for sure? How do we find out?

Our real need, it would appear, is to try to manage libraries by objectives, so that when they change, the staff will be provided with a clearer picture of where we were and are. Top administrators have not taken on the duty of preparing statements of new goals and objectives. McAnally and Downs commented that failure to plan for the future has been one of the major weaknesses of university libraries in general. The administrators have failed to recognize the resultant shakeup in allocation of specific tasks for specific people brought about in an era of change. For this reason I start this paper on library automation systems personnel at the top of the organization chart. As Gunter Grass has said, "In the midst of progress we may find ourselves standing still." Grass called to "the Citizens of Snailville" as I would like, tongue in cheek, to call to the Association of Research Libraries and ALA's Library Administration Division:

> Citizens of Snailville! Changes against which we have long been warning you are threatening to materialize. As we learn from the leaflets of radical innovators . . . the scandalous slogan: "Let us not fear the great leap!" . . . a proposal to rename our beloved Snailville . . . "Snail's Leap" . . . We call upon all citizens to thwart this sacrilege. No leaping for this town. Though we do not reject progress out of hand, we distrust haste. We have always arrived in good time. Often we have owed our survival to arriving too late. . . . Be patient, I'm clinging forward, I'm coming . . . [but] on the way I've forgotten my goal. Now I shall withdraw; what's left of me is fragile. . . .[12]

Lest the message be lost in the satire, I hasten to add that first and foremost we need library administrators who understand how to find and phrase goals and how to obtain satisfactory and satisfying results from people at work in their libraries. Singer's book, *Human Resources*, contains many good suggestions about management by objectives and the management development process (*see* his figure 6.1, especially).[13] In my opinion, there must be an annual review and resetting of objectives in libraries, with an exposition of key results to be obtained by library personnel. Otherwise, can we ever hope to answer the question: Library Systems Personnel: What are our Needs? How can we ever hope to turn around the figures in Presthus's study on the pessimistic attitudes of librarians toward their jobs?

With libraries still in the "new plan syndrome" (described by Hugh W. Calkins in a paper, "An Information System: An Accountability Theory of Policy Analysis," presented at the 1972 annual meeting of the American Political Science Association[14]), there has been no attempt to find out why a previous plan was unsuccessful in meeting its goals, or even if any of the goals were partially or totally met, before taking up a new plan. In other words, we often avoid the difficult but necessary task of finding out why our present plans are not working and we fail to measure the forces producing changes that the old plan and its adminis- tration are unable to cope with. The current planning practice in libraries today does not seem to use information intelligently.

Although I will not concentrate on policy analysis and the manage- ment development process in this paper, they are very important concepts related to personnel aspects of library automation. The recruit- ment, selection, and promotion policies of libraries, the specification of skills, knowledge, experience, and personal qualities required to perform library jobs (which in turn are designed to meet organizational ob- jectives), the job grading and salary structures established, and the identification of development potential within the present library staff (with plans for replacements and additions to insure growth)—all these topics and more are outlined in the management development process literature such as Singer's book,[15] which I urge library administrators to read.

My first point, then, which I want to make loud and clear, is: *The evolutionary extensions of the traditional bound-volume library brought about by technological innovations must be properly assessed by the top managers of these libraries with an eye to accommodating these changes in personnel and they must plan to revise the stated, and in fact, observed objectives of the libraries.* There must be a simpler way to say what I have just said, but so often we miss saying that top administrators need to look at their job of managing differently (*see* the bibliography in the McAnally-Downs article[16] for some notable exceptions to this criti- cism), although we often admonish staff in lower echelons to look at their jobs differently. The probable reason this point has not been made clear is that so much of what is written comes from the top administrators (e.g., Hammer, Weber, Rogers and Weber) themselves![17] I began this paper by concentrating on the workers in the field, but some of the background reading I have done for this paper and the remarks of the ISAD oracles have made me aware that since technological changes have begun in libraries we have not had administrators who appear to be competent enough to plan for successful transitions. Just as Congress has now established a Technology Assessment Office, we in the library field must do the same or find others who can do it for us. Our job satisfaction depends on it and our very existence also may depend on it.

Carlos Cuadra has said that professional librarians and other library personnel are ill-prepared to appreciate or assimilate the capabilities and promise of the new technology, whether in computing, reprography, or communications.[18] He also said that persons skilled in the computing art and in other aspects of the changing technology are rarely equipped to deal with the specific and complex requirements of library operations. He said that in 1969. My ISAD oracles agree with his assessment of professional librarians, circa 1968.

Are library systems personnel any better prepared now than in 1968? Apparently we are. The MARC User Survey[19] in 1972 showed 159 staff members in 52 libraries engaged in MARC *developmental* activity alone (62 of these librarians, 92 "computer people," and 4 a combination of the two). Those engaged in networks and consortia, providing services on an operational basis to external agencies are providing everything from catalog cards, selection, ordering, and circulation control to on-demand searches and SDI. Upwards of 514 external agencies are provided catalog cards or catalogs from 19 operational systems surveyed in the MARC User Survey. Dake Gull's earlier estimated ratio of one systems personnel to every twenty librarians may be very far off mark if we consider all the functions being provided by the systems personnel running the operational systems today. It just may be that we are doing something right by providing new services and doing old routines more efficiently with fewer people running the systems! Although some people are pessimistic, my ISAD oracles are very impressed with the personnel they have hired, by and large, and they are satisfied with their potential to maintain as well as improve the services presently being performed.

Another study, recently completed, corroborates the findings of the MARC User Study. Twice as many operational systems are in existence today as in the years before 1970. A 1972 Inforonics survey of some 27 libraries found about 40 mechanized systems for acquisition, cataloging, and circulation control.[20] The overall trends show libraries increasing their use of on-line systems and basic assembly language programming, and a movement into the area of cataloging mechanization. To plan and direct such large-scale information systems demands personnel with skills in handling complexity and difficult economic and technical considerations. They need to have "a lot of fight" (to quote one ISAD oracle), and to "be fanatics about their work" (to quote another).

Gone are the days of the self-taught librarian-programmer trying to find a free hour of computer time or a computer operator who plans to automate the library in his spare time. We are all aware of the shift in personnel working on library automation efforts. My ISAD oracles confirmed this. They said that today you will find personnel who are library-school trained with some basic understanding of computers and systems analysis. Library clerks have been retrained or replaced with trained keypunchers. The computer center on some campuses or in service bureaus provide some programmers and systems analysts who have been trained by computer manufacturers, or in industry, to handle large files and library operations. A more sophisticated crew is on board in 1973, and their numbers are increasing but at a slower rate. Someone, like Fred Kilgour, still could say in 1972 that there is a "near total absence of librarians possessing an effective knowledge of computation and of systems programmers with experience in designing and programming complex character manipulation systems."[21] So our needs are not yet totally met by any means.

Many organizational charts and task analysis projects reflect the role of the librarian and the nonlibrarian specialist in library automation projects.[22] The Illinois Task Analysis Project clearly delineates between librarian, specialist, and technical assistant, with computer work and data processing enumerated as areas of tasks and skills in their array of some 1800 tasks found in 18 different Illinois libraries.[23] The rating scales developed by the U.S. Department of Labor and used in this task analysis study, which was conducted by SERD (Social, Educational Research & Development, Inc.), confirm the amount of years of training required and the advanced language and math skills required for such tasks. The task environment for such work is described as "very specific" and they state the requirement that a precise attainment of tasks with set limits or tolerances is the norm with evaluation against measurable or verifiable criteria. Would that this were the case for other library tasks!

Most of the writers on the organization of personnel to perform library automation efforts stress the "team approach" but they put the team together in different ways, depending upon which phase (developmental or operational) they are describing, and, more importantly, whether they see the automation aspects integrated with current operations in the library as it is presently operating (from acquisition through reference and readers' services), or as an opportunity to reorganize staff and work procedures. The charts also reflect differences when the automation staff is on the library payroll or the computation center payroll.

The developments in staff realignments are worth watching very carefully. They do reflect one answer to the question: What are the needs for systems personnel? Several of the ISAD oracles commented on the need to differentiate between development (or planning) and operational staff. For instance, the MARC User Survey referred to earlier described the developmental workers separately and the Inforonics study was directed toward operational systems, first and foremost.

A statement on staff needs then might run something like this:

1. For development, we need a leader who understands user requirements thoroughly. "Someone with tact, diplomacy, leadership ability, financial and planning expertise," according to one ISAD oracle. Another oracle mentioned such characteristics as "flexible, open to logical planning procedures." They agree that the development staff should include a systems analyst and perhaps a programmer. Whether there are librarians on this staff is not essential in their opinion.

2. On the operational side, there should be more machine operators, programmers, and systems people who work closely with the staff in the older library departments. Because the flow of work with an automated system can differ quite considerably from the old procedures, going into the operational phase can cause a breakdown of the barriers between departments, resulting in new combinations in order to eliminate duplication of work. The overall organization structure of the library may be materially altered as a library proceeds into its third or fifth operational year of library automation. This should be closely watched. Given the fact in the Inforonics study that systems started in 1970 in the libraries surveyed increased the number in operation by 300 percent, we can safely predict some rather traumatic changes in library organization unless the top administrators prepare *now* for needed organizational changes.

These changes will occur even on the highest levels in the organizational chart. Some libraries, for example, have already reorganized around three assistant directors: for resources, services, and support; or stated differently, as services, collections, and processing. Other libraries have tried to accommodate the relationships they have established with the computer center by assigning an assistant director to automation responsibilities, working within the library through an "automation committee" and outside via a university committee for computer system planning. The planning (or development) function is often accommodated by a line officer for planning.

Most of the organization charts I examined or heard about from my ISAD oracles appear to be quite tentative and untested against the need in the very near future to accommodate the predicted event of *network* systems planning and operations. Except for advisory committees, which contribute greatly to the progress of some consortia and networks, internal staff changes are not yet implemented; many are waiting for retirements of key personnel. Fred Kilgour addresses this problem from the point of view of the director of a computerized regional cooperative. Library administrators must think about and express their views too.

Another change which is not properly accommodated in the present organizational charts is how automation and the reference service or bibliographic functions will be integrated. A loose arrangement via a committee will not provide the proper clout for effecting those needed changes in personnel and objectives in the organization which is implicit in one policy statement: "point of use is point of input." The amount of retraining of staff, systems analysis and redesign of work flow, revision of objectives, and task allocation that this will bring cannot be studied or implemented smoothly if we stay with the present organizational charts existing in most libraries with automation at the present time. One ISAD oracle considers this transfer of personnel to be one of the major problems generated by library automation efforts.

As if these problems regarding library staff weren't enough, Herb Landau opened another can of worms (or sparkling challenge, if you are an optimist) when he pleaded with librarians in 1970 to consider themselves as data base managers.[24] If they didn't, he said, someone else will take on the task for us. Will the proliferation of data bases go on for some time before many librarians perceive the impact such a resource has or can have on their present library systems? Landau highlights the functions that such a data base manager would have to perform, and they are indeed very similar to those enumerated by Weber when he describes library automation efforts.[25] The projected developments in networks and consortia, expanded services, and new data bases could all come together if the top managers of large libraries begin to see their role as ever-expanding rather than status quo. To repeat Gunter Grass: "In the midst of progress we may find ourselves standing still." What are we going to do in Library Snailville this year?

Besides these new challenges, the ISAD oracles see the need for personnel who can maintain and refine existing systems and help to interconnect through software the various regional centers and networks which are not now 100 percent compatible. Most of them agree that we will need many more clerical people for the massive effort underway to automate the entire current bibliographic apparatus at the Library of Congress and elsewhere. The differentiation between systems and application programmers will continue and, of course, this will mean the need for personnel, some who care more, some less, about library problems. Even so, one ISAD oracle saw the merging of the two disciplines by 1978, with librarians and computer people much more appreciative of each other's special skills and knowledge. One oracle said we need people who can understand the potential of the computer *and* the potential of the library. The trend toward use of external services, with trained systems personnel in one location to do work for several libraries (clearly a trend, if the *MARC User Survey* in 1972 is a fair sample), will most likely result in the conclusion on the part of even the staunchest citizens of Library Snailville that we will have to do away with the idea of local self-sufficiency. The fast-response, computerized union catalogs and their ancillary network apparatus will do more to change our goals and attitudes, believe it or not, about *library service* than it has or will change our cataloging procedures. The management details associated with negotiating contracts and planning the execution of library programs dependent on outside services will cause a wholly different approach to library administration. There are many challenges ahead for library personnel on all levels. Fred Kilgour said that the unattainable goal of libraries for economic viability may only be reached with the combination of computation and cooperation.[26] We all hope that this is a true promise!

All of this and more, that even my ISAD oracles did not describe, appears to be waiting for us on the way to 1978. The impact that these predictions have on education for librarianship is just short of tremendous. All of the ISAD oracles commented on this as they reviewed the qualifications they expected staff to have in 1978. They commented on the amount of time they and their systems staff had to spend in on-the-job training since 1968. One ISAD oracle estimated more than 30 percent of their time was spent in training sessions with the library staff! They all expected to do less of this as the library schools turned out graduates who were more sophisticated about data communication, computer technology, microforms, etc., but one oracle said that on-the-job training in the future will be needed to help librarians find new products and services as they concentrate less on changes in their work routines.

Shoffner in 1970 proposed a fellowship program to support any and all librarians for reeducation in computer-based library systems.[27] He estimated that some 15,000 man-years of student time (roughly six man-months for each of 30,000 librarians today) costing some $40 million would be a reasonable investment if you consider that this staff is the manpower now managing some $2 billion each year of library services. Whether the curriculum is that of systems analysis and computer technology or improved management skills, I think we would agree that courses would go far beyond those described by Tell in 1967, namely, programming, systems analysis, flowcharting, operations research, etc.[28] Rauseo thought there were training implications for people who prepared input data, people who ran computer systems, and people who use computer outputs.[29] That is a tall order, especially when one realizes that the staff being retrained are facing dislocation and/or instability of employment, and the teachers realize that these people will place heavy demands on them for different educational experiences than they provided earlier. Landau[30] provides a reading list to help librarians train themselves as data base managers; this includes readings in file design, vocabulary and language processing, search strategy, data base software, hardware and administration. No doubt we need more self-learning packages for everyone, from the top of the organization chart on down. But first, the question is, who will teach the teachers so that they are prepared for the reeducation programs of librarians?[31] I don't have the answer immediately, but I would guess it is related to my suggestion for a change in attitude of the top administrators in libraries. Mary Lee Bundy asks, "Are we like Merton's engineers . . . indoctrinated with an ethical sense of limited responsibilities?"[32] The ISAD oracles agree that we need more questioning, evaluating spirits by 1978. My suggestion is that we look for these people to fill jobs from the top down, in library schools and on the job. Whoever is doing the looking for staff today must help us reverse the trend which Robert Presthus found in 1970: two-thirds of the librarians with "job blahs," top administrators with lower accommodation potential than some of their staff, and education and training patterns which barely represent the status quo, let alone the future.

I hope we are beyond the end of the following story about wisdom which Stafford Beer tells. A young man asked a rabbi, "Rabbi, how do I become wise?" The rabbi replied, "Well, you study, work hard, and gain knowledge." The man said, "But, rabbi, a lot of people study and work hard and gain knowledge and are not wise." The rabbi said, "You study, work hard, gain knowledge, *and* have experience." The man said, "Rabbi, a lot of people study, work hard, gain knowledge, have experience and are not wise." The rabbi said, "Well, you work hard, study, gain knowledge, have experience and good judgment." "Rabbi, how do you have good judgment?" The rabbi said, "By having bad experience."[33]

Can we pool our bad experiences and possibly make an effort to apply wisdom to our needs for systems personnel and to our goal setting for library service? I sincerely hope so.

ACKNOWLEDGMENTS

Anonymous but impeccable sources have been consulted to provide the writer with the proper perspective of the then-now-and-future scene. As with the oracles in ancient Greece and Rome, their answers have hidden meanings but are, nonetheless, very wise answers. Their years of experience and their accomplishments in the library automation field are well documented. Their anonymity here allows them, through me, to reveal some of their impressions of where we have been and where we are going, without a need to defend themselves or protect the institutions which they have served or are serving. I want to thank these ISAD oracles for their help.

DISCUSSION

Harold Roth (Nassau County Reference Library): What is the time frame between development and operational systems in a library?

Veaner: There is no fixed answer to a question like that. I believe it depends entirely on the complexity of the tasks you are attempting, the resources at your disposal, and the environment that you are working in. I just think that there is no canned answer for that question. Anyhow, Pauline, I'm here to make comments, not to answer questions that you are supposed to be answering. I did not have a question—I want to thank you for a very beautiful paper, but you did cite the number "20" associated with the staffs for BALLOTS—and I thought I ought to explicate that number somewhat, because I think it may be slightly misleading. Many of you know that at one time there were actually two projects that were running together at Stanford, BALLOTS and SPIRES, which for a four-year period or so were under combined directorship, and while those two projects were combined, the total development staff ranged from 17 to 20 at various times. Last year SPIRES became a production system, fully supported by the Stanford Center for Information Processing, and subsequent to that the staffing for SPIRES is now two persons on maintenance only, and the staffing for the BALLOTS project is twelve persons, which consists of the following: one program director, one programming manager, two secretarial and support staff, one documentation specialist, four analyst/programmers and three programmers. The analyst/programmers kind of move back and forth between functions from time to time. This number does not include any of the training contributions and other contributions made by the regular library staff, including the director and the heads of the departments and individual users who help specify what's needed, but the correct number at this time for BALLOTS is twelve.

Atherton: Allen, how many staff members are at Stanford, just to get a proportion?

Veaner: How many contributed?

Atherton: No, how many total library staff people are there now, full-time equivalent, at Stanford?

Veaner: Oh, full-time equivalent? The number is about 250 librarians.

Atherton: That's one to twenty; that's magic—that may become a law!

Veaner: I've got it here; the staffing of the University Library is 257 persons, and that does not include 65 FTE casual or hourly employees, nor does it include the twelve persons on the BALLOTS project.

Atherton: To answer the first question, I didn't think I am as qualified to answer as someone with experience, but we have certain landmark dates in library automation. Before 1965 a lot of people didn't even know what the term meant or they were working on something in such a way that there really wasn't much impetus. Certainly you would have to call it exploratory development, if it was development. We are eight years away from 1965, so that I think if you are starting out from scratch (and Allen was right—there are so many different factors involved), you have to feel that there is some kind of time frame, probably two or three years, and that's a very rough estimate of involvement in thinking, objective setting, and planning that will come in along the way. I also think we are borrowing each other's systems, which would of course cut down development time.

Veaner: May I make one more comment, which I think was inherent in your paper, but maybe not explicit, and that is I believe that the development process never really ceases in any live organization, and if any of us believe that once we have passed by this development stage we are all done, that we can tie the ribbon around the package, plug it in and start using it, I think that's a mistake. Investment in development and maintenance is a continuing effort, not a one-shot deal.

Atherton: That's why in the *MARC User Survey* of development efforts there was this blending between the two. Ralph?

Shoffner: Yes, Pauline. First, a clarification on the '70 paper. What I estimated was that it was virtually redoing one-half of the professional librarian's education; that's the way I arrived at the six man-months. What I had in mind was not that it would be necessarily an intensive six months all at one time, but that it was going to be at that kind of level.

Atherton: Or that it would have to be in a classroom, or sitting in with 400 people at the Frontier Hotel.

Shoffner: Quite right. Now a question with respect to your oracles, and it's essential—do you trust them with respect to their statements about the present? Isn't there a certain amount of tendency of the oracles to be very optimistic about the present and somewhat more balanced in view about the things that are long gone, for which the final reports have been written and all justifications have been taken care of?

Atherton: Well, I can tell you this about their personalities. Some of them are rather discouraged where they are presently working, and others are just born optimists. There is no doubt about that. They didn't know that each of the others would be presenting remarks to me. I didn't get them on a conference call and ask them these questions. Each independently answered my questions, and I was surprised to find there was as much corroboration of their estimates of the present staff, future, and things like that. What really hit me between the eyes and caused me to change the whole emphasis of my paper was how they felt about the library administrators. Some of them have been library administrators themselves! Their remarks urge me to strongly encourage ISAD to do some kind of manpower study. When I say manpower study I mean study of attitudes and organizational structures and *staffs* and things like that. There is a lot to be done. No, I feel very queasy about trusting to eight people's comments, and that's all I really heard from, but they are good people and they certainly have more experience than I have handling the changes that have come in the last five years and that are to come in the next five.

Howard Dillon (Sangamon State University, Illinois): I only wanted to ask a few questions, but first of all it struck me: did you not develop and direct a project called "Project LEEP"?

Atherton: Yes, spelled LEEP, which stands for Library Education Experimental Project.

Dillon: It just struck me as you were reading. To make some observations about the possibilities, or potential possibilities for library education: I noticed that your oracles felt that a portion of their time was being taken with staff training and they were saying, "Would you please as a library educator take that burden away from us?"

Atherton: No, they didn't say that; they just said they thought they had less to do because library education was turning out better graduates. No, they still felt the need in their own libraries.

Dillon: Well, I'll ask the question anyway. Can library education meet all of these needs? That is, if you are to graduate persons who have at least a general knowledge in systems and technical matters, they also need to know something about resources development and bibliographical organization; they need to know something about learning theory and how librarians are facilitators for persons learning, what the relationship is there; they need to know more about human skills and interpersonal interaction, and they need to know more about administrative problems—management/labor is a very strong issue in education. I'm going to make my comment that if anyone then, as I did, heard your comment and said that people are trying to remove the need for staff training on the job and put it back in library schools, my feeling is that that's impractical in terms of the broad range of things we have to deal with.

Atherton: No, that would be the wrong interpretation of what my remarks were leading to. Now I see education as a continuous process, I see people in library schools almost overly concentrating on the beginning of that process and not enough balance in blending in with that continuous process. It's difficult to implement but I still think it needs to be worked out somehow. The ISAD committee that's working on seminars has stated the continuous training problem for our profession.

We should try to tap library education educators to help with that process, which may go on in libraries, may go on in regional network staff meetings, or wherever. As far as the beginning of the process is concerned, concentration is on the master's degree in library schools. Some library educators are thinking very seriously of a need for a two-year program, just to get in more skills than one can in one year. No one is more frustrated than I am in a cataloging class when I want to talk about abstracting and indexing services and developing a thesaurus and there just isn't time to do it adequately. I also don't believe that this kind of relationship between you and me is a very effective educational device. I abhor it but still take the opportunity to participate because I think there may be some stimulation. I believe more in self-learning and we haven't done enough in that area, so there are various ways of handling the problem.

Dillon: Let me give you another subject to comment on. You do, to a degree, or your oracles do, to a degree, chastise the administrators of libraries in the '60s for having been baroque and too cautious.

Atherton: No, cautious wasn't the word; they just didn't give any guidance. Yesterday someone came to my table in the evening and said "We are data processing people and we really can't find out from librarians what they want"; that's another way of saying what I said in my paper today. The library administrators responsible for goal-setting in a library, however they want to do it, with their staff involvement, or all by themselves as pronouncements, just did not come through with these statements when they were needed. So that's not caution, that's ineptitude.

Dillon: Do you think in the '70s there is going to be the opportunity to make those leaps; economically, will we have the kind of money we saw in the late '60s and without the money, will we make those leaps?

Atherton: I don't think money is the problem. I think money became the problem when we had too much of it. We have been looking at the Senate Watergate hearings on TV the last couple of weeks hearing of another situation where too much money sometimes causes its own problems. I really believe that we can solve our problems if we tend to do our jobs as well as we can. This includes getting the right person in the right job so that they can really blossom in that job. The evidence both from the library administrators themselves which comes through in the McAnally and Downs article in *College and Research Libraries* for

March and the words of my ISAD oracles just hit me that this is a group of people who for one reason or another (and I'm not a part of them, so as an outsider I can always see them better than they can see themselves, maybe) who really need some reeducation, revitalization. I would like to hear from the administrators in the audience. Am I right about this opinion? Or am I wrong?

James Dolby (R & D Associates): Could a nonadministrator say something? I'm Jim Dolby, I'm a nonadministrator, nonlibrarian, non-computer man. I am a statistician and I would like to say something about my field that applies, I think, to something that you said about yours. In the '30s in statistics something grew up known as mathematical statistics and it did not do away with the old statistics, which was largely census survey methods that of course goes back to Roman times and is as ancient as librarianship in that sense. I recall going to a meeting in the mid-fifties where I stood around talking to a number of statisticians older than I and better known then, and now, for that matter, and it turned out I was not only unique in being the youngest one in this conversation, I was also unique in being the only one who had taken a course in statistics. This whole group had migrated during the '30s and '40s from the mathematical field, from the fields of chemistry, biology, actuarial science, and things of this sort. The result was that a whole new set of statistics courses came into being in the '50s; and statistics degrees came into being that made something very different from the statistics degrees in the '30s and early '40s. It would not surprise me if a rather similar thing would happen here. I am sure that a number of librarians have already migrated over into it.

Atherton: A number of people have done something and wandered off again, but I think you will find that in five or ten years from now, there will be a very significant number of people at an ISAD meeting who still haven't had their first course in librarianship.

Weisbrod: I assumed you called these consultants "oracles" because you used the Delphi Method, but I guess not?

Atherton: It wasn't iterative. I didn't have enough time.

Weisbrod: There is a Delphi Method which involves recycling itera-tively samples anonymously or identified as a source through a panel several times so each can react to the response of the first. One tends to draw a consensus, but amazingly enough you say you started with a consensus. Just one additional thing, if my recollection as to the number of full-time equivalent manpower of the Yale University Library is correct, I think our ratio there was 100 to 1.

Atherton: I think that's the direction we will be going in.

William McGrath: (Southwestern Louisiana University): Well, you asked the question, if you are right or wrong, and I'll respond to that. I think you are right. The goal-setting in libraries is a very important thing. Incidentally, I would like to tell that statistician that I am a library administrator and this summer I'm going to take my sixth course in statistics.

Atherton: You may be a statistician before long.

McGrath: My staff thinks I'm a statistician, but I'm not. W. H. Auden says somewhere, "Thou shalt not sit with statisticians." I think that it might be mentioned that there are several well-known librarians that have done the very thing you are asking them to do: to sit down and set their goals. I think one of the significant efforts in this line recently is that of Cornell University. You might invite Ry Ross to describe that.

Atherton: He is right behind you.

Ryburn Ross (Cornell University): Well, for an entire year the Cornell University Libraries with the help of the American Management Association as a consultant has gone through a very soul-searching process in which we have tried to describe the mission of the library, its objectives, its policies, what it really is made up of, and set a course of action insofar as laying down a strategy of planning for the future, and it's only beginning. It took an entire year, a great deal of staff effort. It's been very well documented by Bill McGrath in a report which will be made available through ERIC, and we have sent some copies out. There is a very limited number of copies that were sent out to the ARL Libraries so if you are a member of an ARL library, get to your library director and see if you can get hold of a copy that was sent to him, which is in printed form, and you will also be able to get the report through ERIC eventually.

I think it carries forward some of the work that was done at Columbia, which, of course, is still going on at Columbia. Now, in data processing, we laid down several objectives, both continuing and specific, in relationship to what we felt would be the direction of the future, and we will be looking at every system that comes along really on a cost benefit basis, and doing it extremely carefully. We did lay down an objective that we would join networks as they come up and we will in August have terminals on the OCLC system and our cataloging system has searching, cataloging, and card production systems already set, all the personnel has been trained, the tie-line is in, the only thing we are waiting for is a brand new terminal that is just being manufactured by Beehive Medical Electronics in Salt Lake City, both for OCLC's use and for FAUL, Five Associated University Libraries. FAUL consists of five of the large schools in central western New York State; we have extended membership in this organization to the State Library of New York and to State University of New York in Albany. I think the process that Bill is speaking of is really a very beginning; it's maybe changed my thinking as an assistant director in the library system; I think it's changed the director's thinking about automation rather drastically, and he allowed me to make some reorganizational changes, which I think will eventually have effect in the field of automation and in data processing in our libraries.

Roth: I'm in a new area, developing a new operation; it's written up in a variety of places, and people respond to it, but you don't get total detail. But what comes out of it is an attempt to build a large operating structure on top of institutions which should have followed rather than preceded it, and in a political milieu where tremendous computer capability is available on a county level, where the responsibility is not given up, and where the relationships are very uncertain because our agency after three-and-a-half years is still an uncertain johnny-come-lately that stands in danger of jeopardizing—or so people think—their operation. As an administrator I am trying to work in a goal-oriented operation; however, we've found out we had to learn to be opportunistic and leave our options open, to draw and derive from. Perhaps that's why I enjoyed Mitch's paper yesterday—because the use of the type of information that is available (and I guess the important part is having available to you the knowledge that this information exists and some evaluation of how it works) is extremely important to help the administrator to make some effective decisions, certainly to keep his goals and objectives up-to-date, because the difficulty we are finding is that interpreting us as librarians to people who are management/information-oriented and who control the computers from an operational point of view is most difficult, including the reason for my earlier question on timing for development. Selling the concept of how much time it takes to develop something is impossible in this situation because they say "We already exist; if you tie in with us, we will tell you how much time it takes." But we may end up with a camel or an elephant or something else—not the kind of service we want. Many of us here have the same problem; maybe we don't speak of it, but it does exist. I know that at many of the academic institutions I visited when I worked for Baker & Taylor and others, the decision was not made by the administrator because the funding available to him restricted how far he could go on his decisions. And I would say, if I were to offer any criticism, that you are talking in a very theoretical way about this end, and when we start applying practice to the theory we run into trouble and start beating up on our confreres, saying, "Why didn't you do it differently?" They didn't do it differently because they didn't have enough information; they don't have the capacity, and worst of all, sometimes they don't have the support from the total group to make it worthwhile to do anyway. I think we are too snobbish in many ways, and I'm concerned with the statement made yesterday which relates to this, to the fact that this will become an elite group again. The day we stop permitting people to come in by keeping our information at a slightly lower level is the day we are going to lose the whole battle to whoever else is strong enough to take it over. My point, nonetheless, is the fact that this is the difficulty of trying to be goal-oriented, yet recognizing that you have to be flexible.

Butler: I had one comment as we close, as a personal comment, as one person who didn't fit into your classifications very readily, my primary responsibility in my company is marketing but, as Jim Dolby says, I poke my nose in various things. It has been my observation, and people like Harold Roth have been on both sides of the fence, that one of the remarkable differences between successful and unsuccessful library automation projects—and it's true of the small ones and more true of the big ones and it's vital with the networks—is the marketing of the project; what we would call in the outside world—marketing the project—and by that I mean improving the communication with the people, if you like, the customers of the center or the individual branch librarians or staff who are going to be the customers of the computer operation and you can do chapter and verse on the ones that have been more successful because of improved communication. It means money, it means more expense, it means a lot more time. I would consider it marketing, there are a lot of other names for it. That kind of communication is something to add to that list of qualities in library automation personnel that was pretty long already.

APPENDIX: QUESTIONNAIRE SENT TO 13
ISAD ORACLES.

As a personal favor to me, would you participate in a Delphic exercise relating to Library Automation Staff Needs? I'm preparing an opinion paper for the ALA Las Vegas Preconference. In it, I will try to present a five year perspective on the occupational outlook of Library Automation Systems Personnel. I HONESTLY NEED YOUR HELP! Like Szilard's *Voice of the Dolphins*, we need the word from an impeccable source! Your remarks will be used anonymously. I will batch the ten Delphic remarks I am soliciting and who knows (!) even you may not be able to recognize your own statement.

You have been chosen because of your clear and present visage through the years that library automation has come into its own. With such a perspective, you can look backwards and forwards, I'm sure. Speak from your present vantage point, or from a previous position you recently left.

Please comment on the following topic and questions. Feel free to use a tape recorder (cassette or reel will be accepted) if you can "predict" or "recall" more fluidly in that way. (I will return tapes if you so desire.) Anything you can provide before May 1 will be greatly appreciated.

I. *Staff Organization for Library Automation Efforts*
   In 1968—Now—and in 1978:
   a) Who did what?
   b) How did "regular" librarians participate?
   c) How was/is obsolescence, termination, and retraining of manpower handled?
   d) How has staff organization chart changed because of library automation?
   e) What *new* skills were/are needed and where did/will this talent come from?

II. *Staff Qualifications*
   A. What personality characteristics and qualifications did you (in 1968) and will you (in 1973) look for?
   B. What kind of training did you expect (in 1968) prospective staff member to have? Has that changed? Should it change by 1978?

C. What kind of on-the-job training did you provide in 1968? in 1972?

III. *Occupational Outlook*

A. By 1978, how many people do you expect will be employed in library automation tasks in:

	Guestimate for 1978	Your 1968 Estimate
a) Individual libraries	_____	_____
b) Consortia, systems, or networks	_____	_____
c) Commercial processing centers	_____	_____

B. What percent will be professional?   _____%

What percent will be clerical?   _____%

C. How will the tasks performed by library automation staff change by 1978?

Thanks a million!
Sincerely,

Pauline A. Atherton
Professor

PAA:kao

REFERENCES

[1] *Occupational Outlook Handbook,* 1959 and 1972–73 eds. (Washington, DC: U.S. Dept. of Labor, Bur. of Labor Statistics).

[2] C. D. Gull, "Personnel Requirements for Automation in Libraries," *in* John Harvey, ed., *Data Processing in Public and University Libraries* (Washington, DC: Spartan, 1966), pp. 125–41.

[3] *Library Automation: A State of the Art Review.* Stephen R. Salmon, ed. Papers presented at Preconference Institute, June 22–24, 1967. (Chicago: American Library Assn., 1969).

[4] *Recruiting Library Personnel: Automation in the Library* (ACRL Monographs no. 17; Chicago: American Library Assn., 1956), p. 27.

[5] Ibid., p. 43.

[6] David C. Weber, "Personnel Aspects of Library Automation," *Journal of Library Automation* 4:27–37 (Mar. 1971).

[7] Donald P. Hammer, "Casting for Automation: New Roles for Administrator, Librarian, Systems Analyst, Programmer," *Library Journal* 94:4492–95 (Dec. 15, 1969).

[8] Philip H. Ennis, "Technological Change and the Professions: Neither Luddite nor Technocrat," *Library Quarterly* 32:189–98 (July 1962).

[9] Robert Presthus, *Technological Change and Occupational Response: A Study of Librarians.* Final Report, Project No. 07–1084. (Washington, DC: Off. of Education, Bur. of Research, 1970).

[10] Arthur M. McAnally and Robert B. Downs, "The Changing Role of Directors of University Libraries," *College and Research Libraries* 34:103–25 (Mar. 1973).

[11] Abraham J. Heschel, "Second Edition: The Abiding Challenge of Religion," *Center Magazine* 6:43–46 (Mar./Apr. 1973).

[12] Gunter Grass, "From *Diary of a Snail,*" *American Scholar* 42:259–61 (Spring 1973).

[13] Edwin J. Singer and John Ramsden, *Human Resources; Obtaining Results from People at Work* (London: McGraw Hill, 1972).

[14] Hugh W. Calkins, "An Information System: An Accountability Theory of Political Analysis," in *Proceedings* of the 1972 Annual Meeting of the American Political Science Assn., Sept. 5–9. The American Political Science Assn.

[15] Singer and Ramsden, *Human Resources.*

[16] McAnally and Downs, "The Changing Role."

[17] Hammer, "Casting for Automation"; Weber, "Personnel Aspects of Library Automation"; Rutherford D. Rogers and David C. Weber, *University Library Administration* (New York: Wilson, 1971), pp. 299–321.

[18] Carlos Cuadra, *Technology in Libraries* (Santa Monica, Calif.: System Development Corp., 1967), pp. 119–20.

[19] *MARC User Survey* (Washington, DC: Library of Congress, 1972).

[20] Inforonics, Inc., "Survey of Automated Library Systems." Phase I. Final Report for California State University and Colleges, Dec. 8, 1972. (mimeographed).

[21] Frederick G. Kilgour, "Computer-Based Systems, a New Dimension to Library Automation," *College and Research Libraries* 34:137–43 (Mar. 1973).

[22] Richard T. Kimber, *Automation in Libraries* (Oxford, Eng.: Pergamon, 1968), pp. 6, 11, 34. *See also* references mentioned in notes 2, 6, and 7.

[23] Myrl Ricking and Robert E. Booth, "Illinois Task Analysis Project: Phase III Handbook." Prepared for the Advisory Committee, Illinois Task Analysis Project, Aug. 1972. (mimeographed).

[24] Herbert Landau,"Can the Librarian Become a Computer Data Base Manager?" *Special Libraries* 62:117–24 (Mar. 1971).

[25] David C. Weber, "Personnel Aspects of Library Automation."

[26] Kilgour, "Computer-Based Systems."

[27] Ralph M. Shoffner, "Economics of National Automation of Libraries," *Library Trends* 18:461–62 (Apr. 1970).

[28] Bjorn V. Tell, "Inclusion of Systems Analysis and Programming in Curricula for Documentalists," *in International Conference on Education for Scientific Information Work, 3-7 Apr. 1967.* FID 422 (The Hague, FID, Sept. 1967), 200–206.

[29] M. J. Rauseo, "Training Implications of Automated Personnel Systems," *American Documentation* 18:248–49 (Oct. 1967).

[30] Landau, "Can the Librarian Become a Computer Data Base Manager?"

[31] Henriette Avram, "Bibliographic and Technical Problems in Implementing a National Library Network," *Library Trends* 18:487 (Apr. 1970); Elizabeth W. Stone, ed., "Personnel Development and Continuing Education in Libraries-Introduction," *Library Trends* 20:1–16 (July 1971).

[32] Mary Lee Bundy, "Libraries, Manpower, and Automation: Shaping the Future of Libraries," *Library Trends* 18:464–86 (Apr. 1970).

[33] Stafford Beer,"Managing Modern Complexity" *in* House Committee on Science and Astronautics, *Management of Information and Knowledge* (Washington, DC: Govt. Ptg. Off., 1970), p. 16.

7 Innovative Strategies in Systems and Automation

Walter Curley

I am a library administrator who formerly was director of a large information system design group for a commercial research firm. Therefore I have been exposed to both the developmental and decision-making side of the process of innovation.

Many of the developments which have occurred in the area of computer service to libraries have taken place in recent years in colleges and universities. My feeling is that this is the case because of:

1. The presence of operation research personnel on campus
2. The view of some college and university administrations that computers are part of the educational process
3. The availability to libraries of an on-campus, computer facility
4. The circumstance that college and university libraries enjoy a discrete borrowing clientele for the most part, a factor which is particularly useful when designing circulation and reserve systems.

With a few exceptions, the public library field is far behind. Many public libraries working with computers are still struggling with batch processing, and many, perhaps most, are still not yet embarked on their first foray into the computer field. Fred Kilgour's operation (OCLC) is allowing many public libraries to have an opportunity to participate in a network, a regional concept, where on their own they were not able to do this kind of thing. The Los Angeles Public Library and the New York Public Library have made major efforts in this field, with the former working on a multipackaged total system of which much is already completed. The Cleveland Public Library, in its venture with mini-computers, is moving in an innovative direction for libraries. Providence Public Library, the Suffolk Cooperative Library System, the Nassau Library System, and others are notable for their experience with com-

Director, Cleveland (Ohio) Public Library

puters. But when you consider the total number of public libraries in the United States added to the number of college, university, school and special libraries in this country, it must be admitted that we have not yet begun to scratch the surface of computer services for libraries.

You may question why a library administrator has been asked to talk to such a technically oriented audience in his highly untechnical way. I have asked myself this question also. Perhaps I am here to provide comic relief after two days of rather ponderous if enlightening discussion. I would like to believe, however, that it has been recognized that the effectiveness of any library computer program ultimately depends upon the library administration's ability to insure that it is doing what it was intended to do for the library's broad purposes. Speaking, therefore, as an administrator, I want to be certain that whatever is attempted by my library will stand up to a cost/benefit analysis; that it will work; that it will perform in a steady, reliable fashion; and that it will fit within the framework of the institution. Also, and perhaps most important of all, because any computer effort will have its negative audience in the public library, and because positive results must be produced quickly to insure smooth operation of the program, any computer operation must become operational fully or in part with a minimum of lead time.

Why is it that the public libraries are so far behind, and I suspect it's probably because of a little bit that I'm going to touch on right now—the philosophy of having a data base, building the retrospective file and placing this file into one machine-readable form or another, developing an ordering system, capturing the current information, adding the retrospective file and the current information together, taking your book ordering system and having that systematically build your inventory over a period of time. Hopefully what will occur in the process is that you will be paying your bills by harnessing and mechanizing your catalog and order department, and other subsidiary efforts: once the inventory is built, from that will come a book catalog and, eventually, circulation control, and it all hangs together. If you can't do that, then maybe you shouldn't do any of it. There is the concept of the total effort and I think really that's the right concept.

It seems to me that the decision-making process should relate to the institution served, and that perhaps it is not necessary to approach it as rigidly as I suggested earlier. To me, at least, there are several developments in the last five years which tend to open up options to the decision-maker. First, of course, is either the minicomputer role or being able to hang terminals on a data base which is stored somewhere else and which enables one to get the information out on demand. And second, regional centers such as those I mentioned just briefly, or networks where you can enter a large data base that's prepared for you, or that you had a part in preparing and that you can take advantage of not only what you have put in, but perhaps what others have put in as well. I think these are two major developments that open options to an administrator who is seeking to do *something*, if he can't do it all. So, if we are talking about strategies for innovation, you probably are suggesting that what I'm really talking about is thinking big. Well, I'm not sure that's the case. I'm suggesting that you can think both big and small at the same time, and that they are not mutually exclusive. As a matter of fact, I think minicomputers and terminals and the regional centers are not mutually exclusive; I think they can operate together and ought to be able to operate together very well.

It occurs to me that the administrative thought processes which led the Cleveland Public Library to the minicomputer may prove useful to this group. The Cleveland Public Library has a collection of 3-1/2 million volumes, including 1-1/2 million titles. It has a computer which was six years old, operating on a batch processing, report-oriented level, costing approximately $160,000 per year. Very little of the program worked well. We first outlined the major objectives of the library, one of which was to have available management information that would be both timely and accurate. We evaluated the capabilities of various computers, measuring their capabilities against the objectives we sought to achieve. We came to the following conclusions:

1. Our operation was continuous in nature and therefore should have the capability of providing information at any step within whatever process was being computerized.
2. The processes involved in our various operations on the computer were physically distributed throughout two large buildings.
3. The Data Processing Department and the batch-oriented process were part of a centralized operation and were remote from the departments which were being served by this system. This was evaluated to be a disadvantage. A public library because of pay scales is not likely to be able to attract high-powered systems design staff and probably should not try to do so. Many of the computer design staff are not only expensive, but for the sake of their own careers move from institution to institution, constantly seeking state of the art challenges. That being the case, developmental effort of a large scale should be performed outside the library with production and first echelon technical effort provided from within.
4. Any system that we might decide upon should allow for upward mobility and, hopefully, be modular in design.

5. The system to be decided upon would have to be timely with the information it provides, so that management would not have to rely upon and make decisions based upon data at least two weeks old rather than up-to-the-minute in its currency.

6. There was a need to do something immediately which would be both productive and economical. It did not seem unreasonable to hope that some other computer program could produce more and better results at an annual expenditure of less than $160,000 per year.

It is a fact of life that the staffs of many sizeable libraries are not very familiar with the important details of their day-to-day operations, a prerequisite before any sound judgment can be made about which way to move with a computer program. I must confess that the digging which led up to our decision to go the minicomputer route was a most educational experience for me in what it taught me and others about the inner workings of many departments at the Cleveland Public Library.

Following a cost comparison of several large computer systems and a proposed mini-computer system, the Library concluded that the proposed mini-computer system offered a better system at a lower cost than any large computer system. The lower hardware cost allowed a change in emphasis in system design. Instead of one large system, individual systems could be made available to particular tasks or groups of tasks on a dedicated on-line basis. Data entries or requests for information could be serviced by the dedicated systems immediately. No waiting for batch processing times, in order to make use of the computer facility, would be required.

The small size of a mini-computer system, coupled with its freedom from environmental constraints, such as air conditioning, or extra power, would allow complete data processing units, roughly the size of an office desk, to be placed in the operating departments, rather than in a separate computer center. These small units, complete with direct access storage, would form an expandable system of data processing capability. Communication with the system in a user-oriented, conversational mode, would allow the system to be used by Library personnel without formal computer training.

With reference to the staffing of a new computer system, the Library concluded that it should concentrate on the overall planning of its information needs, and contract out for the design, programming, and installation of any computer system. Preferably each system would be acquired as a total package, including the equipment and the programming. The Library's acceptance would be based on the ability of the system supplied to carry out the defined tasks. In this way, the Library would be able to enjoy the benefits of modern data processing equipment and techniques without the burden of staffing and maintaining an expensive in-house data processing department or of exorbitant development costs.

The Library selected as its first objective the conversion from its IBM batch-processing system to a mini-computer system of its book acquisitions, payroll, and service to the Braille and Talking Book Department processes. The Library felt that this approach would bring immediate cost benefits, build an acquisitions file as a by-product, and supply a major component of the input required for an accounting system. If, later, a non-book accounts payable system were added, the Library would be able to implement a complete accounting and budgeting system. Also, as the acquisitions file grew, the Library would be able to use it as the starting point for a circulation control system. On the basis of all these considerations, the Library decided to move forward to its first objective, the conversion to a mini-computer system of its payroll, book acquisitions and processing, and service to the Braille and Talking Book Department. Its interest was not, therefore, in whether or not to automate some of its operations, but rather which system would provide the best services at the least cost to the Library. The primary objective of the Library in 1971 was to escape from a batch-processing system, with a separate data processing department and a separate order department, and the many problems that had sprung from split responsibilities. It was desirous of establishing an on-line, in-house, single-department system that was responsive to the Library's real needs. The Library wanted to get away from the massive generation of reports and listings that were of little value for management purposes and gain true management information, such as answers to control questions: What items are delayed? Where are items located? What funds are encumbered? What funds are expended? etc. The present mini-computer system is enabling the Library to keep track of the flow of materials and dollars at a reasonable price.[1]

The annual cost to the library is in the neighborhood of $60,000 per year, or less than half the cost of the previous system.

The primary objective then was to escape from a batch-processing system with a separate data processing department. And, I might add, in an institution of our size—and I realize there is need in many institutions for a separate data processing department (I'm not saying stamp them out everywhere) but in an institution of our size—they are an irritant. They are an irritant because they are different, and because they are different, all sorts of problems develop. They also have tended to act as a middleman; and as a manager, I have been concerned about placing the responsibility for the input and the output on a particular department. Never mind this constant business of saying "Well, you know those people down in the basement"—always in the basement; I suppose it's because the equipment is heavy. They are *really* the bad guys; the report isn't out, and what are they doing, and they are just blowing a lot of money. You go down and find out that it was the order department in the first place that didn't get the stuff down on time. It's that kind of thing. To me there is a need to pinpoint responsibility if you are going to get results. It seems to me that in placing a mini in the order department, the responsibility is the order department's for the input and output—no middleman. This takes a heavy burden off me and enables me to focus my attention on *one* set of individuals.

One of the deterrents to libraries and librarians utilizing a computer is the size of the personal and financial commitment which has customarily been required. There are the large-task and sophisticated computer systems designed either for special purpose or multi-unit relationships. OCLC (Ohio College Library Center) with Fred Kilgour as its Director; the Ohio State University circulation system, with Hugh Atkinson as its designer; the Stanford University System with Allan Veaner in charge are examples of sophisticated and successful systems which few of us need to duplicate. Of special note to public libraries is the effort of New York Public Library in producing a book catalog.

> The N.Y.P.L. automated book catalog subsystem is designed to embrace most aspects of bibliographic control as it deals with cataloging. (Monographs, Serials, Indexing, Nonbook items).
>
> Input to the system is through original cataloging and MARC records provided by the Library of Congress in the MARC II distribution program.
>
> Data is stored in MARC compatible coding. Differences between N.Y.P.L. and MARC were introduced to enhance the MARC II tagging and delimiting scheme. Particular care was taken to keep these variances optional. This provides for use of Library of Congress machine reading cataloging unaltered.
>
> The book catalog system, now operational, has at present two distinct bibliographic data bases. These two, different in scope as well as content, are the prospective collection of the N.Y.P.L. Research Libraries and the complete collection of the N.Y.P.L. Branch Libraries' Mid-Manhattan Library. Plans call for expansion of scope of the Mid-Manhattan catalog to the entire collection of the N.Y.P.L. Branch Libraries.
>
> A third use of the system, now in its last stages of development, is the catalog of the Research Libraries Dance Collection. The bulk of the material in this special collection is nonbook in nature and will prove, we feel, the diverse utility of the software developed and expertise gained at N.Y.P.L.[2]

For most of us, there will probably be a need to seek out and use computer networks which either are or soon will be operational, such as OCLC, and so forth. For management control, I see individual libraries acquiring smaller equipment of their own or using terminals, enjoying the advantage of software packages which will be provided as turnkey operations. This approach can put public libraries and some university libraries in the computer business in a big way and fulfills the requirements stipulated earlier.

I see most institutions adopting what I would call a parasitic approach: utilize networks for bibliographic banks, catalog information, etc., and for internal controls software developed by someone else. Total systems are fine, but it is possible and highly desirable to build your program piece by piece, keeping a total system in mind. Always bear in mind that nothing lasts forever. There are advantages in producing now. The in-house effort can either be performed on in-house equipment or on linkages to large equipment in the area to be utilized on a time-shared basis. This is a local decision. Minicomputers or terminals and networks are not mutually exclusive, but rather complement one another.

There is evidence of a number of agencies beginning to utilize COM (Computer Originated Material) and in the case of New York Public Library, to name only one, book catalogs. Book catalogs have been with us for many years and can be produced either via the route of microfilming or via printout from machine-readable material. COM can either complement or compete with the book catalog. Micropublishing has progressed more slowly in the last five years than expected, particularly due to hardware problems in dealing with fiche on a large scale. A personal opinion only, but for the near term it would seem that microfiche (COM) may hold more promise than dozens of terminals. I'm referring to the next five years only. COM provides the update feature that terminals and remote storage do, but locations may be added for modest financial outlays.

Crucial in the use of already developed software packages is the relationship of in-house staff to the outside vendors. Involvement is the ingredient for success. Care should be taken to purchase a package that will fit your needs, but not necessarily the present system. Mechanization of an antiquated hand-powered system changing little in the process but the method of producing the materials is one of the very real dangers for performing activity in-house. There are, I feel, advantages in utilizing the Howard Johnson approach, although many will not agree with me. The thrust of this argument is that it is the only way that computers can cease operating for the few and be harnessed by and for the proletariat.

Above all, decision-making should relate to the institution served. If you can afford to convert the data base to machine-readable form, do so. In Cleveland we plan to hitchhike on a network; our conversion costs would be too great at this time and we view the larger, more sophisticated network as providing us with our only real opportunity for building our base and remaining operational. We simply do not have $2 million for the conversion process, and if I had $2 million uncommitted, I would spend it to solve other, more immediate problems.

If I were to summarize what it takes to venture into a library computer program and to make it work, it would go like this:

1. Recognize that hardware is the easiest thing to come by and software the most difficult. The equipment must work; must do what it is intended to do.
2. Know that *time* is your enemy until your computer program is up and operational.
3. Have the patience of a saint with your staff, your board, your public, your computer experts. Be supportive of staff and understanding about the adjustments which they must make to a new way of doing things.
4. Develop the guts of a cat burglar—you will need them. Once you have made a decision to be innovative with computers, everyone will be from Missouri until you show the promised and hoped-for results.

Am I trying to discourage innovation and full utilization of computers for libraries? Far from it. I am dedicated to the proposition that we cannot do without them. All I am saying is that if you succeed, you will receive no medals. But if you fail, God help you!

DISCUSSION

Frank Sherborn (Trustee, Herrick Public Library, Holland, Michigan): I know nothing about the computer or the automation of libraries; we are looking for some guidance. The city of Holland does have a computer center and does serve some of the facilities of the city. The question I would like to ask is that in the experience of you librarians with automation, is there some sort of guideline figure which says that if your library is of a certain size, your city of a certain size or smaller, there is a cut-off point at which automation is not feasible? Or does each library have to decide that for itself?

Curley: Well, I think there may be others who can respond to that better than I. If you are talking in terms of a traditional computer, having one in-house and developing a data processing staff and all of the costs that are involved, then I think you probably have to be somewhere at least in the middle-size range of what constitutes a medium-sized public library. However, there are shortcuts. Many small libraries can consider having a terminal to a very sophisticated operation like OCLC, or hang a terminal on a large piece of equipment downtown if you are sort of built into a county computer, use a piece of it and have a piece of software and use it for a specific task. I really think that what's happening is the range of agencies that can use computers is increasing. In other words the threshold above which you have to be in order to use a computer is dropping and dropping, and so no longer is it just a big public library; it certainly includes, I think, the medium-sized public library and maybe even some of those larger small ones. Now there is a weasel-word statement. But I think you ought not to bar yourself without looking into it, or bar yourself on the basis that "we are really too small." I think you ought to take a look at it, and there are pros around who can help you.

Freedman: I've been a librarian for eight years, half of those with research and academic libraries, or services to them, and half with public libraries. One comment I have is you are far too kind to academic libraries. I don't know how experienced you are with them. I haven't been in hundreds, but I have probably been in fifty of them on business of one kind or another, and there are a lot of disasters out there and some extremely dumb things that have been done. Underutilization of computers, poor utilization, nonutilization, poor manual processing—I'd like to ask you, too, if the degree of unkindness to public libraries is justified or warranted in your talk, at least in terms of the experience I've had with an equal basis to our academic colleagues. Another point, it seemed almost like a straw-man argument you raised about the DP shop in your own library. The government, like a university, can have a machine shared by a number of departments and there's nothing implicit in having them do that. We have a pretty large-scale operation in our own place, and we don't have the Mickey-Mouse stuff that you have in terms of money.

Curley: You have a terminal, I suspect, don't you?

Freedman: Well, we are doing that dirty, horrible, batch-processing method that you complained about, but it's worked pretty well for us, and our acquisition billing costs are anywhere from $10,000 a year.

Curley: I had one in the Suffolk library system, a real workhorse, a 1004 Univac, and it's worked very well.

Freedman: We are installing remote-job-entry equipment to do some other tasks. I just wanted to make the point that people in public libraries should not have to feel, or for that matter, university libraries, that you need a computer in your own library; those aren't the only alternatives available. There is sharing.

If you will allow me one other point. I think you have addressed some of the problems that you have to deal with, but didn't address yourself to the problem of filing catalog cards in 52 branch libraries. How do you propose to have the mini or Mr. Kilgour's service help you with that?

Curley: If we do business with OCLC, which we probably will, we will settle for catalog cards, which is what they are offering. I know they are offering catalog cards at this time; they may offer other things as well later on. However, you see, we are building a retrospective file, but I'm in the unfortunate, or fortunate, position of having a strong library that's not demand-oriented and a file of titles that isn't going to go away five or ten or fifteen or twenty years from now.

Freedman: That's only true for the central libraries, isn't that correct?

Curley: That's correct. So, for the time being, I have some choices, and one of the choices might be to continue with cards for a while, or send out to the branches either an updated listing with a cutoff at some point. New York Public Library cut off at a point and went into book catalogs, and from a certain point forward gets printouts, either on COM or in book-catalog form. Frankly, I like the idea of COM because I think the updating is a lot easier. That's my personal feeling, but I'm not quite sold yet that the user (I don't mean the librarian—for just in-house, we would use COM) but for the library patron, I would have to be a little more certain that the library patron could handle it in the branches. We are thinking along these lines, but that is just several steps up the road.

Freedmun: If I can make one last comment, Brett. I didn't want to dwell on Hennepin County yesterday, but the justification for an automation program had nothing to do with the production of cards or any in-house technical services costs. We have a large building program; we spent $20 million over a space of 15 years for buildings and books, and a 10-year projection showed that by going into automation, including a conversion of the entire retrospective shelflist, we would save $100,000 in manual filing, arranging, and revising costs. I think the public libraries have a real opportunity for justifying automation for cost savings because they have unusual catalog-card filing problems.

Curley: You can talk perhaps far better than I on the development that is taking place in the New York Public Libraries.

Freedman: The people here from New York, I think, could do that.

Curley: The fact that they have cut off their filing of catalog cards and have come up with a book catalog, which will be massive and, I think you may have touched on it in your talk, but if you want to say anything about that, I think it's timely to do so.

Freedman: Someone from New York might want to talk about it. That's in effect what we did in Hennepin County. We took out all the card catalogs; there are no more card catalogs.

Butler: You might also mention the number of volumes and titles you've got, as something of a contrast to Cleveland's.

Freedman: Well, it's not in contrast to the branch system though, Brett. We've got more titles than he would have in his combination of branches. We are going to have about 125,000 titles in a few months.

Bruce Bajema (Marin County Library, California): If I might disabuse your comments on COM: we have three public uses of fiche in the county already—in the tax collector's office, the assessor's office, and the recorder's office, I believe. Contrary to your comments, all three instances have found better public acceptance than staff acceptance. The staff is where you had to fight; the public loves it and has found it very easy to use. We are, on that basis and having done a few minor surveys with our public, going ahead with a catalog, a fiche catalog, which I hope will be out next year.

Curley: I'm very glad to know that because I'm always a bit chicken when it comes to the public. If something *can* go wrong, it *will* go wrong, kind of thing. That has been my general philosophy. The staff, I've got a hand on them—sometimes, at least—and so I have approached it on that basis. However, I'm glad to know this because it may get rid of some of the constraints I have, and my constraints ought not to be your constraints, and I think the point he made is well worth making.

Butler: We should mention that Book Catalog Use Committee tomorrow night, which is about microfilm book catalogs. We'll have some people talking about their own libraries where they have had the catalog itself in microfilm for several years, so it is analogous to what Bruce brought up.

Veaner: It takes some time to educate people to actually get a system installed, to train them and, further, I'm assuming that maybe even on a turn-key operation things don't work exactly right the very first time and continue to work 100 percent correctly thereafter. What was the staff's reaction? What kinds of problems did you have and how were they overcome?

Curley: Well, it's the same answer that I have had to use when we are developing innovative programs to minority groups in the city. Move the staff out of the branch and move a new staff in. It's not quite that way, but there are elements of this. First of all, because of a relationship with the union, we offered all the people who were involved in the data processing department downstairs an opportunity—the keypunchers and so forth—to come upstairs and work on the mini, and they all quit in a span of two, three, or four weeks—probably because it required a different set of skills. I expected they would leave anyway, there is a certain repetitive aspect to keypunching where you keep your eye on the ball and keep slogging away, whereas this requires interaction, and it requires a different set of talents, and there was a problem. I guess the answer really was that we had to set up a subdepartment within the order department, composed of individuals who had some degree of enthusiasm for the program, and we really have a department within a department. It works well now that those who really do not want to be associated with the program are elsewhere. There is another factor of fear, there is a factor of noise, there is a factor of doing it differently. Being involved previously, the operation was remote; it was in the basement, and suddenly it's right there at your elbow. There were problems and you had to move your staff around. If you can't move your staff around, then you probably shouldn't go into it because that's a factor. You ought to be able to have some flexibility to be able to move your staff around.

REFERENCES

[1] Used with permission of Richard P. Palmer, Professor, Simmons College School of Library Science, from his book, *Case Studies in Library Automation,* soon to be published by Bowker.

[2] Quoted with permission of James A. Rizzolo, Chief, Systems Analysis & Data Processing Office, New York Public Library.

8   Outlook for the Future

Ralph M. Shoffner

I came prepared to tell you a couple of things that I feel are in the future. I must admit that I am delighted to have the opportunity to do this, because as Allen said at the beginning, it is rather like the dessert. Since research and development is the sort of thing I do, I like to look at events that have occurred already and then to guess what is going to happen at some future time. My present purpose is to share some of my predictions with you. Before doing so, however, I would like to set the stage by first discussing the nature and purpose of prediction and then summarizing the events of the recent past which I consider important, especially in relation to the predictions I'll be making.

Prediction is guessing which is controlled to reduce the risk inherent in guessing and to allow others to understand the basis on which the guess is made. The object of a prediction is some event or state of nature. The common method of prediction is to determine a set of related events wherein one event is likely to occur if some other event occurs. One can then develop the likely event sequence and begin searching for evidence for which events in the chain have occurred. This allows one to position oneself in the chain and to test whether events are occurring and if they are occurring in the predicted order.

If you are performing historical research, you are usually concerned with unreported events in the middle of a chain and searching for evidence of those events having occurred. If you're talking about the future, it's a little different because you have to wait and search for one event in time sequence. Therefore, if you are projecting the future, the important thing is that you tie the projection down to a period of time in which you expect the events to occur.

Now in terms of investigation of the past, you can obviously go in either direction; so a great deal of work is done in trying to take things in the present and work backwards to what the preconditions must have been in order to allow the current events to have taken place. Now, in

Director of Research and Development, Richard Abel Company

talking about the future, I don't quite have that ability, so naturally I have to work in the other time direction. It may be an obvious point, but sometimes when one does this, in projecting the future, one wants to go backward, into the past to find out if perhaps you have the event chained in the wrong order, and whether some things could have occurred long before you expected them to, possibly in another environment than you expected them to have occurred. One of the dangers in talking about the future is that you predict something that occurred a long time ago and you didn't know anything about it.

Prediction then is the key in talking about the future, and to make a prediction means that you make a statement which at least in theory is capable of being proven or of being refuted. If you don't do that, the statement may give you personal gratification, but it won't be helpful in terms of using the prediction for some other purpose because you won't ever know just what it is that you meant. So we have a verifiable prediction about events to occur within a stated period of time.

PREDICTION AND THE GALLICO-
SIKORSKY SYNDROME

Allen did a very nice job in opening the session by pointing out how very bad some predictions are. These bad predictions in general have a common thread through them, namely they tend to be predictions that events will not occur, not predictions of events which *will* occur. The reason for this is that it is much harder to make a negative prediction. In order to make a positive prediction, one need find only one valid event sequence leading to the event that you are predicting. Then from there you can go through a secondary search to see whether there is possibly some other event sequence which will merely move this event up in time, but which in itself would be a valid sequence of events to support the prediction. Only the time span would be different. So, in general, in positive prediction all you have to do is find one valid event sequence. In negative prediction, you have to demonstrate that there exists no valid event sequence which leads to the event you are talking about. That means either you must search through the realm of possibility and the world of reality exhaustively or you have to have an extremely good search algorithm to tell you what parts of that world to search in. Because there are so many people in the world and because so much has happened, in general, any one person making a negative prediction about what are essentially human and technological events had better be extremely well grounded in some very solid theory. While we shouldn't be surprised when people say that such and such will not happen, we might question whether it's worth reading that kind of prediction. As a result, I'm going to refuse to give you any negative predictions about what's going to happen in this area.

Why predict at all? It's for advantage, obviously. You can take the advantage in several different ways. One way is to clarify and understand what is going on now, because quantitative prediction forces a more careful analysis of all the various factors influencing the chain of events. Any specific effect on behavior may be difficult to detect. The next way is that one may want to adjust the activities of an organization or one's individual activities to conform with what will take place. In other words, if we knew what was going to happen on the gambling tables outside, we would use that knowledge to guide our actions in an explicit manner, but not to change the events themselves. The final way that people may use predictions is to attempt to influence the occurrence of particular events. Many predictions in the world of human affairs are really attempts to force a direction of events rather than the passive prediction that one thinks about in relation to the sciences.

Now, in terms of the presentation today, my interests are probably somewhere between the latter two. That is, from a personal and organizational point of view, I have a responsibility for predicting the future in order to try to make the personal and corporate events conform to that future. But, in addition, I don't want to be wrong, and therefore it doesn't hurt at all to try to give my forecasts a focus and hope that by making them, some people will be interested in and will want to work on them and move in those directions. I would like to hope, however, that some of my predictions are among the former—that they are predictions for the sake of prediction. In some of these, it is demonstrable that I have no particular vested interest in whether the predicted events take place.

The time period in which I am interested is four to six years from now. Because of the level of accuracy of the prediction, it is acceptable if the events occur in this period. Also there are some things that I am going to ignore in the predictions and I think you should understand those. One of the areas that I am going to ignore is hardware, and another is networks. In general, I am going to ignore those events which are the responsibility of a single organization, and those where the likelihood of occurrence is the result of the work of an organization with unique capabilities. That means, for example, there will be no prediction about what LC shall or shall not do; that is not my present concern. If you look then at the things that I ruled out, the predictions that I'm going to make will be concerned either with the functions that are going to be performed or with issues having to do with people. Therefore I can safely avoid the issue of the network or the hardware because these things primarily affect the time in which things take place. If they affect the function, we can deal with it more directly by talking about the function itself.

THE PRESENT AND THE PAST

The use of the computer in the field at this point can be summarized without being unduly harsh as being similar to that of a large file cabinet. Its use in the library is almost completely filing records and reporting portions of them with very little in the way of record transformation, with very little in the way of any kind of computational use in order to determine overall operating characteristics, without use of modeling, etc. I consider the systems that have been developed today to be very crude because they do not concentrate on elements of control for the general production and operating processes in a library. The information that we have received in the last two days about automation has been notably lacking with respect to the kinds of information that an administrator would want to have in order to understand what is happening in a library operation. If he were treating that library operation as management treats other kinds of operations in this country, that would be a primary concern of the automation. In other words, there is reflected in the library's automation a major disparity between the nature of current management in libraries and the nature of management in other organizations. There has been some interest, certainly, and there has been some use of circulation data for management and control purposes. While I'm not trying to disparage the specific work that's been done, this is my overall summarization of where the work stands from a point of view of the library community as a whole.

There has been regional cooperation and there have been, for example, operations in which libraries have decided not to buy things on an individual basis because of the existence of the material in the region. There is nothing particular about the use of the computer, however, that is at this time making regional cooperation radically different for the community as a whole. At some point, certainly one of the important functions that it is going to serve is to modify extensively the way in which we make our acquisitions decisions.

It may be my organizational myopia that makes me think that this is important enough to be mentioned, but one thing that has not been mentioned is selective dissemination of books; that is, approval programs. There are several hundred libraries now operating approval programs. These programs simply would not work at the level that they do without the use of the computer, just as selective dissemination of information in general would not work, because of the inherent problems of control of a manual process in which so many individual decisions are being made on a daily basis. While the number of approval programs are going to grow, I'm not going to make any predictions about them.

In the world external to the individual library, the most significant change has been discussed thoroughly, that is, the standardization of catalog record structure. However, it was not mentioned that work is underway to develop many standard formats within the structure for England, France, Germany, Canada, and South America. This is an extremely important trend as far as moving us to a higher level of standardization than we have had in the past. Another important trend which has already been mentioned a number of times is that of contracting outside, or purchasing outside, processes and services that previously had been in-house operations. The strongest trend at present is in cataloging and processing.

I personally am most disappointed with the low rate of progress in automated support to the public services area. With the exception of circulation systems, there is not a great deal of concern about, or investigation of, automation to improve public services. One of the most serious problems in this area has been identified by Resnikoff & Dolby in *Access*. The point that is made is that access to books quite simply isn't good enough because there is a missing level of information between that contained in standard cataloging and the information content of the book. A book is too large a package of information to be represented by standard cataloging. This is a very serious debility for people who are reading for defined purposes and who cannot spend a great amount of time searching current, inefficient catalog descriptions for the information to be found in monographs. Unfortunately, there appears to be a trend to ignore this and keep going with current, standard cataloging. Yet we keep publishing books and we really are not giving the user proper access to those books. I have no quarrel with the size of any book—that is perfectly reasonable—but I quarrel extensively with my access to it. However, this is something I cannot predict because I am saying that nothing is going on. While I'm afraid that this will continue, I hope that you will give your own access some serious consideration in terms of your own personal reading. Possibly this is an area in which we can force some change.

The most important trend in libraries is really not automation as such.

The most important thing is that there is continuing to be a perceptual change within the library about the role of the library and the way in which the library operates. First, there is a growing acceptance of the idea that there *is* an information industry. While we can flay the librarians for being slow to accept the fact that they have a large role in the information industry, a great many of them are not held back by their perception; but they are held back by some of the very tough questions of how to finance, organize, and operate nonstandard, non-traditional services. Though it may exist, I have not yet seen anywhere sound financial planning for routine operational support of these services. But certainly the perception is there, and hopefully the planning will follow.

Second, this perception will be important in attacking the myth of self-sufficiency. It's strange that we should even talk in libraries about self-sufficiency. After all, we don't produce the information; how can we possibly be self-sufficient unless we produce it? We don't obtain all of it; how can we select everything our users want? Invariably we are obtaining materials from somewhere else. In general, a library provides a storage function, and the information community provides an access function to those things which are stored.

The third change in perception is that libraries should have goals, that these should be laid out in terms of clear objectives, that there should be commitment to reaching these objectives, and that there should be times and dollars attached to the commitments to reach these objectives. This is a rather different way of operating. At the present time, this is not the standard way in which libraries are operating, but I believe that it is becoming the perception that they *should* operate in that manner. We have heard a number of comments during this meeting about administrative competence, and it seems generally accepted by this audience that we must have more highly qualified library administrators, not from the point of view of their abilities with respect to librarianship, but from the point of view of their abilities with respect to general management. I think this is now accepted in general. There have been a number of things which have been done to move in that direction, as, for example, the management studies sponsored by the Association of Research Libraries.

Finally, a fourth perception that is beginning to be accepted is that a library must perform active marketing of its services. Many libraries have been doing this, but the nature of this marketing is changing, the degree of activism is increasing, and the acceptability of calling it marketing is increasing.

It's interesting to ask why all these changes in perception. We have heard one of the reasons, and that reason is budget pressure; everybody has been talking about budget pressures which have caused those agonizing reappraisals. I submit that while this may be correct in one sense, in a deeper sense that is not the reason. Budget pressures have always been with us and always will be with us. Budget pressures cannot automatically translate themselves, for example, into the changing perceptions about goals and commitments to objectives. If something else hadn't changed, then the budget pressures would have a simple solution: the budget would simply be cut, and activities would be carried on as well as they could under the reduced budget. But there is a different way of looking at the change. Outside the library community there have been changes in the perceptions of the people who fund the libraries. In general that change indicates that throughout the country we should be developing, on a continuing basis, increases in productivity by changing the products we produce as well as the nature of the processes by which we produce them. The general perception is that each segment of the society *must* be concerned with the nature of their productivity and with the innovation which is possible within that segment. Along with the perception of innovation as the standard way of operating our industries there has been development in management science. The easiest way I can indicate the development in management science is to relate that one of the graduate business schools with a well-known program in management science keeps a regular check on the salaries its graduates receive in their first job. For the graduates of 1971 the average salary for an M.S. in management science with no experience was $15,000. While I wouldn't want to say that businessmen are consistently rational in their salary structures, they do attempt to judge the likely payoff from graduates of business schools just as they do other stuff. I can attest that people think carefully about hiring a young person with no experience at thousands of dollars more than someone else in the organization with experience who is doing a fine job but doesn't have the substantive training desired; yet this is being done because of the belief that it will pay off. I submit to you that if we are serious about management of libraries, we must modify our salary and organizational structures in order to obtain and utilize well qualified management talent. But, to come back to the main point, it is not budget pressures, but the change in management science and in the perception of continuing innovation to obtain continuing improvement in productivity that is driving the libraries. It will continue to drive the libraries no matter whether the budget increases or decreases. It just happens that for a few years in the 1960s the pressure seemed to be off because of the rising budgets. The libraries that are successful in innovation will have the least apparent budget pressures.

SPECIFIC PREDICTIONS

The first prediction concerns collection planning. We now have circulation systems on which we could run analyses of the use of the collection. We could run analyses in terms of patron usage, we could characterize the patrons, we could then make projections about the change in the patron base as a function of community plans, and we could therefore control our acquisitions policy in an overall sense with respect to circulation observed behavior. I predict, therefore, that in four to six years between four and eight libraries will have used a formal model to analyze patron characteristics, patron use, and patron projections in order to decide upon their acquisitions fund allocations.

Acquisitions. There will be between three and seven networks operating. They may be either manual networks or machine networks insofar as their communication structure is concerned, but they will be providing computer algorithms for deciding whether to purchase a particular individual item based upon the libraries which have already decided to obtain it and some quantitative and descriptive characteristics about the item itself.

Cataloging. The Library of Congress is going to decrease as a source for cataloging in a specific area, namely that of materials which are published in other countries. The reason for this is that there will be between five and fifteen new national bibliographies which will be providing MARC data. Now that doesn't mean that LC will stop its cataloging operations. It means that just as BNB (British National Bibliography) tapes come into LC at the present time and are reworked, similarly there most likely will be redistribution of these five to fifteen national bibliographies.

Services. Because I had forgotten about the operations that the public libraries have had for some time with respect to their services for the blind, this could be one of those predictions of an event of the past. However, in terms of general service, between ten and thirty libraries will be routinely running direct mail lending of books to patrons without their being required to come into the library. In another area of service, between one-third and two-thirds of the cities with more than 500,000 people will have for-profit companies providing information search services.

Professional competence. With respect to the increasing mathematical competence in our field, by 1979 less than one in ten articles which deal with the rates of growth of published material will refer to either the exponential growth of publication, or the information explosion. By then both terms will be gauche.

Personnel retraining and reassignment. From Pauline's presentation this morning, you are aware that I had suggested a fellowship program with respect to retraining. It's still a good idea, but I don't think it's in the cards as a federally supported program. If it's done, we are going to have to do it on an individual library basis, and we will have to support extensive retraining. Therefore, between thirty and fifty libraries will have announced an explicit policy of retraining and reassignment with the commitment that there will be no staff reductions except by attrition.

In this sense my next prediction (and you will see why I say I am hopeful about that), I expect that if we won't do that sort of thing rapidly enough, we are going to have major personnel problems in some libraries, especially with the professional staff. I predict that between one and three libraries will have experienced a staff walk-out, strike, or protest of not less than one week in duration in which the central issue will be security of employment in relation to automation and the changing nature of jobs in the library.

Organization of the library. There is going to be change in the organization of library operations. One specific change will be the use of contract library operations, that is, operations of the library facility by personnel who are employed by an organization other than the library itself. We already have elements of this in the operations of an organization like OCLC. When the main portions of the cataloging function are outside the library, it's but a short step to take on the operating responsibility for the connecting terminals, as well as for the central facility. This will happen because, as I also pointed out in the 1970 report, libraries are very small organizations in terms of organization size in this country. At the same time, there has to be a way of distributing innovation to these libraries. There has to be a way of distributing, therefore, not only equipment, but also specialized knowledge with respect to the management sciences. This is going to be necessary and one of the ways that it will happen is by setting up contract operations, that is, facilities management. Within the six years it will not be in the cards that there will be general for-profit libraries operating. That's a different concept and the difference is in who owns the materials. The prediction? Between three and ten libraries with more than $250,000 annual budget will be operated under a facilities management contract. The reprise? It seems to me that all of this represents a change in our perceptions and in the discipline that we put ourselves under in this field.

A final comment with respect to automation: good intentions are not going to be enough. Whereas during the last six years, writing a good-looking proposal (that is, to have good intentions) was often good enough, track record is going to be important over the next six years. Because I work in this field, I believe this change is good, since there really isn't all that much money available, even in the best of industries, that we can afford to be profligate about its expenditure. In this particular industry, as was already pointed out, we have less than the national average. When it comes to research and development, we are a deprived industry and we can expect to continue to be so. This will affect the kind of work we do in automation, and it's going to be terribly important, therefore, that the planning for automation take into consideration how much risk there is in such projects, the goals of the project, and the people who are to be responsible for reaching those goals. That means that for an automation project whose goal is the reduction of unit operating costs, the question should be asked in the planning stage: who in fact is responsible for reducing this cost at the point at which the system is available and operational? If the person responsible for doing that will not commit to the project, one had better be quite certain that his administrator will commit to the project. If that is not available, one had better wonder if it's a useful expenditure of funds, no matter how good it looks on paper. In the final result, the people who work in automation are not responsible for the operating effectiveness of their system. It is the people in line operations who must be responsible for that. The people in research and development are responsible for the definition of what the system is and what it will do, and then they are responsible for the commitment to develop an operational system meeting those specifications within the resources that they defined for it, but again it must be the operating people and the administrators who commit to the overall effectiveness of the system and who ultimately define whether the project will go or not. And once more, good intentions are not enough, and we are going to have to work very hard for our innovations.

DISCUSSION

Butler: Thank you, Ralph, very much. If everyone is not totally suffering from future shock, we will take a few questions.

Bob Erisman (University of Colorado): This management report thing you mentioned, I thought it was something we took for granted, at least from the literature, that when we automated statistics would be a natural by-product. Do you think we are not getting them? Do you think we are ignoring them? Or do you think they are of no quality? What's happening that we don't have the management reports or whatever we need that the computer can provide?

Shoffner: The answer to your first three questions is "yes." In many of the operations we aren't getting them. In most of the operations that I have seen, they are not good enough because they don't really tie into any kind of decision process. I'm not worried about the collection of statistics as such; I'm worried about the hard thinking that has to go into the development of the model, if you will, of the operation of the organization. I don't mean model in the abstract sense; I mean the operating model that the managers are going to use that tells them what they are looking for when they use the data, and therefore most of the data that is being produced, I submit to you, is merely using up our forests.

Erisman: I have a question about money. I believe Pauline said this morning that money wasn't that important; that it didn't matter that much. That may be an extreme view; getting money is important. I'm wondering why, what is missing, what are we doing wrong that librarians or libraries can't convince whoever has the money—the funding agencies—that what we are doing is worthwhile. Of course the question is, is it worthwhile? How can libraries afford to operate unlike profit-making organizations? It's even more ironic that apparently special libraries *are* able to convince their constituencies that it is worthwhile to automate or do whatever needs to be done to do something in the best possible way and get the most out of your money. What's happened?

Shoffner: I've been in the research and development field now since 1960, and as far as I can understand, with the exception of the biomedical and aerospace industries, funding for research is a very short-term process arising out of some kind of immediate political pressure. The funding will last in the range of three to five years; it's used entirely to stimulate the society to move in a particular direction, and after that time it is shut off on the basis that if there is anything to be done in the area, the people have now had a chance to get into it, there are people who are now committed to go in those directions, there will be some people who have been trained to do the work, and it's then up to the society to adjust to that shock. Now that may be a highly skeptical view of the way it operates, but it's a pattern that you can see in many, many places; and I'm afraid that my answer is that I see nothing in the political process today that would say that in the library community as it is presently organized there is the likelihood of renewed federal funding of the kind that was fueling the organization I was with, Allen's organization, and others.

Erisman: Yes, but what I was really talking about was in the context of everyday operation. Let's be simplistic: if it takes 20 people to run something or other, and the machine can do it, and we've got this basic thing I think that everybody is accepting that people are going up in price and machines are going down, how are we still unable often to convince a board of trustees, or any other kind of funding agency that somehow the library can run better with some new things?

Shoffner: Again, at the risk of irritating a lot of people, the analysis isn't real, and no one trusts it: the people who would need to sign off to make it a real commitment of real people who are going to run the library. It would be a different kind of analysis. Most of these things are made up out of whole cloth, and I've made up a lot of them. You know, I understand the process very well. But what I'm saying is that it's going to have to be a kind of work where the people who are ultimately responsible get their oars in early in the game and there is a real decision about who is on the line for each different aspect of the development process and of the operation afterward.

Dolby: You took our name in vain earlier. First, for anyone who is interested, we at R & D Associates no longer have any copies of *Access.* It was published in April of '72 and was a report to the Office of Education and presumably is retrievable through ERIC. I have not found out how to access through ERIC. If all goes well, we are doing a revision this summer and it will be published as a book by Melville some time after the first of the year.

Secondly, you said that nobody was doing anything about filling the gap between the catalog and the book itself. We are trying to do something, as you know, with our cumulative indexes. I think in general that is the way it will have to be done; that is, by publishing things for profit. It seems to me that we should recognize that the information store is built largely through the profit-oriented publishing industry, and although there are a zillion government reports, they are frequently written by profit-making organizations making a profit on government contracts. On the other hand, the access system, the card catalog, is produced by the nonprofit-making library community. I think it is unreasonable to think that the library community can increase its efforts in this direction by an order of magnitude, particularly the way we define an order of magnitude, which says a factor of 30. I think they can get a factor of two or three by various devices, but I don't think they can find enough spare manpower and money to increase it by even a factor of 10, let alone 30. So it seems to me that if we are going to fill this gap, it will have to be by the commercial publishers finding economical ways and means to produce greater access to the existing store and then publishing for a profit.

Shoffner: Is it fair to ask a question of Jim?

Butler: You've got a microphone!

Shoffner: Am I correct that if your model worked out for our current publication, if proper access were provided for everything that is being published and distributed at the present time, it would increase publishing cost by 1/27. Is that the right number?

Dolby: Yes, roughly speaking.

Shoffner: So what we would have is an increase in purchasing of 1/27 or a reduction in the number of individual things bought by that amount in order to pay for those things which were published.

Dolby: That's right.

Shoffner: Now my point in raising this in this audience is that the purchasers of this material would be the libraries. So, what I'm trying to do is create a market, not only for R&D, but for the publishing industry for a different kind of publication.

Dolby: Right. I wholeheartedly aprove.

John Linford (State University of New York at Albany): I think one of the answers to why we are not able to convince management a little better than we do most of the time is because the initial costs are almost always higher for an automated project than for an unautomated one of any kind; so you establish a higher level of cost throughout the system which may at that point then stay level regardless of your increase in work load. I think Ohio State proved that out with their circulation system. The cost of the circulation system as automated was much higher than their manual system, but the increase in work load that the system was able to accept was such that their unit cost has decreased, and I think, as someone else pointed out earlier in the meeting, the automated systems goals are much different than what you have in manual systems. So, what unit is it you are costing? The Ohio State circulation system now has to include in its costs the search factor; I think Ohio College Library Center has the same problem as well. Part of the cost is still the hook-up with terminals that do nothing but search, that do not actually come out with a hard transaction. So, I think that's one of the reasons; but my real point in coming up here was a question to Ralph.

We have been talking about a lot of the internal things in libraries, you know, the management type of things, and so on. I think maybe you could speak to the point of external effects on libraries in the future, which I think are primarily going to come up based on the continuing-education thrust of future shock—the push for retraining of people, people outside the library, the library users who are having to retrain themselves for new jobs, or just for a new interest, the leisure-time type aspect of this thing. Could you speak on that, please?

Shoffner: Before I speak on that I would like to follow up on your comment on OSU because I think there is another important point in OSU that can be easily overlooked. As libraries are organized, in general the attempt to increase circulation is dysfunctional because it increases cost without direct increase in budget, and there are many libraries, of course, which justify their existence on the basis of the circulation and in that area it is not dysfunctional. But if circulation is not in the justification for the budgeting of the library in the first place, then why would anyone ever want to circulate book one? I have been disturbed ever since I came into this field in 1956 to discover that it was not a routine standard operating procedure of academic research libraries to report circulation. I'm not saying it should be the only measure, but I think it's an extremely good sign that OSU justifies its system on the basis of unit cost in a situation, where if I understood you correctly, total cost for the library circulation has indeed gone up. But if one took the total cost of the library operation, not just circulation, but of everything else, and asked what is the total cost per unit item delivered to a person, I think it would show up as a very much better operation than it did before.

Obviously, I haven't done that analysis, but I think it is important to think about circulation and the key role it really plays in the long-term justification of the library as a portion of our society.

Now that takes me then directly to the second part: Continuing education—the school without walls and that sort of thing—is certainly on the increase. Book utilization is on the increase, and the way I see this sort of thing operating is through mail sorts of operations, and that's the reason for my prediction that there are going to be libraries that are going to be doing this sort of thing, because just as with the service for the blind, there is to be a very good operating justification for doing this, even though it increases the cost of the library because it provides the service. In the long run if we don't circulate the materials, if we don't get the people into the building, or if we don't provide telephone reference services, what is our justification going to be? And the whole movement is toward distributing this information and not insisting that the people come into the building.

Bajema: Once again to correct you, I think your mail prediction is off by about six years. I can name four libraries in California that already do that. There is an association of libraries which are doing that, rendering service by mail, and they have been meeting here. They held a meeting last night.

Shoffner: This is direct mail to individuals?

Bajema: Yes, direct mail to individuals.

Shoffner: And it's a standard service?

Bajema: Not only that, but there is a company now that prints catalogs for these libraries to mail out to their patrons as standard operating service.

Shoffner: Excellent! That's one of the hazards of predicting. The present is with us such a short time.

Butler: Ralph, if I understand your implications of positive and negative predictions, it means that we could go on discussing positive and negative predictions forever, so perhaps we ought to cut that part off. I'd like to thank all the speakers for their efforts, written and unwritten, and all those local committee people who helped us put things together. I'd like to thank Sue Martin for her future efforts in doing the proceedings and turn the mike over to her.

Martin: These announcements are very pleasant ones to make. First of all, I would like to introduce two people: the first one is Don Hammer, who three days ago became executive secretary of ISAD, and Fred Kilgour, who recently became president-elect of ISAD, and who, because of Don's becoming executive secretary, therefore becomes president much sooner than he had intended to be. Fred, would you like to say a few words?

Frederick Kilgour (Ohio College Library Center): I interpret Brett's remarks to mean that I am the only person in the whole world that stands between you and the drinks. I have the feeling that the majority of you here came for perhaps two different reasons: (1) to catch up and (2) to answer the question as one New England librarian put it, "How do you make these decisions?" The keeping-up is bothersome to me because there are avenues to do it and I don't think we do it very well, and I'm reasonably sure that none of the speakers told you how to do it. Let me very briefly suggest what you do. I think you've got to start by becoming familiar with and using the abstract journals that exist in the field. I think you've got to spend $30 and invest in *Library and Information Science Abstracts* and read it, and write letters requesting off-prints or documents that are listed there to build your own armamentarium of information; you should also read some computing reviews and do exactly the same thing, and then there is an ASIS publication that also does the same thing. Then as I say, you have to build your reprint file, get your boxes, build the collection, purchase books and read reviews, enter subscriptions to the major journals, of which, of course, the outstanding one is the *Journal of Library Automation*, and there is also of course the *Journal of the American Society for Information Science* that is a must. *Program*, the British publication, is another must, and the *Journal of Documentation* is awfully close to being another must, and is a must for some of you. You have to keep these journals, and you should purchase books and build your own library.

The library profession is changing; information science is a new profession. It's no longer a matter of reading the old essays that appeared in the *Bulletin* of the American Library Association that appeared in the 1930s. There is new information available, information that you have to have as systems people to make your recommendations and information that you need to make the decisions. I'm not going to get into any discussions of trade-off studies and so on, but the administrators are going to have to do this; they are going to have to get down on their hands and knees with pen and paper and do trade-off studies among the various avenues that are available to them, and they have to have adequate data in advance to do that study. And to get that adequate data you have to keep up and go to that perfectly delightful ISAD meeting five years from now on the state of the art.

Now, perhaps I should go back to the New England College whose librarian supplied the text in part for this speech and tell you that some 30 or 40 years ago, I was courting a girl there, and we went to a church on Sunday morning and the minister chose as his text, although he didn't identify it as P. G. Wodehouse, that "the butler entered, a silent procession of one," and I think that I will now so exit.

Library Automation: Bibliography 1973

Martha W. West

This bibliography is a sequel to that compiled by Alice Billingsley and published as "Bibliography of Library Automation" (AMERICAN LI-BRARIES, March 1972). This, in turn, supplemented "Bibliography of Library Automation" (ALA BULLETIN, September 1969), compiled by Charlene Mason, which continued the comprehensive "Bibliography on Library Automation" (ALA BULLETIN, June 1967), compiled by Lois C. McCune and Stephen R. Salmon, and reprinted as part of the Proceedings of the 1967 Preconference on Library Automation (LIBRARY AUTOMATION: A STATE OF THE ART REVIEW [ALA, 1969]).

Coverage is in general limited to North America, as was the Pre-conference Institute, although a few foreign citations are included. The publication period covered is the later half of 1971, all of 1972, and the first half of 1973.

OVERVIEW AND GENERAL

Aman, Mohammed M. "The year's work in international librarianship: 1970," INTERNATIONAL LIBRARY REVIEW 4(2):235–50 (Apr. 1972).

"Are Computer-Oriented Librarians Really Incompetent?" Excerpts from the Proceedings of a LARC meeting held during the ALA Conference in Dallas, Texas, June 24, 1971. Tempe, Ariz.: Library Automation Research and Consulting Assn., 1971. 10p. ED 056 701.

Artandi, Susan. AN INTRODUCTION TO COMPUTERS IN INFORMATION SCIENCE. 2d ed. Metuchen, NJ: Scarecrow Pr., 1972. 190p.

Avram, Henriette D. "Library Automation," in Carlos A. Cuadra, ed., ANNUAL REVIEW OF INFORMATION SCIENCE AND TECHNOLOGY, v. 6. Chicago: Encyclopaedia Britannica, 1971. p.171–217.

Avram, Henriette D. "Library automation: a balanced view," LIBRARY RE-
SOURCES AND TECHNICAL SERVICES 16(1):11–18 (Winter 1972).

Balmforth, C. K., and N. S. M. Cox, eds. INTERFACE: LIBRARY AUTOMA-
TION WITH SPECIAL REFERENCE TO COMPUTING ACTIVITY. Cambridge, Mass.: MIT Press, 1971. 251p.

Becker, Joseph. "Trends in library technology," SPECIAL LIBRARIES 62(10):
429–34 (Oct. 1971).

Becker, Joseph, and J. S. Pulsifer. APPLICATION OF COMPUTER TECH-
NOLOGY TO LIBRARY PROCESSES: A SYLLABUS. Metuchen, NJ: Scarecrow Pr., 1973. 173p.

Beckman, Margaret. "A library computer: need and costs," in AUTOMATION
IN LIBRARIES. Canadian Association of College and University Libraries,
Workshop in Library Automation, Vancouver, BC, 19–20 June 1971. Ottawa:
CACUL, 1972. p. 9.1–9.10.

Bellomy, Fred L. FINAL REPORT OF THE FINDINGS OF THE FEASIBILITY
PHASE. Santa Barbara: Univ. of California, Library Systems Development
Program, 1971. 101p. ED 063 001.

Berman, Sanford. "Let it all hang out," LIBRARY JOURNAL 96(12):2054–58
(15 June 1971).

Buckland, Lawrence F., James L. Dolby, and Mary Madden. SURVEY OF
LIBRARY AUTOMATION SYSTEMS. Phase 1. Final Report, prepared by
Inforonics, Inc., for The California State University and Colleges. Los
Angeles: Off. of the Chancellor, CSUC, 1973.

Council on Library Resources. 15TH ANNUAL REPORT FOR THE YEAR
ENDING JUNE 30, 1971. Washington, DC: Council on Library Resources,
Inc., 1971. 45p. ED 061 966.

_____ 16TH ANNUAL REPORT FOR THE YEAR ENDING JUNE 30, 1972.
Washington, DC: Council on Library Resources, Inc., 1972. 56p.

Cox, N. S. M. "Formalism in library automation," LIBRI 22(4):333–47 (Apr.
1972).

Cuadra, Carlos A., ed. ANNUAL REVIEW OF INFORMATION SCIENCE
AND TECHNOLOGY, v. 7. Washington, DC: ASIS, 1972. 606p.

"Education for automation and teamwork in automating library systems (panel
discussion)," in PROCEEDINGS OF THE LIBRARY ASSOCIATION OF
AUSTRALIA CONFERENCE, 1971. Sydney, Australia: The Association,
1972. p.729–40.

Elias, Arthur W., ed. KEY PAPERS IN INFORMATION SCIENCE. Washington, DC: ASIS, 1971. 230p.

Eyre, John. "Computers and libraries; the implication for management." in
B. Redfern, ed., STUDIES IN LIBRARY MANAGEMENT, v. 1. London,
Eng.: Clive Bingley, 1972. pp.135–68.

Eyre, John, and Peter Tonks. COMPUTERS AND SYSTEMS: AN INTRO-
DUCTION FOR LIBRARIANS. Hamden, Conn., Shoe String Pr., 1972.
127p.

Foskett, A. C. THE SUBJECT APPROACH TO INFORMATION. 2d ed.
Hamden, Conn.: Linnet Books, Shoe String Pr., 1972. 429p.

Gechman, Marvin C. "Control and management of library automation projects," in Jeanne B. North, ed., COMMUNICATION FOR DECISION-MAKERS. Proceedings of the 34th Annual Meeting of the American Society for Information Science, Denver, 7–11 November 1971. Westport, Conn.: Greenwood Publishing Co., 1971. v. 8, p.297–304.

Hamilton, Robert. "Applying technology effectively in library operations," ILLINOIS LIBRARIES 53(9):777–84 (Nov. 1971).

Hayes, Robert M., and Ellsworth Mason. "Hayes and Mason on automation," COLLEGE AND RESEARCH LIBRARIES 32(5):384–88 (Sept. 1971).

Henley, J. P. COMPUTER-BASED LIBRARY AND INFORMATION SYSTEMS. 2d ed. New York: American Elsevier, 1972. 106p.

Hirsch, Richard S. "Functions and economics of an operating automated library system," in L. Vilentchuk and Gila Haimovic, eds., ISLIC INTERNATIONAL CONFERENCE ON INFORMATION SCIENCE, PROCEEDINGS, Tel Aviv, 29 August–3 September, 1971. Tel Aviv: National Center of Scientific and Technological Information, 1972. p.333–38.

Immroth, J. Philip. "Retraining, retreading and repeating," LIBRARY JOURNAL 97(6):982–83 (15 Mar. 1972).

International Business Machines Corp. LIBRARY AUTOMATION: INTRODUCTION TO DATA PROCESSING. White Plains, NY: IBM, 1972. 50p.

_____ Data Processing Division. LIBRARY AUTOMATION—THE I.B.M. SYSTEM/3. White Plains, NY: IBM, 1972. 72p.

Kemeny, John G. "Library of the future," in his MAN AND THE COMPUTER. New York: Scribner, 1972. pp.85–98.

_____ "Library of the future," DARTMOUTH COLLEGE LIBRARY BULLETIN 12:50–60 (Apr. 1972).

Kilgour, Frederick G. "Evolving, computerizing, personalizing," AMERICAN LIBRARIES 3(2):141–47 (Feb. 1972).

Lancaster, F. Wilfrid, ed. APPLICATIONS OF ON-LINE COMPUTERS TO LIBRARY PROBLEMS. Proceedings of the 1972 Clinic on Library Applications of Data Processing. Urbana: Univ. of Illinois, Graduate School of Library Science, 1972. 169p.

Landau, Herbert B. "Can the librarian become a computer data base manager?" SPECIAL LIBRARIES 62(3):117–24 (Mar. 1971).

Livingston, Lawrence. "Technology and the library," in NEW OPPORTUNITIES FOR RESEARCH LIBRARIES. Minutes of the 80th meeting of the Association of Research Libraries, Atlanta, Ga., 12–13 May 1972. Washington, DC: ARL, 1972. p.70–77.

Lucas, Henry G. Jr. "Influencing computer decisions," SPECIAL LIBRARIES 63(7):281–84 (July 1972).

McAllister, Caryl. "On-line library housekeeping systems, a survey," SPECIAL LIBRARIES 62(11):457–68 (Nov. 1971).

Maidment, W. R. "Management information from housekeeping routines," JOURNAL OF DOCUMENTATION 27:37–42 (Mar. 1971).

_____ "Management of libraries and mechanization," in H. A. Whatley, ed., BRITISH LIBRARIANSHIP AND INFORMATION SCIENCE, 1966–70. London, Eng.: Library Association, 1972. p.215–23.

Markuson, Barbara E. "Progress and problems in library automation," in

PROCEEDINGS OF THE LIBRARY ASSOCIATION OF AUSTRALIA CON-
FERENCE, 1971. Sydney, Australia: The Association, 1972. p.39–49.

Markuson, Barbara E., and others. GUIDELINES FOR LIBRARY AUTOMA-
TION: A HANDBOOK FOR FEDERAL AND OTHER LIBRARIES. Santa
Monica, Calif.: Systems Development Corp., 1972. 401p.

Martin, Susan K. "Library automation," in Carlos A. Cuadra, ed., ANNUAL
REVIEW OF INFORMATION SCIENCE AND TECHNOLOGY. Washington,
DC: ASIS, 1972. v. 7, p.243–77.

Mason, Ellsworth. "Perspectives on libraries and computers; a debate: Computers in libraries," LIBRARY RESOURCES AND TECHNICAL SERVICES
16:5–10 (Winter 1972).

Minkel, Vera. DATA TERMINAL AND YOUR LIBRARY. Tempe, Ariz.:
Library Automation Research and Consulting Assn. (LARC), 1972.

Molgaard-Hansen, R., and M. Westring-Nielsen, eds. SEMINAR ON UDC AND
MECHANIZED INFORMATION SYSTEMS, 2d, Frankfurt, 1970. Copen-
hagen: Danish Centre for Documentation, 1971. 230p.

Molz, Kathleen. "Gradus ad Parnassum," ILLINOIS LIBRARIES 53(3):185–91
(Mar. 1971).

National Academy of Sciences. Computer Science and Engineering Board.
Information Systems Panel. LIBRARIES AND INFORMATION TECHNOL-
OGY—A NATIONAL SYSTEMS CHALLENGE. A report to the Council on
Library Resources, Inc. Washington, DC: National Academy of Sciences,
1972. 95p. ED 060 872.

Owen, Jeanne C. "Marriage a la mode: libraries and computers in the U.S.,"
AUSTRALIAN LIBRARY JOURNAL 20(5):16–20 (June 1971).

Patrinostro, Frank S., comp. A SURVEY OF COMMONPLACE PROBLEMS IN
LIBRARY AUTOMATION. Peoria, Ill.: LARC Pr., 1972.

Ravi, A. "Automation and libraries," INDIAN LIBRARIAN 27:19–30 (June
1972).

Resnikoff, H. L., and James L. Dolby. ACCESS: A STUDY OF INFORMATION
STORAGE AND RETRIEVAL WITH EMPHASIS ON LIBRARY INFORMA-
TION SYSTEMS. Final Report. Los Altos, Calif.: R and D Consultants Co.,
Mar. 1972. 280p. ED 060 921.

Ruby, H. V. "A funny thing happened on the way to the computer," ILLINOIS
LIBRARIES 54(3):183–86 (Mar. 1972).

Salton, G. "Computers and libraries—a reply to Ellsworth Mason's 'Stamp out
computers,'" LIBRARY JOURNAL 96(18):3277–82 (15 Oct. 1971).

Schriefer, Kent, and Iva Mostecky. "Compact book storage: mechanized systems," LIBRARY TRENDS 19(3):362–78 (Jan. 1971).

Shera, J. H. "Two decisive decades: documentation into information science,"
AMERICAN LIBRARIES 3:785–90 (July 1972).

Shumilak, E. E. AN ONLINE INTER-ACTIVE BOOK-LIBRARY-MANAGE-
MENT SYSTEM. Houston, Texas: NASA Manned Spacecraft Center, March
1971. N71-20526.

Stephens, D. R. "Information conglomerates, a needed trend," IOWA LIBRARY
QUARTERLY 21:288–91 (July 1972).

Stevenson, C. G. "Impact of automation on library building design," in

LIBRARY BUILDINGS: INNOVATION FOR CHANGING NEEDS. Proceedings, Library Building Institute, San Francisco, 1967. Chicago: American Library Assn., 1972. p.277–83.

Swihart, Stanley J., and Beryl F. Hefley. COMPUTER SYSTEMS IN THE LIBRARY: A HANDBOOK FOR MANAGERS AND DESIGNERS. Los Angeles: Melville, 1973. 338p.

Vagianos, Louis. "Information science: a house built on sand," LIBRARY JOURNAL 97(2):153–57 (15 Jan. 1972).

———— "Libraries: leviathanic vagrants on a 'Titanic' trip," LIBRARY JOURNAL 98(9):1449–51 (1 May 1973).

Valentine, Violet. "So—data processing never fails?" AMERICAN LIBRARIES 3(3):313–14 (Mar. 1972).

Veaner, Allen B. "Approaches to library automation," LAW LIBRARY JOURNAL 64(2):146–53 (May 1971).

Vickery, Brian C. INFORMATION SYSTEMS. Hamden, Conn.: Shoe String Pr., 1973. 350p.

Wall, R. A. "Computer applications in libraries," INTERNATIONAL JOURNAL OF MATHEMATICAL EDUCATION IN SCIENCE AND TECHNOLOGY 2(1):51–74 (Jan./Mar. 1971).

Warheit, I. A. "The automation of libraries: some economic considerations," SPECIAL LIBRARIES 63(1):1–7 (Jan. 1972).

———— "Computer service agencies and the needs of libraries," LAW LIBRARY JOURNAL 64(2):133–36 (May 1971).

White, Howard S. "Library technology in the '70s," WILSON LIBRARY BULLETIN 47(9):748–52 (May 1973).

Woods, R. G. "Electronic data processing in libraries," JOURNAL OF DOCUMENTATION 28(1):93–94 (Mar. 1972).

BIBLIOGRAPHIES AND INFORMATION SOURCES

Billingsley, Alice, comp. "Bibliography of library automation," AMERICAN LIBRARIES 3(3):289–312 (Mar. 1972).

CUMULATIVE INDEX TO THE ANNUAL REVIEW OF INFORMATION SCIENCE AND TECHNOLOGY, v. 1–7. Washington, DC: ASIS, 1972. 171p.

Defense Documentation Center. INFORMATION SCIENCES: CONFERENCES, SYMPOSIA, REVIEWS, SUPPORTING RESEARCH AND STINFO ACTIVITIES. v. 4. (Report bibliography Jan. 1953–Feb. 1971). Alexandria, Va.: The Center, Mar. 1972. 232p. AD 739 630.

———— INFORMATION SCIENCES: DATA AND INFORMATION HANDLING, STORING, RETRIEVING, AND DISSEMINATION. v. 1 (Report bibliography June 1955–Sept. 1971). Alexandria, Va.: The Center, Mar. 1972. 274p. AD 739 600.

_____ INFORMATION SCIENCES: INFORMATION CENTERS AND SPECIAL LIBRARIES. v. 2 (Report bibliography Sept. 1959–Feb. 1969). Alexandria, Va.: The Center, Mar. 1972. 157p. AD 739 610.

Fong, Elizabeth. A SURVEY OF SELECTED DOCUMENT PROCESSING SYSTEMS. Washington, DC: National Bur. of Standards, Systems Development Div., Oct. 1971. 67p. COM–71–50399.

Library of Congress. National Referral Center for Science and Technology. SELECTED INFORMATION RESOURCES ON LIBRARY AUTOMATION. 1972. 7p. ED 065 155.

Patrinostro, Frank S., comp. AVAILABLE DATA BANKS FOR LIBRARY AND INFORMATION SERVICES. Tempe, Ariz.: LARC Assn., Jan. 1973. 40p. ED 076 219.

Patrinostro, Frank S., comp., and Nancy P. Sanders, ed. A BIBLIOGRAPHY OF LITERATURE ON PLANNED OR IMPLEMENTED AUTOMATED LIBRARY PROJECTS. pt. 1, v. 9, World Survey Series; Tempe, Ariz.: LARC Assn., 1973. 69p. ED 076 209.

_____ A BIBLIOGRAPHY OF LITERATURE ON PLANNED OR IMPLEMENTED AUTOMATED LIBRARY PROJECTS, pt. 2, v. 10, World Survey Series; Tempe, Ariz.: LARC Assn., 1973. 70p. ED 076 210.

_____ A SURVEY OF AUTOMATED ACTIVITIES IN THE LIBRARIES OF THE UNITED STATES. v. 1, World Survey Series; Tempe, Ariz.: LARC Assn., 1971. 154p. ED 060 904.

_____ A SURVEY OF AUTOMATED ACTIVITIES IN THE LIBRARIES OF GREAT BRITAIN AND THE COMMONWEALTH COUNTRIES. v. 2, World Survey Series; Tempe, Ariz.: LARC Assn., 1973. 93p. ED 060 873.

_____ A SURVEY OF AUTOMATED ACTIVITIES IN EUROPEAN LIBRARIES. v. 3, World Survey Series; Tempe, Ariz. LARC Assn., 1972. 48p.

_____ A SURVEY OF AUTOMATED ACTIVITIES IN THE LIBRARIES OF MEXICO, CENTRAL AMERICA AND SOUTH AMERICA. v. 4, World Survey Series; Tempe, Ariz.: LARC Assn., 1972. 85p. ED 063 005.

Schneider, John Hoke, and others. SURVEY OF COMMERCIALLY AVAILABLE COMPUTER-READABLE BIBLIOGRAPHIC DATA BASES. Washington, DC: ASIS, 1973. 181p.

Schutze, Gertrude. INFORMATION AND LIBRARY SCIENCE SOURCE BOOK; a supplement to Documentation Source Book. Metuchen, NJ: Scarecrow Pr., 1972. 492p.

Wasserman, Paul, ed. LIST 1971: library and information science today. New York: Science Associates/International, Inc., 1971. 397p.

_____ LIST 1972: library and information science today. New York: Science Associates/International, Inc., 1972. 519p.

_____ LIST 1973: library and information science today. New York: Science Associates/International, Inc., 1973. 536p.

Wellman, Barry Stephen. COMMUNITY-NETWORK-COMMUNICATION: AN ANNOTATED BIBLIOGRAPHY. Monticello, Ill.: Council of Planning Librarians, 1972. 138p.

STANDARDS

American National Standards Institute. AMERICAN NATIONAL STANDARD
FORMAT FOR BIBLIOGRAPHIC INFORMATION INTERCHANGE ON
MAGNETIC TAPE, Z39.2–1971. New York: ANSI, 1971.
Association of Research Libraries. "Ad Hoc Committee on Specifications for a
Study of Automation in Research Libraries," in MINUTES. Association of
Research Libraries, 77th Meeting, Los Angeles, Calif., 17 January 1971.
Washington, DC: ARL, 1971. Appendix C, p.79–83.
International Federation of Library Assns. Committee on Cataloguing. Working
Group on the International Standard Bibliographic Description. INTER-
NATIONAL STANDARD BIBLIOGRAPHIC DESCRIPTION: FOR SINGLE
VOLUME AND MULTI-VOLUME MONOGRAPHIC PUBLICATIONS. Lon-
don, Eng.: International Federation of Library Assns., Committee on Catalogu-
ing, 1972. 30p.
INTERNATIONAL STANDARDIZATION OF LIBRARY AND DOCUMEN-
TATION TECHNIQUES. Paris: UNESCO, 1972. 284p.

MARC

Avram, Henriette D. RECON PILOT PROJECT; FINAL REPORT. Washington,
DC: Library of Congress, 1972. 49p.
Avram, Henriette D., and Kay D. Guiles. "Content designators for machine-
readable records; a working paper," JOURNAL OF LIBRARY AUTOMA-
TION 5(4):207–16 (Dec. 1972).
Avram, Henriette D., and Lenore S. Maruyama. "RECON pilot project; a
progress report, April–September 1970," JOURNAL OF LIBRARY AUTO-
MATION 4(1):38–51 (Mar. 1971).
_____ "RECON pilot project; a progress report, October 1970–May 1971,"
JOURNAL OF LIBRARY AUTOMATION 4(3):159–69 (Sept. 1971).
Avram, Henriette D., Lenore S. Maruyama, and John C. Rather. "Automation
activities in the processing department of the Library of Congress," LIBRARY
RESOURCES AND TECHNICAL SERVICES 16(2):195–239 (Sept. 1972).
Buhr, L. R. "Selective dissemination of MARC: a user evaluation," JOURNAL
OF LIBRARY AUTOMATION 5(1):39–50 (Mar. 1972).
Chauveinc, Marc. "Some remarks on the MONOCLE format in relation to the
MARC II format," in INTERNATIONAL SEMINAR ON THE MARC FOR-
MAT AND THE EXCHANGE OF BIBLIOGRAPHIC DATA IN MACHINE
READABLE FORM, 1971, Berlin. Munich: Verlag Dokumentation, 1972.
p.59–62.
Chisholm, Margaret. "Machine-readable cataloging—what is MARC?" AUDIO-
VISUAL INSTRUCTION 16(2):9–11 (Feb. 1971).
Corbett, Lindsay, and Janice A. German. "AMCOS project stage 2; a computer

aided integrated system using BNB/MARC literature tapes," PROGRAM 6(1):1–35 (Jan. 1972).

Coward, R. E. "BNB/MARC and the international MARC network," in PROCEEDINGS OF THE LIBRARY ASSOCIATION OF AUSTRALIA CONFERENCE, 1971. Sydney, Australia: The Association, 1972. p.747–58.

Crittenden, Victor. "The problem of perfection: Library of Congress cataloging, MARC tapes and their use in Australian libraries," AUSTRALIAN LIBRARY JOURNAL 20(4):20–22 (May 1971).

Griffin, Hillis L. "The cataloger's white knight? MARC," SPECIAL LIBRARIES 63(5–6):235–39 (May/June 1972).

Henderson, Kathryn L., ed. MARC USES AND USERS. Proceedings of the 1970 Clinic on Library Applications of Data Processing. Urbana: Univ. of Illinois, Graduate School of Library Science, 1971. 110p.

INTERNATIONAL SEMINAR ON THE MARC FORMAT AND THE EX-CHANGE OF BIBLIOGRAPHIC DATA IN MACHINE READABLE FORM, 1971, Berlin. Munich: Verlag Dokumentation, 1972. 196p.

Irvine, Ruth. "MARC tagging studies: local variations at Southampton University Library," PROGRAM 6(4):286–99 (Oct. 1972).

Jacob, M. E. "MARC in the University of Sydney Library," in PROCEEDINGS OF THE LIBRARY ASSOCIATION OF AUSTRALIA CONFERENCE, 1971. Sydney, Australia: The Association, 1972. p.759–66.

Kennedy, John P. "File size and the cost of processing MARC records," JOURNAL OF LIBRARY AUTOMATION 4(1):1–12 (Mar. 1971).

Library of Congress. MARC Development Off. BOOKS: A MARC FORMAT; specifications for magnetic tape containing catalog records for books. 5th ed. Washington, DC: Govt. Print. Off., 1972. 106p.

———— MARC USER SURVEY, 1972. Washington, DC: Govt. Print. Off., 1972. 58p.

———— FILMS: A MARC FORMAT; addendum 1, specifications for magnetic tapes containing catalog records for motion pictures, filmstrips, and other pictorial media intended for projection. Washington, DC: Govt. Print. Off., 1972. 13p.

———— INFORMATION ON THE MARC SYSTEM. 2d ed. Washington, DC: Govt. Print. Off., 1972. 34p.

———— MANUSCRIPTS: A MARC FORMAT; specifications for magnetic tapes containing catalog records for single manuscripts or manuscript collections. Washington, DC: Govt. Print. Off., 1973. 51p. ED 073 791.

"Machine-readable cataloging (MARC)," in S. Herner and M. J. Vellucci, eds., SELECTED FEDERAL COMPUTER-BASED INFORMATION SYSTEMS. Washington, DC: Information Resources Pr., 1972. p.185–90.

"MARC begins map catalog services," LIBRARY OF CONGRESS INFORMA-TION BULLETIN 32:3–4 (5 Jan. 1973).

"MARC development office designs automated process information file," LI-BRARY OF CONGRESS INFORMATION BULLETIN 31:272 (16 June 1972).

"MARC institutes format recognition," LIBRARY OF CONGRESS INFORMA-TION BULLETIN 31(5):54 (3 Feb. 1972).

"MARC to offer data base in MARC II format," LIBRARY OF CONGRESS INFORMATION BULLETIN 31:167, (10 Mar. 1972).

"MARC uses reported," LIBRARY OF CONGRESS INFORMATION BULLETIN 31:229–30, (19 May 1972).

Maruyama, Lenore S. "Format recognition: a report of a project at Library of Congress," JOURNAL OF THE AMERICAN SOCIETY FOR INFORMATION SCIENCE 22(4):283–87 (July 1971).

Mauerhoff, Georg R., and Richard G. Smith. "A MARC-II based program for retrieval and dissemination," JOURNAL OF LIBRARY AUTOMATION 4(3): 141–58 (Sept. 1971).

National Library of Canada. MARC Task Group. CANADIAN MARC: A REPORT OF THE ACTIVITIES OF THE MARC TASK GROUP RESULTING IN A RECOMMENDED CANADIAN MARC FORMAT FOR MONOGRAPHS AND A CANADIAN MARC FORMAT FOR SERIALS. Ottawa: The National Library of Canada, 1972. 242p.

Rather, John C., and Henriette D. Avram. NATIONAL ASPECTS OF CREATING AND USING MARC/RECON RECORDS. Washington, DC: Library of Congress, 1973.

Stockard, Joan. "Selective survey of MARC literature," LIBRARY RESOURCES AND TECHNICAL SERVICES 15(3):279–89 (Summer 1971).

Taylor, P. "MARC in practice," ASSISTANT LIBRARIAN 65:72–73 (May 1972).

Tucker, A. M. "Experiences with MARC-based systems at Trinity College, Dublin," in INTERNATIONAL SEMINAR ON THE MARC FORMAT AND THE EXCHANGE OF BIBLIOGRAPHIC DATA IN MACHINE READABLE FORM, 1971, Berlin. Munich: Verlag Dokumentation, 1972. p.157–71.

Veaner, A. B. "Applications of MARC at Stanford University, Stanford, Calif., and at Information Design, Inc., Menlo Park, Calif." in INTERNATIONAL SEMINAR ON THE MARC FORMAT AND THE EXCHANGE OF BIBLIOGRAPHIC DATA IN MACHINE READABLE FORM, 1971, Berlin. Munich: Verlag Dokumentation, 1972. p.191–96.

Wainwright, Jane M. "BNB/MARC users in the U.K.: a survey," PROGRAM 6(4):271–85 (Oct. 1972).

Woods, R. G. "Use of the MARC format at Southampton University Library," in INTERNATIONAL SEMINAR ON THE MARC FORMAT AND THE EXCHANGE OF BIBLIOGRAPHIC DATA IN MACHINE READABLE FORM, 1971, Berlin. Munich: Verlag Dokumentation, 1972. p.173–89.

SYSTEMS ANALYSIS

Burgis, G. C. "A systems development concept of organization and control for large university libraries," CANADIAN LIBRARY JOURNAL 28(1):24–29 (Jan./Feb. 1971).

Burns, Robert W., Jr. "A generalized methodology for library systems analysis," COLLEGE AND RESEARCH LIBRARIES 32(4):295–303 (July 1971).

de Boer, Aeint. CENTER FOR INFORMATION SERVICES, PHASE II: DE-

TAILED SYSTEMS DESIGN AND PROGRAMMING, PART 1—A MODU-LAR COMPUTER PROGRAM FOR REFERENCE RETRIEVAL. Phase IIA, Final Report. Los Angeles: Univ. of California, Institute of Library Research, Mar. 1971. 45p. ED 057 806.

Lancaster, F. Wilfrid, ed. "Systems design and analysis for libraries," LIBRARY TRENDS 21(4):463–603 (Apr. 1973).

Lubans, John, Jr. SYSTEMS ANALYSIS, MACHINEABLE CIRCULATION DATA AND LIBRARY USERS AND NON-USERS. Paper prepared for American Society for Engineering Education Annual Meeting, U.S. Naval Academy, Annapolis, Md., 21–24 June 1971. 12p. ED 060 911.

FILE STRUCTURE

"Bibliographic data in machine readable form," in PROCEEDINGS OF THE LIBRARY ASSOCIATION OF AUSTRALIA CONFERENCE, 1971. Sydney, Australia: The Association, 1972. p.482–97.

Dimsdale, J. J., and H. S. Heaps. "File structure for an on-line catalog of one million titles," JOURNAL OF LIBRARY AUTOMATION 6(1):37–55 (Mar. 1973).

Guthrie, Gerry D., and Steven D. Slifko. "Analysis of search key retrieval on a large bibliographic file," JOURNAL OF LIBRARY AUTOMATION 5(2): 96–100 (June 1972).

Kilgour, Frederick, and others. "Title-only entries retrieved by use of truncated search keys," JOURNAL OF LIBRARY AUTOMATION 4(4):207–10 (Dec. 1971).

Long, P. L., and F. G. Kilgour. "Truncated search key title index," JOURNAL OF LIBRARY AUTOMATION 5(1):17–20 (Mar. 1972).

Lynch, Michael F. "Compression of bibliographic files using an adaptation of run-length coding," INFORMATION STORAGE AND RETRIEVAL 9(4): 207–14 (Apr. 1973).

Palmer, Foster M. "Automatic processing of personal names for filing," JOURNAL OF LIBRARY AUTOMATION 4(4):185–97 (Dec. 1971).

Sherman, Don. "Converting bibliographic data to machine form," in Melvin J. Voigt, ed., ADVANCES IN LIBRARIANSHIP, v. 3. New York: Seminar Pr., 1972. p.221–43.

West, Martha W., Rowena Koch, and Brett Butler. "Computer filing vs. ALA filing rules," CALIFORNIA LIBRARIAN 34(3):47–56 (Apr. 1973).

SOFTWARE

Gold, Jack A. "PRECIS: an analysis," CANADIAN LIBRARY JOURNAL 29(6): 460–69 (Nov./Dec. 1972).

Heath, John Thomas. INPUT: A GENERALISED IBM 360 MARC FILE HAN-
DLING SYSTEM. London: British National Bibliography, 1971. 99p.
"Translation program for MARC tapes available from Drexel," JOURNAL OF
LIBRARY AUTOMATION TECHNICAL COMMUNICATIONS 3(3):2
(May/June 1972).

TECHNICAL PROCESSING

Avram, Henriette D. "Automation in technical processing at the Library of
Congress," in THE BOWKER ANNUAL OF LIBRARY AND BOOK TRADE
INFORMATION, 1972. New York: Bowker, 1972. p.80–85.
Chvatal, Donald P., and Gary L. Olson. "A computer-based acquisitions
system for libraries," in Jeanne B. North, ed., COMMUNICATION FOR
DECISION-MAKERS. Proceedings of the 34th Annual Meeting of the Ameri-
can Society for Information Science, Denver, 7–11 Nov. 1971, v. 8. Westport,
Conn.: Greenwood Publishing Co., 1971. p.217–26.
Fischer, Mary, comp. LOS ANGELES PUBLIC LIBRARY DESCRIPTION OF
THE AUTOMATED LIBRARY TECHNICAL SERVICES (ALTS) PRO-
GRAM. Los Angeles Public Library, Jan. 1973.
Kountz, John C. "BIBLIOS revisited," JOURNAL OF LIBRARY AUTOMATION
5(2):63–86 (June 1972).
Melcher, Daniel. "Cataloging, processing, and automation," AMERICAN LI-
BRARIES 2(7):701–13 (July/Aug. 1971).
Shipman, George W. "The relation of the Card Division to library technical
processing," ILLINOIS LIBRARIES 53(3):182–84 (Mar. 1971).
Stevens, L. C. "Computerized acquisitions and cataloguing," NEW ZEALAND
LIBRARIES 35:19–22 (Fall 1972).
Ungerleider, S. Lester. STUDY OF USEABILITY OF COMPUTER OUTPUT
MICROFILM IN THE TECHNICAL PROCESSING AREA OF THE YALE
UNIVERSITY LIBRARY. New Haven, Conn.: Yale Univ. Library, 1971.
Woods, R. G. ACQUISITIONS AND CATALOGUING SYSTEMS: PRELIMI-
NARY REPORT. Southampton, Eng.: Southampton Univ. Library, 1971.
52p. ED 059 744.

ACQUISITIONS

Carter, Ruth C. "Automation of acquisitions at Parkland College," JOURNAL
OF LIBRARY AUTOMATION 5(2):118–36 (June 1972).
COLLEGE BIBLIOCENTRE ACQUISITION AND ACCOUNTING SYSTEM
OPERATING MANUAL. Don Mills, Ontario: College Bibliocentre, 1971.
54p. ED 056 691.

Fristoe, Ashby J., and Rose E. Myers. "Acquisitions in 1970," LIBRARY RESOURCES AND TECHNICAL SERVICES 15:132–42 (Spring 1971).

International Business Machines Corp. ONLINE ACQUISITIONS: SANTA CLARA COUNTY FREE LIBRARY. White Plains, NY: IBM, 1973. 13p.

_____ ONLINE LIBRARY ACQUISITIONS SYSTEM AT THE UNIVERSITY OF MASSACHUSETTS. White Plains, NY: IBM, 1972. 12p.

Library of Congress. MARC Development Office. ORDER DIVISION AUTOMATED SYSTEM. 1972. 74p.

Melcher, Daniel. MELCHER ON ACQUISITION. Chicago: American Library Assn., 1971. 169p.

Sheehan, P. M. Cost-responsive acquisitions system," in Jeanne B. North, ed., COMMUNICATION FOR DECISION-MAKERS, Proceedings of the 34th Annual Meeting of the American Society for Information Science, Denver, 7–11 November 1971. v. 8. Westport, Conn.: Greenwood Publishing Co., 1971. p.311–19.

Post, M. "Computer checking of Scarborough's acquisitions," ONTARIO LIBRARY REVIEW 56:238–39 (Dec. 1972).

CATALOGING

Arms, William S., and Caroline R. Arms. ACCESS TO UNION CATALOGUES MAINTAINED BY COMPUTER. London, Eng.: National Central Library, 1972. 47p.

Bakewell, K. G. B. "Cataloguing and indexing activities," LIBRARY ASSOCIATION RECORD 73(3):49–50 (Mar. 1971).

_____ "Cataloguing and indexing activities," LIBRARY ASSOCIATION RECORD 73(10):189–90 (Oct. 1971).

Brown, Ann T. "Use of the MT/ST at a remote facility to produce catalog cards," SPECIAL LIBRARIES 63(5–6):235–39 (May/June 1972).

Buckland, Lawrence F., and Mary Madden. INVESTIGATION OF THE SEARCHING EFFICIENCY AND COST OF CREATING A REMOTE ACCESS CATALOG FOR THE NEW YORK STATE LIBRARY. Final Report. Maynard, Mass.: Inforonics, Inc., Dec. 1972. 77p. ED 073 782.

"Catalog production," THE OHIO COLLEGE LIBRARY CENTER NEWSLETTER no.54:2 (1 Nov. 1972).

Chen, Simon P. J. "Automated cataloging and reclassification by ATS," SPECIAL LIBRARIES 64(4):193–97 (Apr. 1973).

CREATION OF MACHINE READABLE CATALOG ENTRIES; AN ADAPTATION OF THE "DATA PREPARATION MANUAL: MARC EDITORS." Columbus: Ohio College Library Center, May 1971. 72p. ED 060 858.

Fox, Ann M. THE AMENABILITY OF A CATALOGING PROCESS TO SIMULATION BY AUTOMATIC TECHNIQUES. Final Report. Urbana: Univ. of Illinois, Graduate School of Library Science, 1972. 477p. ED 076 225.

Galloway, M. "Cataloguing for the tri-regional book catalog," ONTARIO

LIBRARY REVIEW 57:21-23 (Mar. 1973).

Grosch, Audrey N. "Computer-based subject authority files at the University of Minnesota Libraries," JOURNAL OF LIBRARY AUTOMATION 5(4): 230-43 (Dec. 1972).

Hallsworth, P. P. "Tri-regional computer produced book catalogue," ONTARIO LIBRARY REVIEW 57:18-20 (Mar. 1973).

Halm, Joh. van. "Use of the UDC in a mechanized system," SPECIAL LIBRARIES 63(10):482-86 (Oct. 1972).

Hazelton, Robert S. "Cataloging geometry," JOURNAL OF LIBRARY AUTOMATION 5(1):12-16 (Mar. 1972).

Hopkins, Judith. MANUAL FOR OCLC CATALOG CARD PRODUCTION. Rev. and enl. Columbus: Ohio College Library Center, Feb. 1971. 69p. ED 046 471.

Irvine, R., and G. Nicholas. "MARC-produced cards: production of cards from MARC-compatible cataloguing tapes before computer input," CATALOGUE AND INDEX 25:8-9 (Spring 1972).

Kniemeyer, Justin M. "Computerized production of library catalogs," in L. Vilentchuk and Gila Haimovic, eds., ISLIC INTERNATIONAL CONFERENCE ON INFORMATION SCIENCE, PROCEEDINGS, Tel Aviv, 29 August-3 September 1971. Tel Aviv: National Center of Scientific and Technological Information, 1972. p.729-35.

Kniesner, Dan L., and Betty J. Meyer. "On-line computer techniques in shared cataloging," LIBRARY RESOURCES AND TECHNICAL SERVICES 17(2): 225-30 (Spring 1973).

Landram, Christina O. "Increasing production in a small university catalog department," LIBRARY RESOURCES AND TECHNICAL SERVICES 15(3): 380-84 (Summer 1971).

Lipetz, Ben-Ami. "Catalog use in a large research library," LIBRARY QUARTERLY 42(1):129-39 (Jan. 1972).

MacDonald, Robin W., and J. McRee Elrod. "An approach to developing computer catalogs," COLLEGE AND RESEARCH LIBRARIES 34(3):202-8 (May 1973).

Malinconico, S. Michael, and James A. Rizzolo. "The New York Public Library automated book catalog subsystem," JOURNAL OF LIBRARY AUTOMATION 6(1):3-36 (Mar. 1973).

Martin, David. UNION CATALOG OPERATIONS MANUAL FOR A SIMPLIFIED ATS (Administrative Terminal System). Columbia, Mo.: Univ. of Missouri, May 1971. 58p. PB 205 946.

Massonneau, Suzanne. "The main entry and the book catalog," LIBRARY RESOURCES AND TECHNICAL SERVICES 15(4):499-512 (Fall 1971).

Morse, Susan S., Larry R. Rowland, and D. A. B. Lindberg. DESIGN FOR A COMPUTER SYSTEM FOR A LARGE LIBRARY BOOK CATALOG. Technical description of the internal architecture of the retrieval system. Columbia, Mo.: Univ. of Missouri, 1971. PB 205 995.

NATIONAL CONFERENCE ON CATALOGUING STANDARDS, Ottawa, 19-20 May 1970. Ottawa: National Library of Canada, Mar. 1971. 176p. ED 058 901.

Nixon, Roberta, and Ray Bell. "The U.C.L.A. Library catalog supplement," LIBRARY RESOURCES AND TECHNICAL SERVICES 17(1):28–31 (Winter 1973).

Ohio College Library Center. STANDARDS FOR INPUT CATALOGING. Columbus: OCLC, June 1972. 28p. ED 063 965.

Palmer, Richard P. COMPUTERIZING THE CARD CATALOG IN THE UNIVERSITY LIBRARY: A SURVEY OF USER REQUIREMENTS. Research Studies in Library Science, no. 6. Littleton, Colo.: Libraries Unlimited, 1972. 141p.

Pfeifer, Ruth Ann. "Shared cataloging," CATHOLIC LIBRARY WORLD 42(10): 650–53 (July 1971).

Port, Idelle. "Developing a strategy for retrospective conversion of the card catalog to a machine readable data base in three academic libraries (small, medium and large): two alternatives considered," INFORMATION STORAGE AND RETRIEVAL 9(5):267–80 (May 1973).

Sargent, C. W., and D. A. B. Lindberg. "Computer-based union catalog project for the University of Missouri," SPECIAL LIBRARIES 63(3):121–29 (Mar. 1972).

Stiles, Helen J., and Joan M. Maier. "Automated cataloging of technical reports via optical scanning," SPECIAL LIBRARIES 63(12):576–87 (Dec. 1972).

Tauber, Maurice F., and Hilda Feinberg. BOOK CATALOGS. Metuchen, NJ: Scarecrow Pr., 1971. 572p.

———— "Book catalogs," in Conrad H. Rawski, ed., TOWARD A THEORY OF LIBRARIANSHIP: PAPERS IN HONOR OF JESSE HAUK SHERA. Metuchen, NJ: Scarecrow Pr., 1973. p.350–77.

Waldron, Helen J. BOOK CATALOGS: A SURVEY OF THE LITERATURE ON COSTS. Santa Monica, Calif.: Rand Corp., May 1971. 27p. ED 053 775.

Wassom, Earl E. ON-LINE CATALOGING AND CIRCULATION AT WESTERN KENTUCKY UNIVERSITY: AN APPROACH TO AUTOMATED INSTRUCTIONAL RESOURCES MANAGEMENT. Bowling Green: Western Kentucky Univ., Div. of Library Services, 1973. 78p.

Woods, R. G. THE COST OF CATALOGING: THREE SYSTEMS COMPARED. Southampton, Eng.: Southampton Univ. Library, 1972. 39p. ED 071 707.

SERIALS

Blair, J. "Routing slips from the computer," SPECIAL LIBRARIES 63(2): 82–84 (Feb. 1972).

Bloch, Earl. "Serials processing system reference manual," LARC REPORTS 5(3):1–16, Appendixes A–E, 1972.

Bosseau, Don L. "The computer in serials processing and control," in Melvin

J. Voigt, ed., ADVANCES IN LIBRARIANSHIP, v. 2. New York: Seminar Pr., 1971. p.103–64.

Budington, William. "Research library expectations of a national serials data program," in MINUTES. Association of Research Libraries 77th Meeting, Los Angeles, California, 17 January 1971. Washington, DC: ARL, 1971. p.21–25.

Campbell, D. J., and M. Morton. "Computerising the recording and control of periodical circulation in an industrial information service," PROGRAM 5(1):19–25 (Jan. 1971).

Condit, Anna R. "Optical mark sensing of serials check-in records: a new approach to serials automation," in Jeanne B. North, ed., COMMUNICATION FOR DECISION-MAKERS. Proceedings of the 34th Annual Meeting of the American Society for Information Science, Denver, 7–11 November 1971, v. 8, Westport, Conn.: Greenwood Publishing Co., 1971. p.287–90.

Fayollat, James. "On-line serials control system in a large biomedical library, pt. 1. Description of the system," JOURNAL OF THE AMERICAN SOCIETY FOR INFORMATION SCIENCE 23(5):318–22 (Sept./Oct. 1972).

_____ "On-line serials control system in a large biomedical library, pt. 2. Evaluation of retrieval features," JOURNAL OF THE AMERICAN SOCIETY FOR INFORMATION SCIENCE 23(6):353–58 (Nov./Dec. 1972).

_____ "On-line serials control system in a large biomedical library, pt. 3. Comparison of on-line and batch operations and cost analysis," JOURNAL OF THE AMERICAN SOCIETY FOR INFORMATION SCIENCE 24(2):80–86 (Mar./Apr. 1973).

Hammer, Donald P. "HELP: the automated binding records control system," JOURNAL OF LIBRARY AUTOMATION 5(2):137–45 (June 1972).

Hickey, Doralyn J. "The serials catalog becomes machine-readable," in PROBLEMS IN ORGANIZING LIBRARY COLLECTIONS. New York: Bowker, 1972. p.133–38.

"The international serials data system," CANADIAN LIBRARY JOURNAL 29(6):458 (Nov./Dec. 1972).

Johnson, Donald W. "The national serials pilot project," in MINUTES. Association of Research Libraries 77th Meeting, Los Angeles, California, 17 January 1971. Washington, DC: ARL, 1971. p.11–16.

_____ TOWARD A NATIONAL SERIALS DATA PROGRAM: FINAL REPORT OF THE NATIONAL SERIALS PILOT PROJECT. Washington, DC: ARL, 1972. 94p.

JOINT SERIALS CONTROL SYSTEM PROJECT FOR THE LIBRARIES OF CORNELL UNIVERSITY, UNIVERSITY OF ROCHESTER AND THE STATE UNIVERSITY OF NEW YORK AT BUFFALO. Phase 1 Feasibility Study. Final Report. Syracuse, NY: Five Associated University Libraries, Feb. 1971. 141p. ED 051 827.

Koenig, Michael E. D., and others. "SCOPE: a cost analysis of an automated serials record system," JOURNAL OF LIBRARY AUTOMATION 4(3):129–40 (Sept. 1971).

Kraft, D. H., and T. W. Hill, Jr. "A journal selection model and its implications for a library system," INFORMATION STORAGE AND RETRIEVAL 9(1):1–11 (Jan. 1973).

Krieger, Tillie. "The national serials pilot project," in L. Vilentchuk and Gila Haimovic, eds., ISLIC INTERNATIONAL CONFERENCE ON INFORMATION SCIENCE, PROCEEDINGS, Tel Aviv, 29 August–3 September 1971. Tel Aviv: National Center of Scientific and Technological Information, 1972. p.699–708, 737–43.

Lazerow, Samuel. "The national serials system: concept and commitment," in MINUTES. Association of Research Libraries 77th Meeting, Los Angeles, California, 17 January 1971. Washington, DC: ARL, 1971. p.17–21.

"National serials data program report is given," LIBRARY OF CONGRESS INFORMATION BULLETIN 31:513–14 (1 Dec. 1972).

Pound, Mary. "Serials: a review of 1970," LIBRARY RESOURCES AND TECHNICAL SERVICES 15(2):143–49 (Spring 1971).

Roberts, Stephen A. A MACHINE READABLE DATA BASE OF SOCIAL SCIENCE SERIALS. Bath, Eng.: Bath Univ. of Technology, Univ. Library, (Nov.) 1971. 27p.

Roth, Dana L. "Scientific serial lists," JOURNAL OF LIBRARY AUTOMATION 5(1):51–57 (Mar. 1972).

Sawyers, E. J. "Union list development: control of the serial literature," MEDICAL LIBRARY ASSOCIATION BULLETIN 60(3):427–31 (July 1972).

Surace, Cecily J. "PEARL, an automated periodicals control system," SPECIAL LIBRARIES 63(9):385–93 (Sept. 1972).

Thompson, V. "Computerized serials list at Mossly University Library," NEW ZEALAND LIBRARIES 35(2):9–12 (Feb. 1972).

"Tri-college libraries Union List of Serials system," LARC REPORTS 5(4): 1–80 (1972).

Wilkinson, W. A., and Loretta A. Stock. "Machine-assisted serials control. Bindery preparation and claims control," SPECIAL LIBRARIES 62(12):529–34 (Dec. 1971).

Yerkey, A. N. "Computer-assisted periodical routing and renewal audit," SPECIAL LIBRARIES 64(3):126–29 (Mar. 1973).

CIRCULATION

Aagaard, James S. "An interactive computer-based circulation system: design and development," JOURNAL OF LIBRARY AUTOMATION 5(1):3–11 (Mar. 1972).

Allred, John R. "Data capture devices and stock control in libraries: some recent trends," NEW LIBRARY WORLD 73:189–91 (Jan. 1972).

Buckland, Michael K., and Bernard Gallivan. "Circulation control: off-line, on-line, or hybrid," JOURNAL OF LIBRARY AUTOMATION 5(1):30–38 (Mar. 1972).

Crowe, A. J., and H. I. Hammond. AN AUTOMATED STOCK CONTROL SYSTEM. Shrewsbury, Eng.: Shropshire Central Library, 1973. 22p.

Downing, J. "Computer controlled circulation system," COMPUTER JOURNAL 14(1):2–6 (Feb. 1971).

Fuller, Donald F. "Santa Clara Public Library's computerized circulation system," NEWS NOTES OF CALIFORNIA LIBRARIES 67(2): 283–86 (Spring 1972).

Gallivan, Bernard, R. N. Bamver and Michael K. Buckland. COMPUTER LISTING OF A RESERVE COLLECTION. Occasional papers no. 6. Lancaster, Eng.: Univ. of Lancaster Library, 1972. 68p.

Guthrie, Gerry D. "An on-line remote access and circulation control system," in Jeanne B. North, ed., COMMUNICATION FOR DECISION-MAKERS. Proceedings of the 34th Annual Meeting of the American Society for Information Science, Denver, 7–11 November 1971. v. 8. Westport, Conn.: Greenwood Publishing Co., 1971. p.305–9.

International Business Machines Corp. Data Processing Div. ON-LINE REMOTE CATALOG ACCESS AND CIRCULATION CONTROL SYSTEM. Pt. 1. Functional specifications; Pt. 2. User's manual. Columbus: Ohio State Univ. Libraries, 1971.

Kozumplik, William A. "Circulation mechanized," SPECIAL LIBRARIES 62(7–8):287–88 (July/Aug. 1971).

"Library computer," AMERICAN SCHOOL AND UNIVERSITY 44(2):15–16 (Oct. 1971).

Lin, S. H. "Library fines and their effects on users: study of the automated fines system of the University of Kansas," MOUNTAIN-PLAINS LIBRARY QUARTERLY 16:3–5 (Fall 1972).

McGee, Robert S. "Analysis of manual circulation systems for academic libraries," JOURNAL OF THE AMERICAN SOCIETY FOR INFORMATION SCIENCE 24(3):210–17 (May/June 1973).

_____ "Key factors of circulation system analysis and design," COLLEGE AND RESEARCH LIBRARIES 33(2):127–39 (Mar. 1972).

_____ A LITERATURE SURVEY OF OPERATIONAL AND EMERGING ON-LINE LIBRARY CIRCULATION SYSTEMS. Chicago: Univ. of Chicago Library, Library Systems Development Off., 1972. 64p.

_____ "Two types of designs for on-line circulation systems," JOURNAL OF LIBRARY AUTOMATION 5(3):184–202 (Sept. 1972).

Miller, Jean K. "Computer assisted circulation control at Health Sciences Library SUNYAB," JOURNAL OF LIBRARY AUTOMATION 5(2):87–95 (June 1972).

Peake, D. G., and P. Glock. "IBM 357 circulation system at the University of New South Wales," AUSTRALIAN ACADEMIC AND RESEARCH LIBRARIES 3:21–32 (Mar. 1972).

Piatkowski, T. F. REVIEW OF THE ON-LINE REAL-TIME CIRCULATION DESK PROJECT. Hanover, NH: Thayer School of Engineering, Dartmouth College, 1971. 28p.

Rao, Paladugu V., and B. Joseph Szerenyi, "Booth Library on-line circulation system (BLOC)," JOURNAL OF LIBRARY AUTOMATION 4(2):86–102 (June 1971).

Rivoire, H., and M. Smith. BUCKNELL LIBRARY ON-LINE CIRCULATION SYSTEM (BLOCS). Bucknell Univ. Library, March 1971. 17p.

Ross, John, and Jane Brooks. "Costing manual and computerized library circulation systems," PROGRAM 6(3):217–27 (July 1972).

Simmons, Peter. COLLECTION DEVELOPMENT AND THE COMPUTER: A CASE STUDY IN THE ANALYSIS OF MACHINE READABLE LOAN RECORDS AND THEIR APPLICATION TO BOOK SELECTION. Vancouver: Univ. of British Columbia, School of Librarianship, 1971. 63p. ED 054 817.

———— "Reserve collections: some computer assistance for the perennial problems," CANADIAN LIBRARY JOURNAL 29(3):82–87 (Mar./Apr. 1972).

Surace, Cecily J. "Library circulation systems: an overview," SPECIAL LIBRARIES 63(4):177–88 (Apr. 1972).

Veneziano, Velma. "Interactive computer-based circulation system for Northwestern University—the library puts it to work," JOURNAL OF LIBRARY AUTOMATION 5(2):101–17 (June 1972).

INTERLIBRARY LOAN

Scholz, William H. INTRASYSTEM LOANS AT TIMBERLAND REGIONAL LIBRARY; A STUDY AND COMPUTER SIMULATION. Olympia: Washington State Library, 1972.

Stevens, Rolland E. A FEASIBILITY STUDY OF CENTRALIZED AND REGIONALIZED INTERLIBRARY LOAN CENTERS. Washington, DC: Assn. of Research Libraries, April 1973. 65p. ED 076 206.

REFERENCE

Carville, M., L. D. Higgins, and F. J. Smith. "Interactive reference retrieval in large files," INFORMATION STORAGE AND RETRIEVAL 7(5):205–10 (Dec. 1971).

Finzi, J. C. "Computer-based reference services, a pre-conference institute of the Reference Services Division of the ALA," LIBRARY OF CONGRESS INFORMATION BULLETIN 30(A):111–14 (8 July 1971).

"Hypothetic dialogues: the RSD preconference," LIBRARY JOURNAL 96(14): 2450–51 (Aug. 1971).

Mathies, M. Lorraine, and Peter G. Watson. "Computer-based reference service: a pre-conference institute of the Reference Services Division, American Library Association, Dallas, Texas, 18–19 June 1971." Tutor's manual. Reference Services Div., American Library Assn., 1971. 199p. mimeo.

Maxwell, Margaret. "The machine in the reference room," RQ 11(1):23–25 (Fall 1971).

Negus, A. E., and J. L. Hall. "Towards an effective on-line reference retrieval system," INFORMATION STORAGE AND RETRIEVAL 7(6):249–70 (Dec. 1971).

Winik, Ruth. "Reference function with an on-line catalog," SPECIAL LIBRARIES 63(5–6):217–21 (May/June 1972).

SDI AND CURRENT AWARENESS

Altmann, Berthold. AUTOMATED SDI SERVICES. Washington, DC:Harry Diamond Laboratories, 1972. 16p.

Barker, F. H., and others. "Towards automatic profile construction," JOURNAL OF DOCUMENTATION 28(3):44–55 (Mar. 1972).

Byrne, J. G., P. J. Currivan, and F. V. Mahon. "A current awareness system based on INSPEC tapes," INFORMATION STORAGE AND RETRIEVAL 8(4):177–90 (Aug. 1972).

Cawkell, E. E. "Cost-effectiveness and benefits of SDI systems," INFORMATION SCIENTIST 6(4):143–48 (Dec. 1972).

Duncan, Elizabeth E. CURRENT AWARENESS AND THE CHEMIST. Metuchen, NJ: Scarecrow Pr., 1972. 150p.

Roberts, Anita B., and others. "Development of a computerized current awareness service using Chemical Abstracts Condensates," JOURNAL OF CHEMICAL DOCUMENTATION 12(4):221–23 (Nov. 1972).

Scheffler, F. L., and others. "Experiment to study the use of Boolean "not" logic to improve the precision of selective dissemination of information," JOURNAL OF THE AMERICAN SOCIETY FOR INFORMATION SCIENCE 23(1):58–65 (Jan. 1972).

Wolters, P. H., and J. E. Brown. "CAN/SDI system: user reaction to a computerized information retrieval system for Canadian scientists and technologists," CANADIAN LIBRARY JOURNAL 28(1):20–23 (Jan./Feb. 1971).

INDEXING AND ABSTRACTING

Axhausen, Walter E. A., and Andrew E. Wessel. "Machine-aided indexing and analysis for document and fact retrieval," in L. Vilentchuk and Gila Haimovic, eds., ISLIC INTERNATIONAL CONFERENCE ON INFORMATION SCIENCE, PROCEEDINGS, Tel Aviv, 29 August–3 September, 1971. Tel Aviv: National Center of Scientific and Technological Information, 1972. p.777–83.

Broxis, P. F. "Indexing and abstracting services," in H. A. Whatley, ed.,

BRITISH LIBRARIANSHIP AND INFORMATION SERVICE, 1966–1970. London: Library Association, 1972. p.90–102.

Charen, Thelma. MEDLARS INDEXING MANUAL. Bethesda, Md.: National Library of Medicine, 1972. 511p.

Christ, John M. CONCEPTS AND SUBJECT HEADINGS: THEIR RELATION IN INFORMATION RETRIEVAL AND LIBRARY SCIENCE. Metuchen, NJ: Scarecrow Pr., 1972. 174p.

Collison, Robert L. INDEXES AND INDEXING. New York: John de Graff, Inc., 1972. 232p.

Dataflow Systems, Inc. AN INTRODUCTION TO INDEXING AND AB-STRACTING FOR TECHNICAL INFORMATION SYSTEMS. Bethesda, Md.: Dataflow Systems Inc., 1972. 56p.

Edwards, Tom. "LISA and the comprehensive control of library and information science literature," INTERNATIONAL LIBRARY REVIEW 4(1):67–70 (Jan. 1972).

Hines, Theodore C., and Jessica L. Harris. "Columbia University School of Library Service system for thesaurus development and maintenance," IN-FORMATION STORAGE AND RETRIEVAL 7(1):39–50 (June 1971).

Hoyle, W. G. "Automatic indexing and generation of classification systems by algorithm," INFORMATION STORAGE AND RETRIEVAL 9(4):233–42 (Apr. 1973).

Keenan, S., and M. Elliot. "World inventory of abstracting and indexing services," SPECIAL LIBRARIES 64:145–50 (Mar. 1973).

Lancaster, F. W. VOCABULARY CONTROL FOR INFORMATION RE-TRIEVAL. Washington, DC: Information Resources Pr., (July) 1972. 233p. ED 075 999.

MEDLARS INDEXING AND SEARCHING AIDS. Bethesda, Md.: National Library of Medicine, 1972. 385p.

Salton, G. "A new comparison between conventional indexing (MEDLARS) and automatic test processing (SMART)," JOURNAL OF THE AMERICAN SOCIETY FOR INFORMATION SCIENCE 23(2):75–84 (Mar./Apr. 1972).

Schippleck, S. "Impossible indexing, or looking for ERIC," RQ 11:352–55 (Summer 1972).

Smith, Kingsley R., and Theodore M. Judy. "Correcting author, title and multiple-term index entries in mechanized bibliography preparation," JOUR-NAL OF THE AMERICAN SOCIETY FOR INFORMATION SCIENCE 23(6): 279–83 (Nov./Dec. 1972).

UDC IN RELATION TO OTHER INDEXING LANGUAGES. Proceedings of the International Symposium, Herceg Novi, Yugoslavia, 28 June–1 July 1971. Belgrade: Yugoslav Center for Technical and Scientific Documentation, 1971. 422p.

Vickery, Brian C. "The many uses and forms of subject representation," in L. Vilentchuk and Gila Haimovic, eds., ISLIC INTERNATIONAL CONFER-ENCE ON INFORMATION SCIENCE, PROCEEDINGS, Tel Aviv, 29 August–3 September 1971. Tel Aviv: National Center of Scientific and Technological Information, 1972. p.189–97.

AUTOMATED RETRIEVAL AND DATA BASES

ACCESS TO MACHINE READABLE BIBLIOGRAPHIC DATA, a proposal to MERIT. Detroit: Wayne State Univ.; Michigan Univ. Libraries, 1972. 16p.

Adams, Scott. "The way of the innovator: notes toward a prehistory of MEDLARS," BULLETIN OF THE MEDICAL LIBRARY ASSOCIATION 60(4):523-33 (Oct. 1972).

Aiyer, Arjun K. THE CIMARON SYSTEM: MODULAR PROGRAMS FOR THE ORGANIZATION AND SEARCH OF LARGE FILES. Final Report. Berkeley: Univ. of California, Institute of Library Research, September 1971. 62p.

Bennertz, Richard K. DEVELOPMENT OF THE DEFENSE DOCUMENTATION CENTER REMOTE ON-LINE RETRIEVAL SYSTEM—PAST, PRESENT AND FUTURE. Alexandria, Va: Defense Documentation Center, March 1971. 52p. AD 720 900.

Borman, Lorraine, and Benjamin Mittman. "Interactive search of bibliographic data bases in an academic environment," JOURNAL OF THE AMERICAN SOCIETY FOR INFORMATION SCIENCE 23(3):164-71 (May/June 1972).

Bradley University. SEARCH OF THE LIBRARY INFORMATION COLLECTION 1972. Peoria, Ill.: Bradley Univ., Computer Center, 1972. 38p.

Buginas, S. J., and N. B. Crow. "Computerized file management systems: a tool for the reference librarian," SPECIAL LIBRARIES 64(1):12-17 (Jan. 1973).

Byrum, J. D., and J. S. Rowe. "Integrated user-oriented systems for the documentation and control of machine-readable data files," LIBRARY RESOURCES AND TECHNICAL SERVICES 16(3):338-46 (Summer 1972).

Carmon, James L., and Margaret K. Park. "User assessment of computer-based bibliographic retrieval services," JOURNAL OF CHEMICAL DOCUMENTATION 13(1):24-27 (Feb. 1973).

Chauveinc, Marc. "MONOCLE," JOURNAL OF LIBRARY AUTOMATION 4(3):113-28 (Sept. 1971).

Cuadra, Carlos A. "Are computer services agencies responding to the needs of libraries?" LAW LIBRARY JOURNAL 64(2):126-32 (May 1971).

_____ "On-line systems: promise and pitfalls," JOURNAL OF THE AMERICAN SOCIETY FOR INFORMATION SCIENCE 22(2):107-14 (Mar./Apr. 1971).

Gechman, Marvin C. "Machine-readable bibliographic data bases," in Carlos A. Cuadra, ed., ANNUAL REVIEW OF INFORMATION SCIENCE AND TECHNOLOGY. v. 7. Washington, DC: ASIS, 1972. p.323-78.

Goffman, W. "On information retrieval systems," in Conrad H. Rawski, ed., TOWARD A THEORY OF LIBRARIANSHIP: PAPERS IN HONOR OF JESSE HAUK SHERA. Metuchen, NJ: Scarecrow Pr., 1973. p.234-42.

Ironside, Diana J. "Some thoughts on uses of data banks," CANADIAN LIBRARY JOURNAL 28(1):30-35 (Jan./Feb. 1971).

Keenan, Stella, ed. KEY PAPERS ON THE USE OF COMPUTER-BASED BIBLIOGRAPHIC SERVICES. Washington, DC: National Federation of Abstracting and Indexing Services and the American Society for Information Science, 1972.

Kehl, W. B., and others. CENTER FOR INFORMATION SERVICES, FINAL REPORT. Phase IIB; Detailed design and prototype development, 1 January 1971 to 30 June 1972. Los Angeles: Univ. of California, Center for Information Services, 1972. 80p. ED 073 795.

Klempner, Irving M. "Librarianship and the use of machine-readable bibliographic data bases," in L. Vilentchuk and Gila Haimovic, eds., ISLIC INTERNATIONAL CONFERENCE ON INFORMATION SCIENCE, PROCEEDINGS, Tel Aviv, 29 August–3 September 1971. Tel Aviv: National Center of Scientific and Technological Information, 1972. p.769–76.

Kuo, Franklin F. CRANFIELD CONFERENCE ON INFORMATION RETRIEVAL REPORT. London, Eng.: Office of Naval Research, November 1971. AD 734 388.

Lancaster, F. W. EVALUATION OF ON-LINE SEARCHING IN MEDLARS (AIM-TWX) BY BIOMEDICAL PRACTITIONERS. Urbana, Ill.: Univ. of Illinois, Graduate School of Library Science, 1972. 20p.

Lauterback, Guy. A CATALOGING SYSTEM FOR MACHINE READABLE DATA BASES. Corvallis: Oregon State Univ., June 1971. 15p. ED 071 678.

Mauerhoff, Georg R. "Science-oriented and MARC II tape services," SPECIAL LIBRARIES 64(3):135–40 (Mar. 1973).

Moody, D. W., and Olaf Kays. "Development of the U.S. Geological Survey Bibliographic System using GIPSY," JOURNAL OF THE AMERICAN SOCIETY FOR INFORMATION SCIENCE 23(1):39–49 (Jan./Feb. 1972).

Mott, Thomas H., Jr., Susan Artandi, and Leny Struminger. INTRODUCTION TO PL/1 PROGRAMMING FOR LIBRARY AND INFORMATION SCIENCE. New York: Harcourt, Academic Pr., 1972. 231p.

O'Donohue, C. H. "Comparison of service centers and document data bases— a user's view," JOURNAL OF CHEMICAL DOCUMENTATION 13(1):27–29 (Feb. 1973).

Park, M. K. "Computer-based bibliographic retrieval services," SPECIAL LIBRARIES 64(4):187–92 (Apr. 1973).

PROJECT INTREX: A BRIEF DESCRIPTION. Cambridge, Mass.: Massachusetts Institute of Technology, 1971. 26p.

_____ Semiannual activity report, 15 March 1971–15 September 1971. Cambridge, Mass.: Massachusetts Institute of Technology, September 1971. 124p. ED 053 772.

_____ Semiannual activity report, 15 September 1971–15 March 1972. Cambridge, Mass.: Massachusetts Institute of Technology, March 1972. 111p. Ed 060 899.

_____ Semiannual activity report, 15 March 1972–15 September 1972. Cambridge, Mass.: Massachusetts Institute of Technology, September 1972. 69p. ED 066 207.

Salton, G. "Automatic processing of current affairs queries," INFORMATION STORAGE AND RETRIEVAL 9(3):165–80 (Mar. 1973).

_____ DYNAMIC DOCUMENT PROCESSING. Ithaca, NY: Cornell Univ., Dept. of Computer Science, 1972. 35p.

Schieber, William D. ISIS (INTEGRATED SCIENTIFIC INFORMATION SYS-
TEM); A GENERAL DESCRIPTION OF AN APPROACH TO COMPU-
TERISED BIBLIOGRAPHICAL CONTROL. Geneva (Switzerland): Inter-
national Labour Office, 1971. 120p. ED 054 801.

Shoffner, Ralph M. "Some implications of automatic recognition of bibliographic elements," JOURNAL OF THE AMERICAN SOCIETY FOR IN-
FORMATION SCIENCE 22(4):275–82 (July 1971).

Shoffner, Ralph M., and Jay L. Cunningham. THE ORGANIZATION AND
SEARCH OF BIBLIOGRAPHIC RECORDS: COMPONENT STUDIES. Final
Report. Berkeley: Univ. of California, Institute of Library Research, Sept.
1971. 319p.

Shoffner, Ralph M., Jay L. Cunningham, and Allan J. Humphrey. THE
ORGANIZATION AND SEARCH OF BIBLIOGRAPHIC RECORDS IN ON-
LINE COMPUTER SYSTEMS: PROJECT SUMMARY. Berkeley: Univ. of
California, Institute of Library Research, 1971.

Smith, Stephen F., and William Harrelson. IMS: A TERMINAL MONITOR
SYSTEM FOR INFORMATION PROCESSING. Final Report. Berkeley: Univ.
of California, Institute of Library Research, Sept. 1971. 131p. ED 060 920.

Smither, P. R. EXPLOITING MACHINE READABLE BIBLIOGRAPHIC
DATA. Ottawa, Canada: Defense Science Information Service, 1972. 24p.

Vásárhelyi, Paul. DARE; UNESCO COMPUTERIZED DATA RETRIEVAL
SYSTEM FOR DOCUMENTATION IN THE SOCIAL AND HUMAN
SCIENCES (Including an Analysis of the Present System). Paris: UNESCO,
1972. 43p.

Watson, Peter G. "Planning a center for information services for the university library," LAW LIBRARY JOURNAL 64:154–60 (May 1971).

Watson, Peter G., and R. B. Briggs. "Computerized information services for
the university community," INFORMATION STORAGE AND RETRIEVAL
8(1):21–33 (Feb. 1972).

Weisman, Herman M. INFORMATION SYSTEMS, SERVICES AND CEN-
TERS. New York: Wiley/Becker and Hayes, 1972. 288p.

NETWORKS AND COOPERATION

Becker, Joseph, ed. PROCEEDINGS OF THE CONFERENCE ON INTER-
LIBRARY COMMUNICATIONS AND INFORMATION NETWORKS.
American Library Association and the U.S. Office of Education. Airlie House,
Warrenton, Virginia, 28 September–2 October 1970. Chicago: American
Library Assn., 1971. 347p.

Bhat, Narayan U. INFORMATION NETWORKS: A PROBABILISTIC MODEL
FOR HIERARCHICAL MESSAGE TRANSFER. Dallas: Southern Methodist
Univ., Computer Science/Operations Research Center, Nov. 1971. 19p.

Clemmer, Dan, and Russell Shank. "Library and information networks," in

THE BOWKER ANNUAL OF LIBRARY AND BOOK TRADE INFORMA-
TION, 1972. New York: Bowker, 1972. p.90–95.

Cummings, M. M., and M. E. Corning. "Biomedical communications: developing a mechanized library network," in: UNIVERSITY AND RESEARCH
LIBRARIES IN JAPAN AND THE UNITED STATES. Japan-U.S. Conference on Libraries and Information Science in Higher Education, Tokyo,
Japan, 1969. Chicago: American Library Assn., 1972. p.224–33.

Duggan, Maryann. FINAL REPORT OF A LIBRARY INTER-NETWORK
STUDY DEMONSTRATION AND PILOT MODEL (LIB-NAT). Dallas:
Southern Methodist Univ., 1971.

Epstein, A. H., Douglas Ferguson, and Eleanor Montague. "An on-line network
—cooperative planning with several libraries," in Jeanne B. North, ed.,
COMMUNICATION FOR DECISION-MAKERS. Proceedings of the 34th
Annual Meeting of the American Society for Information Science, Denver,
7–11 November 1971. v. 8. Westport, Conn.: Greenwood Publishing Co.,
1971. p.227–31.

Fasana, Paul J. "Collaborative library systems development: an experiment
in the joint design of automated library systems," in Jeanne B. North, ed.,
COMMUNICATION FOR DECISION-MAKERS. Proceedings of the 34th
Annual Meeting of the American Society for Information Science, Denver,
7–11 November 1971. v. 8. Westport, Conn.: Greenwood Publishing Co.,
1971. p.233–36.

Fasana, Paul J., and Allen Veaner, eds. COLLABORATIVE LIBRARY SYSTEMS
DEVELOPMENT. Cambridge, Mass.: MIT Press, 1971.

Greenberger, Martin, and others, eds. NETWORKS FOR RESEARCH AND
EDUCATION—SHARING COMPUTER AND INFORMATION RE-
SOURCES NATIONWIDE. Cambridge, Mass.: MIT Press, 1973.

Hammer, Donald P., and Gary C. Lelvis, eds. INDIANA SEMINAR ON
INFORMATION NETWORKS (ISIN) PROCEEDINGS. 26–28 October 1971.
West Lafayette, Ind.: Purdue Univ. Libraries, 1972. 91p.

Kilgour, Frederick G. "Computer-based systems, a new dimension to library
cooperation," COLLEGE AND RESEARCH LIBRARIES 34(2):137–43 (Mar.
1973).

_____ "Computerized cooperation," in NEW OPPORTUNITIES FOR RE-
SEARCH LIBRARIES. Minutes of the 80th Meeting of the Association of
Research Libraries, Atlanta, Georgia, 12–13 May 1972. Washington, DC:
ARL, 1972. p.54–61.

Kilgour, Frederick G., and others. "The shared cataloging system of the Ohio
College Library Center," JOURNAL OF LIBRARY AUTOMATION 5(3):
157–83 (Sept. 1972).

Korfhage, Robert R., and others. GRAPH MODELS FOR LIBRARY INFOR-
MATION NETWORKS. Dallas: Southern Methodist Univ., Computer
Science/Operations Research Center, August 1971. 33p. ED 060 861.

"Libraries may operate national computer-based network," LIBRARY JOURNAL
97:1226–27 (1 Apr. 1972).

LIBRARY COOPERATION: A SYSTEMS APPROACH TO INTERINSTITU-
TIONAL RESOURCE UTILIZATION. Report and recommendations. Sacra-

mento: State of California, Dept. of Finance, June 1973. 75p. Report no. PR-70.

Lyons, P., and M. Northcroft. "Ohio College Library Center: a user's viewpoint," CATHOLIC LIBRARY WORLD 44:265-68 (Dec. 1972).

McCarn, D. B. "Networks with emphasis on planning an on-line bibliographic access system," INFORMATION STORAGE AND RETRIEVAL 7(6):271-79 (Dec. 1971).

Miller, Ronald F. "NELINET: a regional network," in NEW OPPORTUNITIES FOR RESEARCH LIBRARIES. Minutes of the 80th Meeting of the Association of Research Libraries, Atlanta, Georgia, 12-13 May 1972. Washington, DC: ARL, 1972. p.62-69.

Montague, Eleanor. SUMMARY OF A FEASIBILITY STUDY ON THE PARTICIPATION OF FOUR COLLEGES AND UNIVERSITIES IN A STANFORD UNIVERSITY LIBRARY AUTOMATION NETWORK. Stanford: Stanford Univ., SPIRES/BALLOTS Project, 1971. 72p.

Nance, Richard E. INFORMATION NETWORKS: DEFINITIONS AND MESSAGE TRANSFER MODELS. Dallas: Southern Methodist Univ., Computer Science/Operations Research Center, July 1971. 28p.

Nance, Richard E., W. Kenneth Wickham, and Maryann Duggan. A COMPUTER SYSTEM FOR EFFECTIVE MANAGEMENT OF A MEDICAL LIBRARY NETWORK: AN OVERVIEW. Dallas: Southern Methodist Univ., 1971. 13p. + appendix.

New England Board of Higher Education. A PROPOSAL TO TEST THE TRANSFERABILITY OF THE OHIO COLLEGE LIBRARY CENTER COMPUTER SYSTEM TO THE NEW ENGLAND LIBRARY INFORMATION NETWORK. Submitted to the Council on Library Resources, Inc. Washington, DC: National Academy of Sciences, 1972. 95p.

NETWORKS AND DISCIPLINES. Proceedings of the EDUCOM Fall 1972 Conference. Princeton, NJ: EDUCOM, 1972.

NETWORKS FOR HIGHER EDUCATION. Proceedings of the EDUCOM Spring 1972 Conference. Princeton, NJ: EDUCOM, 1972.

THE NEXT STEP FOR NORTH CAROLINA LIBRARIES: A LIBRARIES SERVICES NETWORK. The report of a feasibility study of the North Carolina Libraries. Raleigh: North Carolina State Board of Higher Education 1971. 18p.

Ohio College Library Center. ANNUAL REPORT 1971/72. Columbus: OCLC, 1972.

Shank, Russell. A LIBRARY NETWORK FOR WESTERN CANADA; AUTOMATION FOR RATIONALIZATION IN COLLEGE AND UNIVERSITY LIBRARIES IN ALBERTA, SASKATCHEWAN, AND MANITOBA. Kent State Univ., Ohio: Center for Library Studies, February 1971. 78p. ED 053 773.

Sinclair, Michael P. "A typology of library cooperatives," SPECIAL LIBRARIES 64(4):181-86, April 1973.

SLICE/MARC-O CATALOGING DATA SEARCH AND PRINT SERVICE: USER'S MANUAL. 2d ed. Dallas, Texas: SLICE; Oklahoma City: MARC-O, Oklahoma Dept. of Libraries, 1972. 12p.

SLICE/MARC-O DESCRIPTION OF SERVICES. Dallas, Texas: SLICE; Oklahoma City: MARC-O, Oklahoma Dept. of Libraries, 1972. 20p.

SLICE OFFICE QUARTERLY REPORT FOR THE PERIOD 1 JANUARY TO 31 MARCH 1973. Dallas: Southwestern Library Interstate Cooperative Endeavor, Apr. 1973. 72p. ED 075 034.

Spicer, Michael W. A COMPARATIVE ANALYSIS OF FIVE REGIONAL REFERENCE AND INFORMATION NETWORKS. Columbus: Ohio State Univ. Library, 1972. ED 071 667.

Tolliver, Don. L., and Miriam Drake. A SURVEY OF THE INDIANA LIBRARY TWX NETWORK SYSTEM AS IMPLEMENTED BY THE INDIANA STATE LIBRARY AND THE FOUR STATE UNIVERSITY LIBRARIES. Lafayette, Ind.: Purdue Univ., Instructional Media Research Unit, Jan. 1973. 21p. ED 073 778.

Veaner, Allen. COLORADO ACADEMIC LIBRARY BOOK PROCESSING CENTER CONSULTING REPORT. Boulder, Colo.: CALBPC, 1972. 133p.

TELECOMMUNICATIONS

Niehaus, Carl A. UTILIZATION OF TELECOMMUNICATIONS BY ACADEMIC AND SCHOOL LIBRARIES IN THE UNITED STATES. St. Louis: Washington Univ., Program on Application of Communication Satellites to Educational Development, Mar. 1972. 58p. ED 064 901.

Oettinger, Anthony G., and Nikki Zapol. WILL INFORMATION TECHNOLOGIES HELP LEARNING: AN ANALYSIS OF SOME POLICY ISSUES. Cambridge, Mass.: Harvard Univ., Program on Technology and Society, Dec. 1971. 104p. ED 064 902.

Ohlman, Herbert. COMMUNICATION MEDIA AND EDUCATIONAL TECHNOLOGY: AN OVERVIEW AND ASSESSMENT WITH REFERENCE TO COMMUNICATION SATELLITES. St. Louis: Washington Univ., May 1971. 252p. ED 053 540.

COSTS

Axford, H. William. "An approach to performance budgeting at the Florida Atlantic University Library," COLLEGE AND RESEARCH LIBRARIES 32(2): 87–104 (Mar. 1971).

_____ PROCEEDINGS OF THE LARC COMPUTER-BASED UNIT COST STUDIES INSTITUTE, 16–17 September 1971. Tempe, Ariz.: LARC Assn., 1972. 91p.

Barr, William J. COST EFFECTIVE ANALYSIS OF NETWORK COMPUTERS. Master's Thesis. Urbana, Ill.: Univ. of Illinois, Dept. of Computer Science, 1972. 74p.

CONCEPTUAL REPLACEABILITY ANALYSIS FOR ORDER AND STANDARD LOAN TASKS. Santa Barbara: Univ. of California, Library Systems Development Program, Feb. 1971. 60p. ED 061 972.

DuBois, Dan. LIBRARY LABOR COST ACCOUNTING SYSTEM. Los Angeles: California State Univ. and Colleges, Off. of the Chancellor, 1972. 104p. ED 075 063.

Skov, Helge J. "The cost of documentation services based on magnetic tapes," in L. Vilentchuk and Gila Haimovic, eds., ISLIC INTERNATIONAL CONFERENCE ON INFORMATION SCIENCE, PROCEEDINGS, Tel Aviv, 29 August–3 September 1971. Tel Aviv: National Center of Scientific and Technological Information, 1972. p.659–65.

West, Martha W. REPORT ON A COST STUDY OF SPECIFIC TECHNICAL PROCESSING ACTIVITIES OF THE CALIFORNIA STATE UNIVERSITY AND COLLEGES LIBRARIES. Los Angeles: CSUC, Off. of the Chancellor, Feb. 1973.

Wilson, John H. "Costs, budgeting and economics of information processing," in Carlos A. Cuadra, ed., ANNUAL REVIEW OF INFORMATION SCIENCE AND TECHNOLOGY, v. 7. Washington, DC: ASIS, 1972. p.39–67.

NATIONAL AND FOREIGN STUDIES

"Automation in New Zealand libraries: state of the art reports on New Zealand university library automation," NEW ZEALAND LIBRARIES 35:3–22 (Feb. 1972).

Baker, L. R. "United we stand, divided we . . . : the case for cooperation among CAE libraries," AUSTRALIAN LIBRARY JOURNAL 20(8):15–22 (Sept. 1971).

Bryant, Philip, and Maurice B. Line. "Cataloguing and classification at Bath University Library," LIBRARY ASSOCIATION RECORD 73:225–27 (Dec. 1971).

Bryant, Philip, Gillian M. Venner, and Maurice B. Line. THE BATH MINI-CATALOGUE: A PROGRESS REPORT. Bath, Eng.: Bath Univ. Library, Feb. 1972.

Chauveinc, Marc. "Automation in French libraries," PROGRAM 5(4):179–90 (Oct. 1971).

Coblans, Herbert. "National reports and information policy," ASLIB PROCEEDINGS 23(1):24–32 (Jan. 1971).

DEVELOPMENT AND TESTING OF AUTOMATED LIBRARY PROCESSES: REPORT ON OSTI-SUPPORTED PROJECT, APRIL 1968 TO MARCH 1971. Summary. Loughborough Univ. of Technology, 1971. 27p. ED 059 724.

Downey, M. W. "Data collection and transcription in the cataloging section: report on a pilot project in the ETHZ library, Zurich," LIBRI 22(1):58–76 (1972).

Hein, Morten. "Scandinavian Conference on Data Processing Libraries," SCANDINAVIAN PUBLIC LIBRARY QUARTERLY 1:47–50 (1971).

Jacob, Mary Ellen L. "Background to automated library systems—the Australian context," AUSTRALIAN LIBRARY JOURNAL 20(5):5–11 (June 1971).

Line, Maurice B. "Automation and the British Library," LIBRARY ASSOCIA-TION RECORD 74(11):213–15 (Nov. 1972).

_____ "The developing national library networks in Great Britain," LIBRARY RESOURCES AND TECHNICAL SERVICES 16(1):61–73 (Winter 1972).

Line, Maurice B., and A. Phillips, eds. SCOPE FOR AUTOMATIC DATA PROCESSING IN THE BRITISH LIBRARY. Department of Education and Science. London: HMSO, 1972. 2 v. 641p.

Lugenberg, W. "Central organization for libraries in the German Federal Republic," LIBRI 22(2):55–62 (Feb. 1972).

MacKenzie, A. Graham. "Library research at the University of Lancaster," LIBRARY ASSOCIATION RECORD 73(5):90–92 (May 1971).

MacLean, H. "Automation in the National Library," NEW ZEALAND LI-BRARIES 34(2):54–57 (Apr. 1971).

Munn, R. F. "Use of modern technology in the improvement of information resources and services in developing countries," INTERNATIONAL LIBRARY REVIEW 3(1):9–13 (Jan. 1971).

Roberts, Norman. "University libraries," LIBRARY ASSOCIATION RECORD 73(6):110–12 (June 1971).

Sylvestre, Guy. "The developing national library network of Canada," LIBRARY RESOURCES AND TECHNICAL SERVICES 16(1):48–60 (Winter 1972).

Tyskevic, N. I. "Mechanization and automation of information and library operations in the U. S. S. R. and their development prospects," UNESCO BULLETIN FOR LIBRARIES 26(5):247–96 (Sept./Oct. 1972).

"UNESCO's Information and Documentation Programme for 1971–72," UNESCO BULLETIN FOR LIBRARIES 25(3):122–33 (May 1971).

Whyte, Jean P., ed. PROGRESS AND POVERTY; Library Association of Australia Proceedings of the 16th Biennial Conference, Sydney, August 1971. Sydney, Australia: Library Assn. of Australia, 1972. 790p. ED 061 986.

Wilson, A. "Typewriter terminals: their use in the National Library of Australia's ANB/MARC system," LASIE 3:2–13 (Sept. 1972).

GOVERNMENT LIBRARIES

Clayton, Fred W. "The toxicology information program of the National Library of Medicine," CLINICAL TOXICOLOGY 5(2):283–94 (Feb. 1972).

Corning, Mary E. "The U.S. National Library of Medicine and international MEDLARS cooperation," INFORMATION STORAGE AND RETRIEVAL 8(6):255–64 (Dec. 1972).

Cuadra, Carlos A., and Karl M. Pearson, Jr. "Status and prospects of auto-mation in the federal library community," in Jeanne B. North, ed., COM-MUNICATION FOR DECISION-MAKERS. Proceedings of the 34th Annual

Meeting of the American Society for Information Science, Denver, 7–11
November 1971. v. 8. Westport, Conn.: Greenwood Publishing Co., 1971.
p.291–95.

Henderson, Madeline M. "Library automation in the federal government," in
THE BOWKER ANNUAL OF LIBRARY AND BOOK TRADE INFORMA-
TION, 1972. New York: Bowker, 1972. p.75–80.

Radford, N. J. "Federal Library Committee's Task Force on Automatioh,"
LIBRARY OF CONGRESS INFORMATION BULLETIN 30:393–94 (1 July
1971).

VanDyke, Vern J., and Nancy L. Ayer. "Multi-purpose cataloging and index
system (CAIN) at the National Agricultural Library," JOURNAL OF LI-
BRARY AUTOMATION 5(1):21–29 (Mar. 1972).

Welsh, William J. "The Processing Department of the Library of Congress in
1970," LIBRARY RESOURCES AND TECHNICAL SERVICES 15(2):191–214
(Spring 1971).

COLLEGE AND UNIVERSITY LIBRARIES

Bommer, Michael R. W. THE DEVELOPMENT OF A MANAGEMENT SYS-
TEM FOR EFFECTIVE DECISION MAKING AND PLANNING IN A
UNIVERSITY LIBRARY. Philadelphia: Wharton School of Finance and
Commerce, Dec. 1972. 344p. ED 071 727.

COMPUTING IN HIGHER EDUCATION 1971. Proceedings of the EDUCOM
Fall 1971 Conference. Princeton, NJ: EDUCOM, 1972. 127p. ED 061 992.

Dahnke, Harold L., and others. ACADEMIC SUPPORT FACILITIES. Higher
Education Facilities Planning and Management Manual Four. rev. Athens,
Ohio: American Assn. of Collegiate Registrars and Admissions Officers,
May 1971. 74p. ED 061 625.

DiLucca, J. S. "Library automation at Villanova University," CATHOLIC
LIBRARY WORLD 44:260–64 (Dec. 1972).

Dyson, Sam A., ed. PLANNING AND IMPLEMENTING ACADEMIC LI-
BRARY AUTOMATION PROGRAMS: PROCEEDINGS OF THE LIBRARI-
ANSHIP TRAINING INSTITUTE HELD AT LOUISIANA TECHNICAL
UNIVERSITY 14–28 June 1970. Ruston, La.: Louisiana Technological Univ.,
1971. 224p. ED 054 836.

Ellsworth, Dianne. "The academic library looks at union lists," COLLEGE
AND RESEARCH LIBRARIES 32(6):475–78 (Nov. 1971).

Ely, Donald P. "The contemporary college library: change by evolution or
revolution?" EDUCATIONAL TECHNOLOGY 11(5):17–19 (May 1971).

Epstein, A. H. "BALLOTS-MARC operations at Stanford University," LIBRARY
OF CONGRESS INFORMATION BULLETIN 32:130–31 (13 Apr. 1973).

Epstein, A. H., and others. BIBLIOGRAPHIC AUTOMATION OF LARGE
LIBRARY OPERATIONS USING A TIME-SHARING SYSTEM: PHASE

II, PART I (July 1970–June 1971). Final Report. Stanford: Stanford Univ. Libraries, 1972. 287p.

Epstein, A. H., and Allen B. Veaner. A USER'S VIEW OF BALLOTS. Stanford: Stanford Univ. Libraries, BALLOTS Project, 1972. 31p. ED 071 723.

Ferguson, Douglas. THE LIBRARY, THE RESEARCHER, AND COMPUTERIZED INFORMATION AT STANFORD UNIVERSITY; A REPORT TO THE DIRECTOR OF LIBRARIES. Stanford: Stanford Univ., October 1971. 23p. ED 060 913.

Fussler, H. H. "Some aspects of technology and change in relation to university libraries," in UNIVERSITY AND RESEARCH LIBRARIES IN JAPAN AND THE UNITED STATES. Japan-U.S. Conference on Libraries and Information Science in Higher Education. Tokyo, Japan, 1969. Chicago: American Library Assn., 1972. p.214–24.

Kessler, Myer M. "The computer and the MIT Library," in L. Vilentchuk and Gila Haimovic, eds., ISLIC INTERNATIONAL CONFERENCE ON INFORMATION SCIENCE, PROCEEDINGS, Tel Aviv, 29 August–3 September 1971. Tel Aviv: National Center of Scientific and Technological Information, 1972. p.709–13.

LEARNING RESOURCES OPERATIONAL MODEL. Fort Worth, Texas: Tarrant County Junior College District, June 1971. 102p. ED 051 859.

Logan, Timothy, A. H. Epstein, and Wayne Davison. A USER'S VIEW OF BALLOTS, NO. 2: THE IPF MODULE. Stanford: Stanford Univ. Libraries, June 1973.

Mason, Ellsworth. "Along the academic way," LIBRARY JOURNAL 96(10): 1671–76 (May 1971).

Meredith, W. B. "Automation in the Dartmouth College Libraries," DARTMOUTH COLLEGE LIBRARY BULLETIN 13:39–44 (Nov. 1972).

Montague, Eleanor. A USER'S VIEW OF BALLOTS, NO. 3: THE CDF MODULE. Stanford: Stanford Univ. Libraries, June 1973.

Payne, Charles T., and Robert S. McGee. THE UNIVERSITY OF CHICAGO LIBRARY BIBLIOGRAPHIC DATA PROCESSING SYSTEM: DOCUMENTATION AND REPORT SUPPLEMENT. Chicago: Univ. of Chicago Library, 1971. 159p.

Payne, Charles T., Robert S. McGee, and Ellen R. Fisher. THE UNIVERSITY OF CHICAGO LIBRARY BIBLIOGRAPHIC DATA PROCESSING SYSTEM: DOCUMENTATION AND REPORT AS OF 31 OCTOBER 1969. Chicago: Univ. of Chicago Library, Oct. 1970. 287p.

Price, Bronson, and Doris C. Holladay. LIBRARY STATISTICS OF COLLEGES AND UNIVERSITIES. FALL 1969; ANALYTIC REPORT. Washington, DC: National Center for Educational Statistics (D-HEW/OE), 1971. 93p. ED 055 614.

Oddy, R. N. COMPUTER PROCESSING OF LIBRARY FILES AT DURHAM UNIVERSITY; AN ORDERING AND CATALOGING FACILITY FOR A SMALL COLLECTION USING AN IBM 360/67 MACHINE. Durham, England: University Library, 1971. 202p.

Shively, D. "Automation at the Stabley Library, Indiana University of Pennsylvania," PENNSYLVANIA LIBRARY ASSOCIATION BULLETIN 26:85–91 (Mar. 1971).

Sokoloski, James S. "Data processing at the University of Massachusetts Library." (Unpublished paper presented at the meeting of the Information Science and Automation Division, COLA Discussion Group.) American Library Assn., 20 June 1971.

"University of Maryland expedites library service with computer help," BULLE-TIN OF BIBLIOGRAPHY 29:23–24 (Jan. 1972).

SCHOOL AND PUBLIC LIBRARIES

Ball, Arzell L. "A superintendent's view of a computer system," SCHOOL MANAGEMENT 15(12):12–14 (Dec. 1971).

Black, Donald V., and Ann W. Luke. "A comprehensive automated instructional materials handling system for school districts," in Jeanne B. North, ed., COMMUNICATION FOR DECISION-MAKERS. Proceedings of the 34th Annual Meeting of the American Society for Information Science, Denver, 7–11 November 1971. v. 8. Westport, Conn.: Greenwood Publishing Co., 1971. p.279–85.

Brown, W. L. "Computers and the public library," in PROCEEDINGS OF THE LIBRARY ASSOCIATION OF AUSTRALIA CONFERENCE, 1971. Sydney, Australia: The Association, 1972. p.279–89.

Maidment, W. R. "Computer applications for public libraries: achievement and possibilities," in PROCEEDINGS, PAPERS, AND SUMMARIES OF DIS-CUSSIONS AT THE PUBLIC LIBRARIES CONFERENCE HELD AT BRIGHTON, 25TH SEPTEMBER TO 28TH SEPTEMBER 1972. London, Eng.: The Library Association, 1972. p.8–14.

Miller, Ellen W. "Sensible steps toward library automation," SCHOOL LI-BRARY JOURNAL 97(4):37–39 (15 Feb. 1972).

"O.E. computer grant to L. A. schools; project AIMS will be model," SCHOOL LIBRARY JOURNAL 97(4):10 (15 Feb. 1972).

Prostano, Emanuel T., and Joyce S. Prostano. THE SCHOOL LIBRARY MEDIA CENTER. Littleton, Colo.: Libraries Unlimited, 1971. 256p. ED 073 628.

SPECIAL LIBRARIES AND INFORMATION CENTERS

Bauer, Charles K. "Automation and its lessons," SPECIAL LIBRARIES 63(2): 47–53 (Feb. 1972).

Bratton, Rose J. "A building and construction industry urban affairs information center," SPECIAL LIBRARIES 64(3):121–25 (Mar. 1973).

Carmon, J. L. "A computer-based information center," SPECIAL LIBRARIES 64(2):65–69 (Feb. 1973).

Chicago Assn. of Law Libraries. "Seminar on law library problems: law libraries and automation," LAW LIBRARY JOURNAL 64:113–212 (May 1971).

Corbett, L. "Problems in using external information services: attitudes of the special library and its users," ASLIB PROCEEDINGS 24:96–110 (Feb. 1972).

Douville, Judith A. "Technical information centers: specialized services to science and technology. An overview," JOURNAL OF THE AMERICAN SOCIETY FOR INFORMATION SCIENCE 23(3):176–84 (May/June 1972).

Foskett, D. J. "Special Libraries." Paper prepared for presentation at the International Conference on Librarianship held in Kingston, Jamaica, 23–29 April 1972. ED 061 995.

Griffin, Hillis. "Computer applications for small libraries," LAW LIBRARY JOURNAL 64(2):161–66 (May 1971).

Jackson, Eugene. "Toward information centers," SPECIAL LIBRARIES 62(5–6): 238–41 (May/June 1971).

Landau, Herbert B. "Contract services in the special library," SPECIAL LIBRARIES 64(4):175–80 (Apr. 1973).

Lowry, W. R. "Use of computers in information systems; new information system developed at Bell Telephone Laboratories leans heavily on computers," SCIENCE 175:541–46 (25 Feb. 1972).

Malley, Patricia Munson. "Development of a technical library to support computer systems evaluation," JOURNAL OF LIBRARY AUTOMATION 4(4):173–84 (Dec. 1971).

Neufeld, I. H. "Computer application in the United Aircraft Corporation library system," SPECIAL LIBRARIES 64(5–6):235–38 (May/June 1973).

O'Leary, Martha H., ed. AUTOMATED FUNCTIONS AND EQUIPMENT IN LIBRARIES AND INFORMATION CENTERS OF GREATER NEW YORK. 2d ed. New York: Documentation Group, Special Libraries Assn., New York Chapter, 1972. 22p.

A PROPOSAL TO DEVELOP AND IMPLEMENT A NORTHEAST ACADEMIC SCIENCE INFORMATION CENTER (NASIC). Wellesley, Mass.: New England Board of Higher Education, 1972.

Randall, G. E. "The inventory of a special library collection," SPECIAL LIBRARIES 63(3):130–34 (Mar. 1972).

Randall, G. E., and J. G. Oxton. "Mechanized library ten years later," SPECIAL LIBRARIES 64(2):76–80 (Feb. 1973).

Simkins, M. A. "The use of external services in a small research information department," ASLIB PROCEEDINGS 25(1):22–26 (Jan. 1972).

Slater, Frank, ed. COST REDUCTION FOR SPECIAL LIBRARIES AND INFORMATION CENTERS. Washington, DC: ASIS, 1972.

Weinert, Hartmut H. "A keyword system for small information centers," JOURNAL OF THE AMERICAN SOCIETY FOR INFORMATION SCIENCE 24(3):180–92 (May/June 1973).

Weisman, Herman M. "Technical libraries and the National Standard Reference Data System," SPECIAL LIBRARIES 63(2):69–76 (Feb. 1972).

MEDICAL LIBRARIES

Cheshier, Robeert G. "Fees for service in medical library networks," BULLETIN OF THE MEDICAL LIBRARY ASSOCIATION 60(2):325–32 (Apr. 1972).

Fenske, Ruth E. "Mechanization of library procedures in the medium-sized medical library: correlations between National Library of Medicine classification numbers and MeSH headings," BULLETIN OF THE MEDICAL LIBRARY ASSOCIATION 60(2):319–24 (Apr. 1972).

Howard, Ellen, and Gloria Kharibian. "Mechanization of library procedures in the medium-sized medical library: computer applications in hospital departmental libraries," BULLETIN OF THE MEDICAL LIBRARY ASSOCIATION 60(7):455–66 (July 1972).

Key, J. D., and K. J. Sholtz. "Mayo Clinic author catalog: a living repository of medical knowledge," BULLETIN OF THE MEDICAL LIBRARY ASSOCIATION 61:228–37 (Apr. 1973).

Monroe, Elizabeth Jean. LENDING PATTERNS AMONG LARGE BORROWING INSTITUTIONS (Kentucky, Ohio, Michigan Regional Medical Libraries). Bethesda, Md.: National Library of Medicine, 1972. ED 071 670.

INFORMATION TECHNOLOGY

"Audiovisual cataloging automated," LIBRARY OF CONGRESS INFORMATION BULLETIN 31(4):37 (27 Jan. 1972).

Alanso, P. A. "Feasibility study on computer-produced map catalogues," AUSTRALIAN LIBRARY JOURNAL 21:243–52 (July 1972).

Buckle, D. G. R., and Thomas French. "The application of microform to manual and machine-readable catalogs," PROGRAM 6(3):187–203 (July 1972).

Fischer, Mary L. "The use of COM at the Los Angeles Public Library," JOURNAL OF MICROGRAPHICS 6(5):205–10 (May/June 1973).

Gilbert, Leslie A., and Jan W. Wright. NON-BOOK MATERIALS: THEIR BIBLIOGRAPHIC CONTROL. London, Eng.: National Council for Educational Technology, 1971. 84p. ED 064 933.

Hyer, Anna L. EDUCATIONAL TECHNOLOGY: A CHALLENGE FOR LIBRARIANS. Washington, DC: National Education Assn., Div. of Instruction and Development, Feb. 1972. 19p. ED 058 752.

LIBRARY DEMONSTRATION–DIAL ACCESS RETRIEVAL SYSTEM. Narrative Report. Mitchell, SD: Independent School District 45, June 1971. 27p. ED 052 870.

Liao, Robert C., and Phillip J. Sleeman. "Inexpensive computerized cataloging of educational media . . . a mini-system," AUDIOVISUAL INSTRUCTION 16(2):12–14 (Feb. 1971).

McGrath, William E., and Donald Simon. "Regional numerical union catalog on computer output microfiche," JOURNAL OF LIBRARY AUTOMATION 5(4):217–29 (Dec. 1972).

McNally, Paul Terence. A GUIDE TO THE PRACTICE OF NON-BOOK LIBRARIANSHIP. Canberra, Australia: Commonwealth Advisory Committee on Advanced Education, 1972. 137p. ED 064 949.

Marland, S. P., Jr. EDUCATIONAL TECHNOLOGY—A VOTE OF CONFIDENCE. Washington, DC: U. S. Dept. of Health, Education, and Welfare, Off. of the Commissioner of Education, April 1972. 16p. ED 063 777.

Morrison, Alta Bradley, ed. MICROFORM UTILIZATION: THE ACADEMIC LIBRARY ENVIRONMENT. Report of Conference held at Denver, Colorado, 7–9 December 1970. Denver, Colo.: Univ. of Denver, April 1971. 241p. ED 048 901.

"MULTIMEDIA: cataloging, indexing, and inventory functions," JOURNAL OF MEDICAL EDUCATION 46(7) pt. 2:51–57 (July 1971).

Ristow, Walter W., and David K. Carrington. "Machine readable map cataloging in the Library of Congress," SPECIAL LIBRARIES 62(9):343–52 (Sept. 1971).

Rufsvold, Margaret I., and Carolyn Guss. "Software: bibliographic control and the NICEM indexes," SCHOOL LIBRARIES 20(2):11–20 (Winter 1971).

Spigai, Frances G. THE INVISIBLE MEDIUM: THE STATE OF THE ART OF MICROFORM AND A GUIDE TO THE LITERATURE. ERIC/CLIS and ASIS (SIG/RT). Washington, DC: ASIS, Mar. 1973. ED 075 029.

Wall, R. A. "COMP: computer output microfilm peek-a-boo," LIBRARY ASSOCIATION RECORD 79:44 (Mar. 1972).

TEACHING LIBRARY USE AND LIBRARIANSHIP

Atherton, Pauline. "Putting knowledge to work in today's library schools," SPECIAL LIBRARIES 63(1):31–36 (Jan. 1972).

Belzer, Jack, and others. "Curricula in information science: analysis and development," JOURNAL OF THE AMERICAN SOCIETY FOR INFORMATION SCIENCE 22(3):193–223 (May/June 1971).

Borko, Harold. "Data processing in the library: a course description," in Jeanne B. North, ed., COMMUNICATION FOR DECISION-MAKERS. Proceedings of the 34th Annual Meeting of the American Society for Information Science, Denver, 7–11 November 1971. v. 8. Westport, Conn.:Greenwood Publishing Co., 1971. p 137–41.

Culkin, Patricia B. "Computer-assisted instruction in library use," DREXEL LIBRARY QUARTERLY 8(3):301–11 (July 1972).

Donohue, Joseph C. "Research on information seeking—its place in the teaching of librarians," INTERNATIONAL LIBRARY REVIEW 4(1):97–101 (Jan. 1972).

Dyson, Sam A. LIBRARY AUTOMATION; A "FIRST COURSE" TEACHING SYLLABUS. Ruston, La.: Prescott Library Publications, 1971. 121p.

Hansen, Lois. "Computer-assisted instruction in library use: an evaluation," DREXEL LIBRARY QUARTERLY 8(3):345–55 (July 1972).

Horn, Robert E., and others. INFORMATION MAPPING FOR COMPUTER-BASED LEARNING AND REFERENCE. Cambridge, Mass.: Information Resources, Inc., Mar. 1971. 167p. ED 056 494.

Jacob, M. E. "Library in-service training systems analysis and programmers," in PROCEEDINGS OF THE LIBRARY ASSOCIATION OF AUSTRALIA CONFERENCE, 1971. Sydney, Australia: The Association, 1972. p.719–23.

Jahoda, G., and Ferol A. Foos. THE USE OF AN ON-LINE SEARCHED AND PRINTED COORDINATE INDEX IN TEACHING. Tallahassee: Florida State Univ., Computer-Assisted Instruction Center, July 1971. 62p. ED 060 881.

Kurmey, W. J. "Data processing in a library science curriculum," in AUTOMATION IN LIBRARIES. Canadian Association of College and University Libraries, Workshop in Library Automation, Vancouver, British Columbia, 19–20 June 1971. Ottawa, Canada: CACUL, 1972. p.6.1–6.19.

Lubock, Georgette, ed. PROCEEDINGS OF THE INTERNATIONAL CONFERENCE ON TRAINING FOR INFORMATION WORK, ROME, ITALY, 15TH–19TH NOVEMBER 1971. Joint publication of the Italian National Information Institute, Rome, and the International Federation for Documentation, The Hague. Rome: The INI Institute, Sept. 1972. 510p.

Maguire, C. "Integration of data processing in formal education for librarianship," in PROCEEDINGS OF THE LIBRARY ASSOCIATION OF AUSTRALIA CONFERENCE, 1971. Sydney, Australia: The Association, 1972. p.741–46.

Maron, M. E., and Don Sherman. AN INFORMATION PROCESSING LABORATORY FOR EDUCATION AND RESEARCH IN LIBRARY SCIENCE: PHASE II. Final Report. Berkeley: Univ. of California, Institute of Library Research, Sept. 1971. 121p. ED 060 916.

Meredith, Joseph C. REFERENCE SEARCH SYSTEM (REFSEARCH) USERS' MANUAL. Final Report. Berkeley: Univ. of California, Institute of Library Research, Apr. 1971. 124p. ED 060 918.

Mignon, Edmond, ed. DIRECTIONS IN EDUCATION FOR INFORMATION SCIENCE; proceedings of a seminar sponsored by ALA/ISAD and ASIS, Denver, 11–13 November 1971. 177p. ED 061 947.

―――― "Information science in the teaching of traditional reference service," in Jeanne B. North, ed., COMMUNICATION FOR DECISION-MAKERS. Proceedings of the 34th Annual Meeting of the American Society for Information Science, Denver, 7–11 November 1971. v. 8. Westport, Conn.: Greenwood Publishing Co., 1971. p.143–46.

Mignon, Edmond, and Irene Travis. LABSEARCH: ILR ASSOCIATIVE SEARCH SYSTEM TERMINAL USERS' MANUAL. Final Report. Berkeley:

Univ. of California, Institute of Library Research, Sept. 1971. 87p. ED 060 917.

Rao, P. V. "Library automation: a team teaching approach at Eastern Illinois University," ILLINOIS LIBRARIES 54(3):210–12 (Mar. 1972).

Rayward, W. Boyd. "The new technology and education for librarianship," AUSTRALIAN LIBRARY JOURNAL 20(5):12–15 (June 1971).

Silver, Steven S. and Joseph C. Meredith. DISCUS INTERACTIVE SYSTEM USERS' MANUAL. Final Report. Berkeley: Univ. of California, Institute of Library Research, Sept. 1971. 173p. ED 060 919.

Starks, David D., Barbara Horn, and Thomas P. Slavens. "Two modes of computer assisted instruction in a library reference course," JOURNAL OF THE AMERICAN SOCIETY FOR INFORMATION SCIENCE 23(4):271–77 (July/Aug. 1972).

Zachert, Martha Jane K., and Veronica Pantelidis. SIBE: A SEQUENTIAL IN-BASKET EXERCISE TECHNIQUE. Tallahassee: Florida State Univ., Computer-Assisted Instruction Center, 1971. 153p. ED 056 469.